Simon & Schuster's

Guide to
Saltwater
Fish and
Fishing

Angelo Mojetta

A FIRESIDE BOOK
PUBLISHED BY SIMON & SCHUSTER INC.
New York London Toronto Sydney Tokyo Singapore

NOTES ON THE ENTRIES

The entries are arranged in alphabetical order according to the Latin name of the species and are divided into two sections. The first contains the species recognized by the International Game Fish Association (IGFA), the organization that awards prizes for sporting angling. The second comprises species which, although not officially classified, are of particular sporting or food interest. Similar species are dealt with under the same entry. Average and maximum lengths are given for every species.

FIRESIDE
Simon & Schuster Building
Rockefeller Center
1230 Avenue of the Americas
New York, New York 10020

copyright © 1992 Arnoldo Mondadori Editore S.p.A., Milan
copyright © 1992 in the English translation Arnoldo Mondadori Editore S.p.A., Milan

English translation by John Gilbert

Designed by Studio Cancelli, Milan, Italy

Drawings by Lino Simeoni (introduction); Vittorio Salarolo (entries 25 (a), 65 (b), 90 (b), 91 (a), 104 (br), 107 (a), 126 (a); FAO (Food and Agriculture Organization) (all other entries)

Symbols by Studio Cancelli, Milan, Italy

Editorial production by O.A.F. S.r.l., Milan, Italy

Typeset by Tradespools Ltd, Frome, Somerset, England

Printed and bound in Spain by Artes Graficas, Toledo
D.L.TO:747–1992

10 9 8 7 6 5 4 3 2 1

Library of Congress Cataloging-in-Publication Data
Mojetta, Angelo.
   Simon & Schuster's guide to saltwater fish and fishing/by Angelo Mojetta.
       p.   cm.
   "A Fireside book."
   Translated from Italian.
   ISBN 0-671-77947-8
   1. Saltwater fishing.   2. Marine fishes.   3. Marine ecology.
   I. Title.   II. Title: Simon and Schuster's guide to saltwater fish
   and fishing.
   SH457.M58   1992   91-45324
   798.1'6—dc20   CIP

CONTENTS

KEY TO SYMBOLS — page 6

FOREWORD — page 7

INTRODUCTION — page 9

IGFA CLASSIFIED SPECIES — page 99
entries 1–67

OTHER SPECIES — page 171
entries 68–131

GLOSSARY — page 250

BIBLIOGRAPHY — page 252

INDEX OF ENTRIES — page 253

KEY TO SYMBOLS

Type of fishing

From left to right: Big-game fishing or medium trolling, boat fishing (bottom, light trolling, drifting), coastal fishing (casting, surf-casting, fly fishing).

Habitats

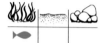

From left to right: Bottoms of *Posidonia* or a prevalence of algae, sandy and/or muddy bottoms, rocky bottoms.

From left to right: Over 6 miles from coast, from 1 to 6 miles from coast, up to 1 mile from coast.

From left to right: Deep waters, intermediate waters, surface waters.

Food value

excellent

good

edible

NOTES ON THE SYMBOLS

In this book each entry devoted to a species is furnished with a series of symbols that indicate, as appropriate, the type of habitat, the depth of the sea, the distance from the coast, the most effective fishing method, and the food value of the species. The need to summarize the distribution and habits of the fish is often at variance with their actual biology, given that they do not always occupy a single habitat. For this reason the symbol indicates, in many instances, the predominant or most characteristic environment for that species. Similarly, the symbol relating to the fishing method refers to that principally used.

FOREWORD

This book by Dr Angelo Mojetta underlines his reputation as a naturalist and as a writer capable of appealing to a wide, non-specialized readership. Little more need be added, save to point out that the book stands out, among others in the same field, for its scientific clarity and balanced approach to the vast subject of saltwater fishing.
As his teacher, and I say it with all humility, I am both proud of Dr Mojetta's achievements to date and full of hope for what he still promises to achieve. I consider this book, with its lucid text and fine illustrations, will be important to many thousands of enthusiasts all over the world.

Professor Menico Torchio
Lecturer in Marine Biology, University of Pavia, Italy

SEAS AND OCEANS

Viewed from satellites, our Earth fully merits the name "Blue Planet," given to it by astronauts. Those of us who do not regularly roam the oceans, whether for pleasure or by profession, or who have not taken a close look at a planisphere may find it difficult to conceive that water occupies the greater part of the planet's surface. Probably this is because we ourselves are essentially land animals. Yet about 70 percent of our body is made up of water; and it is now accepted that the salt content of our most important fluid—blood—corresponds more or less to that of the primitive ocean in which (failing any other more plausible theory) life on Earth began. Moreover, testimony to our aquatic nature is offered by the fact that human gestation occurs in a safe and comfortable watery environment, with the fertilized egg-cell emulating step by step the evolution of all vertebrates, encompassing a "fish" stage during which the embryo breathes through gills. Perhaps it is this affinity that impels many of us to venture out to sea, to discover something of its life forms and to seek contact with its inhabitants, if only by means of a tenuous line of nylon filament. Somehow, maybe unconsciously, the relationship between fisherman and fish recalls the bond forged at the time of our mysterious beginnings.

For this reason alone, it seems important to become acquainted with the sea in all its essential aspects, to understand and appreciate the laws which govern it—laws which necessarily influence its living forms and, indirectly, ourselves.

Seas and oceans

The oceans of planet Earth cover an area of some 138 million square miles (360 million square kilometers), roughly 70 percent of its surface, and occupy a volume of about 1,170 million cubic miles (1,370 million cubic kilometers). The average depth of this layer of water is around 12,500 ft (3,800 m), rising to a

Right: A conveyor belt discharging salt from a salt-works. Opposite: This satellite photograph of the Earth clearly shows the predominance of the ocean and sea areas.

maximum of 35,600 ft (10,850 m) in the Guam (Mariana) Trench. The terms ocean and sea are often used arbitrarily as if they were one and the same thing, but this is incorrect. Strictly speaking, the sea is an intracontinental basin and the ocean an intercontinental basin of saltwater. If this definition were applied to the letter, very few seas would nowadays remain in the atlases. The bounds of the Pacific, Atlantic, and Indian Oceans would be enormously extended. The Mediterranean Sea, for example, would become an appendage of the Atlantic Ocean, which is not so strange a proposition when one considers the affinities between the fauna of these two bodies of water; and the same would be true of the Red Sea and the Indian Ocean.

This fine distinction is useful as an aid to understanding that, fundamentally, the waters of the globe are all connected with one another, and for this reason are uniform in composition, particularly in terms of the principal components of salinity. The immense currents that course through the world's oceans, similar to rivers with unimaginable rates of flow, tend to balance the physical and chemical characteristics of this interconnected mass of water. Yet each body of water presents its own individual features, responsible both for the climatic conditions of the various zones ranged consecutively from the Poles to the Equator, and for the interactions of the oceans with the atmosphere and the continents. The opposing action of these forces in which cause and effect are often indistinguishable, coupled with specific biological populations, helps to differentiate and identify seas and oceans.

Chemical and physical characteristics of marine waters

The most obvious feature of sea water is that it is salty. All water flows into the sea, and in it are dissolved, sometimes in infinitesimal quantities (millionths of milligrams per liter), practically all known elements. Nevertheless, only eleven elements come together to produce more than 99 percent of the entire saline

11

complex, particularly chlorine and sodium which, when combined, form sodium chloride or common kitchen salt. It is especially interesting to note that the percentage of chlorine to be found in marine waters is virtually constant everywhere, so much so that by applying a simple formula it becomes possible to determine the salinity of any body of sea water merely by knowing how much chlorine is present.

According to the definition given at the Second Conference of the International Council for the Exploration of the Seas (1902), salinity is equivalent to the total weight in grams of solid substance dissolved in 1,000 grams of sea water. For this reason salinity is expressed by a number followed by the notation ‰, which signifies "per thousand." For example, 35‰ indicates that the sea water in question contains 35 g of salt to every 1,000 g of water.

The uniform composition of marine water should be challenged as a general rule because differences often occur among masses of water within the same ocean or, for more obvious reasons, between enclosed seas and open oceans. This has consequences for the biological populations which, in some instances, differ not so much as a result of varying levels of salinity in one basin and another as of changing proportions in the concentrations of certain salts. Apart from such differences, there are likely to be variations in salinity as determined, first, by the flow of freshwater, notably at the mouth of major rivers, and, secondly, by the intense evaporation which occurs in tropical zones and enclosed bodies of water such as the Mediterranean Sea and the Red Sea, where the salinity level reaches 43–45‰. As we shall see, such differences are extremely important factors in the lives of fishes, selecting their areas of distribution and delineating impassable boundaries.

Another parameter closely linked to salinity is so-called density, which depends on temperature and pressure, although the latter becomes significant at greater depths.

Temperature

The temperature of the water has a considerable influence both on the chemistry of the water and on the lives of its animal inhabitants. In fact, most of these animals have the same temperature as that of their surroundings. For this reason, fish are commonly described as "cold-blooded animals" or, scientifically, as "poikilotherms."

Variations in the sea's temperature do not merely influence the water density. They also modify the solubility of solids and gases. Particularly important among these is oxygen, of which the quantity in sea water is not uniform, varying from 0 to 8·5 ml/l. The largest quantities of this gas, which is indispensable to life, are found close to the surface, thanks to continuous interchange with the atmosphere. A part, sometimes a considerable part, of this oxygen, however, stems from the photosynthetic activity of plants, although the latter are confined to the well-illuminated surface layers. Temperature is also important in that it regulates the quantity of available oxygen, principally influencing its solubility. The amount of oxygen in cold water is, in fact, greater than that in warm water.

Earth and the atmosphere are heated by radiation from the Sun and cooled by an almost identical percentage of energy dispersed in space. Heating and cooling are obviously not uniform everywhere on Earth: the tropics are warmer and the lower latitudes are cooler. Yet, strange as it may seem, the average temperature of the seas is slightly below 39°F (4°C), even in equatorial waters. Such low mean temperatures are comprehensible only if we take into consideration the mass of oceans in their entirety.

Ocean currents

Mention of ocean currents probably conjures up, for most of us, an image of colossal but invisible rivers ploughing their courses across the world's oceans. Actually the role played by these currents is on a par with that of the winds on dry land, for they are essential elements in the exchange and circulation of ocean waters. Currents are determined by the combination of three forces: solar heat, the Coriolis force—which causes the currents to flow in a clockwise direction in the northern hemisphere and a counter-clockwise direction in the southern hemisphere—and the winds. As these forces interact, they create an intricate pattern of surface, intermediate, and deep currents. The principal currents of the Atlantic and the Pacific are the Gulf and Kurishio Streams respectively, both of them warm.

Near the Equator, in all three oceans, two currents—the North Equatorial and South Equatorial—flow westward, each of them separated by an equatorial counter-current which flows toward the east.

Currents are differentiated not only by direction but also by temperature. As a rule, those that flow along the eastern coasts of continents are warm, originating at the Equator (e.g. the Gulf Stream) and working their way up to the high latitudes, whereas whose along western coasts are cold (e.g. the Bengal Current off the west coast of central-southern Africa), flowing to the Equator.

The quantities of water carried by these various currents is immense: the warm Agulhas Current of the southeast coast of Africa carries some 1,400 million cubic ft (39 million cubic m) of water per second, while the comparable figure for

the Gulf Stream is about 2,500 million cubic ft (70 million cubic m). Very often the boundaries of two currents overlap, and the meeting point of these gigantic masses of water creates tracts of ocean that teem with life. The most notable instance of this occurs on the Banks of Newfoundland where the warm Gulf Stream (first studied scientifically by Benjamin Franklin) meets the cold Labrador Current to create one of the richest fishing zones in the world.

As marine biologists know, ocean currents can influence fish in various positive ways. Thus they may give direction to their general movements and migrations, affect their behavior, or cause them, directly or indirectly, to group together according to the availability of food. The last phenomenon is particularly evident close to "upwelling" zones where deep currents, characterized by cold water rich in nutrients, rise to the surface by reason of favorable local conditions (winds or continental masses which rear up to form a barrier to the currents), and create veritable oases of life, such as those to be encountered off the shores of Peru, California, northwest and southeast Africa, and along the Equator. Many of these zones are especially prized for their excellent deep-sea fishing.

The tides

All seas are powerfully influenced by tides. These phenomena are the reactions of the ocean to the gravitational attraction of the Sun and Moon. Indeed, there is hardly any body of water that does not obey this natural law. Every visitor to the seaside knows that the sea level appears to be higher or lower at different times of day, as the tides come in and go out, covering or exposing tracts of beach. In fact, there are two maximum and two minimum levels, at six-hourly intervals, every 24 hours, these levels varying over the course of a month with the alternation of major and minor tides.

The greatest variation of range (i.e. the biggest rise and fall) occurs at periods of full Moon and new Moon (spring tide), and the least during the first and last quarters (neap tide).

14

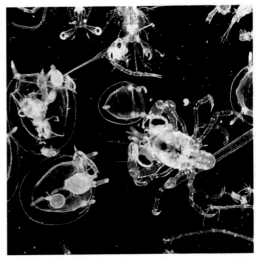

Right: A microscopic photograph of plankton. Opposite: A group of fishing boats left beached by the outgoing tide. On page 16: The shaded zone shows the ocean areas that are potentially richest in life forms.

In some cases the gravitational pull is strong enough to raise the water 50–65 ft (15–20 m) above the mean sea level. Such a height may be difficult to believe, yet in the Bay of Fundy, on the Atlantic coast of Canada, it is the norm. Another astonishing sight occurs in France, on the Channel coast, where the ancient monastery of Mont St Michel is regularly left high and dry on its island by the outgoing tide.

In the Mediterranean, on the other hand, the average range of tidal rise and fall is less than 20 in (50 cm), except in the Adriatic where the difference is more than 3 ft (1 m), all too familiar to the inhabitants of Venice, which is often flooded at high tide.

The constant rise and fall of sea level has yet another effect, causing shifts and transfers of water masses that sometimes produce raging currents. The monsters of Scylla and Charybdis, mentioned by Homer in the *Odyssey*, are actually tidal currents to be found in the Straits of Messina, the effects of which can to this day be felt by passengers on modern ocean liners.

As many books on navigation attest, tides that occur in enclosed areas battered by contrary winds may create currents of uncontrollable violence. Typical examples are those which form around the Aleutians in the Pacific and between the Orkney and Shetland Islands off the coast of Scotland. And the celebrated Maelstrom, familiar to readers of Edgar Allan Poe, is a huge whirlpool caused by a strong current running between the islands of Mosken and Moskenaes in the Lofoten group off the northwest coast of Norway.

Nutrients

These are essentially phosphorus- and nitrogen-based compounds (phosphates and nitrates) distributed non-uniformly in the sea, the presence of which is a determining factor on the abundance of life therein.

These substances (which in excessive amounts are agents of water pollution) are fundamental to the development of algae which constitute the first stage of any food chain. Their abundance in the sea depends upon a number of

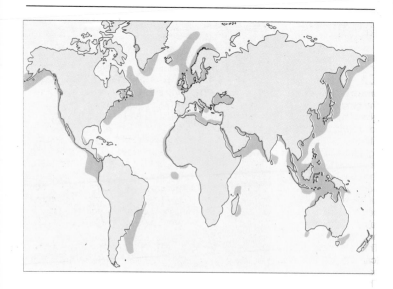

variables but it has been estimated that, on average, the concentration (at the surface) of nitrates fluctuates between 1–120, and that of phosphates between 0–20, micrograms per liter.

These quantities are considerably increased (up to four or five times at the maximum) in the ocean depths where they tend to accumulate as a result of sedimentation and transportation, their consumption being impossible because of absence of light and, hence, of plants. This explains clearly why the afore-mentioned zones of upwelling, where such nutrients are constantly being carried to the surface, are especially rich. Such areas of water are therefore predominantly green and yellow-brown in color, with none of the blue, glassy transparency which distinguishes zones that are poor in life forms. But nutrients are not confined to these zones, for they are cyclically made available to phytoplankton, the sea's most minute plant component. In temperate seas and along the coasts, as a result of dynamic processes which occur regularly each year following the cooling of the water, this phytoplankton makes up veritable ocean prairies.

Falling temperatures bring about an increase in water density; as the surface layers become deeper, they shift the masses of water underneath, gradually eliminating the temperature barriers which normally prevent the free circulation of the water. Within this turbulence, buffeted additionally by winter winds, currents and whirlpools bring up the nutrients in suspension from the depths, in regular preparation for the revival of marine life in spring. Thus currents, sunlight, temperature, and other factors are, in conjunction, fundamental to the life processes of the sea.

RODS

Before the introduction of modern materials, fishing rods were made exclusively of bamboo or soft cane. The woods had to be of the highest quality and dried with care: working with natural materials, it was not possible to attain the precisely uniform characteristics that we would expect today. Nowadays glass fiber and graphite have replaced the older rods and enabled the industry to experiment with ever improved techniques.

These materials make it possible to produce extremely reliable rods which are light (for example, there are rods of more than 40 ft [12 m] which weigh only about 2 lb [900 g], which last virtually forever and which are capable of retaining their qualities of elasticity and resistance for a very long time. Graphite rods, in particular, and especially those required for heavy duty, are nevertheless intrinsically fragile and have been superseded, in some instances, by the use of ceramic materials. This does not imply the manufacture of ceramic rods but rather the application of a sector of technology already employed in aeronautics and Formula 1 racing cars.

The various types of carbon fibers normally used in the making of graphite rods (carbon-vanadium, carbon-molybdenum and carbon-titanium) are impregnated with resins which contain dispersed short fibers of ceramic material. These, when heated, scatter in every direction to form a kind of web which increases the graphite's resistance and gives homogeneity to the fiber. The result is a rod which is lighter, more solid and flexible, and more quickly responsive.

Which rod to choose

Before examining in detail the characteristics of tackle designed for this or that type of fishing, it may be helpful to give a brief description of the kinds of rod that are nowadays available and some ways in which they can be easily classified. The choice of one rod or another will then depend, inevitably, on the requirements and expectations of the individual angler, and personal preference must be the final guide to such a decision. There is no single rod that performs equally well in all waters.

Rods available for sea fishing fall into three general categories: one-piece rods, telescopic rods, and connected rods. The difference among rods used in inland and coastal waters is often so slight that many anglers, whether fishing from the shore or from boats, will use the same type of rod normally employed for rivers and lakes. Consequently, fixed cane rods of varying length are perfectly suitable for fishing from the bank or from rocks in a sheltered bay for small grouper, saddled bream, ox-eye bream or salpa.

It is more convenient to classify rods according to the type of action involved in the flexing movement, which is affected to some extent both by the material used and on its length and form, particularly as it tapers toward the tip, and which may be rapid, normal or slow.

For example, if you want a rod which is sensitive to touch, you would be well advised to choose one with parabolic action. This method of flection causes the rod to bend gradually and is ideal for contending with the largest fish. Moreover, as the entire rod curves, the tension is wholly transferred to the tip. One disadvantage may be that it requires more physical effort while fishing. This type of rod is very effective in deep drift fishing for swordfish, where the main problem is to recognize the exact moment the fish bites.

A rod with tip action concentrates sensitivity in the tip without any great sacrifice of power. It makes for an immediate, clean catch. Short one-piece rods also lend themselves to this type of action, as do rods for fly fishing at sea (a system which is often successful for catching tarpon, marlin, and flying fish).

It is worth bearing in mind that a flexible rod is always preferable to one that is too rigid, because tension is distributed along the entire length of the tip and does not overtax the line.

A third type is the so-called continuous action rod, which offers a certain measure of strength at the expense of a slight loss in sensitivity of touch. This type of rod also has the advantage of guaranteeing a safe catch, especially when nylon monofilament is used, as is almost always the case nowadays, and where it is not absolutely necessary to extend the elasticity of the line to the tip, even if the rigidity of the latter means losing contact with the fish. It is in such situations that the sensitivity of the angler's hands and his knowledge of the fish are of fundamental importance in gauging just how and when to retrieve or check the line without awaiting any signs from the tip.

Integral parts of sea-fishing rods are the guide systems, which may be of the pulley or ring type.

The function of these fittings is to allow the line to operate freely both when casting and when retrieving. Obviously this is not just a matter of the line running smoothly but also, and more importantly, with the least possible amount of friction, which may become very considerable immediately after hooking a fish which shows fighting spirit and a good turn of speed in its efforts to break free, unwinding tens, even hundreds, of feet of line from the reel in a matter of seconds.

It is essential that rings or pulleys be perfectly aligned, and thus positioned along the "spine," as it were, of the rod. There is nothing worse that trying to retrieve a zig-zagging line; it is virtually certain to snap. Rings must be well distanced from the rod, so that the line does not touch it even when it is in the

Right: Two systems of ring guides. Below: Various models of telescopic fishing rods. Opposite: A set of big-game fishing rods ready for action.

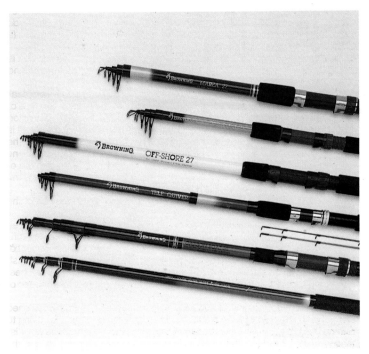

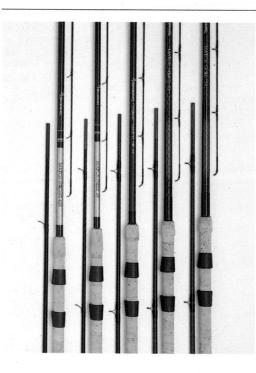

A group of connected rods. Below: Various bags for carrying rods. Careful maintenance can prolong the life of rods, the guide systems, and the reel. On page 23: A rod and reel in action.

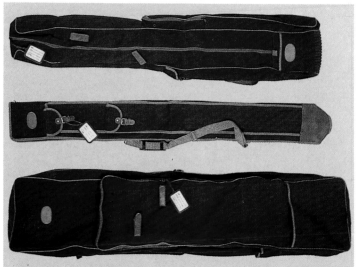

water. Equally important is the number of rings, which will vary according to their distance from the rod and its degree of flexibility, so that the line describes a harmonious curve and does not collapse into a series of practically useless sections. As a rule they are mounted every 12 in (30 cm) or so, becoming farther apart and larger away from the tip.

The selection of ring or pulley guides depends above all on the type of fishing. In surf-casting, the choice will almost exclusively be rings, whereas for trolling and big-game fishing it is better to use rods with pulleys (up to six) or a combination of rings and pulleys. The latter, with a double drive, are positioned at the tip (roller top) and near the butt. This device is indispensable when a metallic line is fitted.

As for the trolling rod, pulley guides are again the norm (those considered best are the AFTCO and Fin-Nor), although they are being superseded by rings of Japanese make (e.g. the Fuji) in materials with a low rate of friction such as semi-precious stone (ceramic, agate), although this description often conceals the fact that they are sometimes mixed with silica, titanium or aluminum. It is hardly surprising that such rods are normally used with the loops turned upward. This is not a caprice of the deep-sea fisherman but a sheer necessity. Indeed, if the line faced downward, the pull exercised by the prey and the constant strains on the line would tear the fastenings off the rings; turned upward, they allow the pressure on the line to be distributed evenly along the entire curve of the rod.

In contrast to rings, pulleys must be frequently checked both at time of purchase and during use. The purpose of such an examination is to make sure they are moving perfectly. A pulley which is blocked or is slow moving can cause the line to break. Sometimes the blockage can be due to tiny blobs of glue or varnish used in trimming the rod. A thorough cleaning, followed by the application of a good lubricant, will soon get the pulley working smoothly again. Some experts advise testing the pulleys by running through a length of wire and pulling it to either side.

MAINTENANCE

1. *Check the guide system for any signs of wear and tear. No matter how strong the materials, any kind of fishing will make constant demands on the tackle being used.*
2. *Inspect for signs of corrosion on the most exposed metal parts, protecting them with suitable sprays or lubricants.*
3. *Check the reel and the brake functioning.*
4. *Keep your tackle protected right up to the moment you use it so as not to expose it unnecessarily to sea water.*
5. *After a day's fishing, rinse your rods in fresh water, apply a lubricant to the pulleys and dry everything off carefully.*
6. *To clean the reel, tighten the brake fully, polish with a rag soaked in fresh water and dry.*
7. *If you do not intend to fish for some time, slacken the brake so that there is no prolonged contact between the brake and the lateral guides. Remove the entire line to ensure that no residues of sea water corrode the internal mechanism.*
8. *Keep the rods in a dry place, using separate containers for each of them.*

Rods for trolling

Many of us enjoy the game of soccer and are familiar with its rules, even if we do not play it ourselves. Fishing for sport also has its rules, which anyone can get to know, even superficially. These rules have resulted in a general codification that governs equipment, to which all manufacturers adhere.

Rods are categorized according to their strength, i.e. the weight necessary to bend its tip downward through 90°, thus forming a quarter of a circle. On the basis of this criterion, and according to the prescription of the International Game Fish Association (IGFA), rods are divided into classes:
—ultra-light (6, 12, and 20 lb);
—light (30 lb);
—medium (50 lb);
—heavy (80 lb);
—ultra-heavy (130 lb)
—without limit (130–180 lb).

These are the classified rods, and if made according to the dictates of the IGFA, they are always of two parts: the tip, which is the rod proper, with a minimum length of 40 in (101·4 cm) and with five guides plus the final one at the very tip, and the butt, no longer than 27 in (68·58 cm).

The butt or the handle may be straight or curved, especially in stronger models designed for catching large fish such as tuna or marlin. Tips may be made of glass fiber or graphite, while butts are of artificial fiber or metal and covered with neoprene, cork or leather to facilitate the grip. Fixed to the butt is the reel, and stronger models terminate in a cross, partially or wholly covered with a rubber plug, so that the rod can be held firmly and attached to suitable slots in the belt or the fighting seat. Such a term may seem somewhat belligerent when applied to a sport such as fishing, but anyone who has summoned up the energy to bring in a large, wounded fish will agree that the word "fighting" is fully justified. Although the rods described here are made of two pieces, there are nevertheless one-piece rods (Tuna Stick and Browning's Special Senator de Luxe) which many anglers prefer for strength.

Rods for bottom fishing

Bottom fishing refers to the types of fishing which entail the use of an anchored or drifting boat. Rods for such purposes, made of tubular glass fiber, sometimes mixed with graphite, are about 10 ft (3 m) long, either in two pieces or telescopic. They are classified, according to the IGFA weight categories, as of 6, 12, 20, and 30 lb, given that they are designed to catch smaller fish. The majority of species fished in this manner are small fish, although the technique is also acceptable for sharks, large rays, and others which are comparable in size to those caught by trolling, in which case heavier rods are required. It is also possible to use the strong and fairly rigid types of rod suitable for catching the larger freshwater species such as pike and carp.

Other types of fishing, such as casting and fly fishing, can also be practiced from a boat some distance from shore. Casting, as a rule, requires a 30-lb rod, while fly fishing requires a rod similar to that used for large trout or salmon, capable of taking fly lines of classes varying from 7 to 12, depending on the species likely to be encountered (see chapters on individual fishing techniques).

Rods for casting

In this very broad category, where sea fishing is concerned, the tackle used is applicable to spinning and surf-casting. The basic aim of this form of angling is

to cast the bait a long distance in order to enjoy the widest possible field of action. A skillful angler equipped with a powerful rod can cast a line more than 200 ft (60 m). Rods for use at sea are divided, according to length, into two categories: medium and long. The former measure 6–10 ft (2–3 m), the latter up to 16 ft (5 m). The ideal types are those made in two pieces from glass or graphite or from phenolic resins. The last two materials are chiefly used for surf-casting rods; graphite, in particular, guarantees increased casting distance.

There is a further differentiation on the basis of the weight cast, with a series of standardized categories that are essential knowledge for the correct choice of tackle.

At sea, given the characteristics of the environment, it is rare to engage in spinning of the minor categories (ultra-light, light, and medium), whereas it is common to practice heavy spinning with rods 6–10 ft (2–3 m) in length, with a strength of 2–5½ lb (1–2·5 kg), capable of casting weights of ¾–1¾ oz (20–50 g).

Surf-casting, on the other hand, is a typical sea-fishing technique and is divided into four categories:

—super-light, requiring rods of 8–10½ ft (2·5–3·2 m), with a strength of 2¼–5½ lb (1–2·5 kg), casting weights of ¾–1 oz (20–25 g);

An angler engaged in casting. With this type of fishing, skillful anglers using the strongest tackle can cast 650 feet 200 meters) and more.

24

—light, requiring rods of 11½–12½ lb (3·5–3·8 m), with a strength of 2¾–3½ lb (1·25–1·6 kg), casting weights of 1–2¾ oz (25–80 g);

—semi-heavy, requiring rods of 13–15 ft (4–4·5 m), with a strength of 4½–6¾ lb (2–3 kg), casting weights of 2¾–3½ oz (80–100 g);

—heavy, requiring rods of 16½ ft (5 m), with a strength of over 6¾ lb (3 kg), casting weights of over 3½ oz (100 g).

It should be mentioned that in most manufacturers' catalogs these distinctions are not strictly adhered to and the strength of individual rods actually refers to the casting weight.

In the author's opinion, however, it is useful to indicate the strength of the rod because this provides a clearer definition between this value and the casting weight. The stronger the rod, the heavier the casting weight, which represents a minimum of ¹⁄₁₀₀ and a maximum of ¹⁄₅₀ of the indicated rod strength.

Bearing in mind this simple rule, it is easier to choose your rod, but it must always remain within these limits. While lower weights will not bend the rod, higher weights may cause it to break.

LINES AND TERMINAL TACKLES

Choosing the ideal fishing rod is essential, but almost as important is choosing the right line, for this represents the link between the fish and the angler. As with rods, lines have developed and improved over the years, both in materials and characteristics, so that today the degree of specialization may, at first glance, appear incredible. The angler can select from a vast range of bobbing, floating, and sinking lines; in black, green, brown, white with dark spots, dichroic; with added silicon; for competition; etc.—lines capable, in fact, of dealing with any problem likely to be encountered.

As far as materials are concerned, lines of braided flax, not very elastic but strong and fast-acting, have all but vanished, to the regret of some anglers, having been replaced by synthetic fibers. For those who still look for, or can even find, flax lines, it is worth noting that their strength depends on the number of threads that make them up. Multiplying this number by three will enable you to calculate the line's strength in pounds. For instance, a 5-thread material gives a strength of 15 lb (7 kg).

The most widely used material nowadays is nylon monofilament, obtained by stretching a raw thread and augmenting its strength and elasticity to the required values. The qualities of nylon monofilament are now such as to satisfy the angler's every need, especially in terms of breaking strength. Each thread has a different diameter and, as is obvious, the greater the diameter, the greater the strength. The breaking point may be expressed in grams or pounds, particularly in the case of IGFA classified baits, i.e. 2–130 lb (0·9–59 kg).

Breaking strength

The breaking strength should be taken into account at time of purchase. Fishing tackle is a combination of different pieces; it is therefore important that rods, lines, and reels should always be chosen in relation to one another. Nylon monofilament, even if used for small and medium trolling (types of 8–12 lb [4–5 kg] to 130 lb [59 kg]), should be selected mainly for casting and needs to have elasticity, little torsion, softness, and uniformity.

These features, nowadays present in all monofilaments, can be tested experimentally by the angler. All that has to be done is to take a piece of line and pull it; if it tends to lengthen (a nylon monofilament may stretch by 20–30 percent, which explains how strains are reduced when fishing) it may be regarded as good and elastic; if it remains taut it should be discarded. Pulled even more, to its yielding point, the ideal line should remain straight once released. If it tends to kink or twist, it is best to throw it away.

These tests, perhaps unnecessary at time of purchase, should be carried out on lines at intervals to ascertain whether the moment has arrived or is approaching to change it. In fact, even if nylon as such is regarded as almost everlasting, this cannot be said of the mechanical properties of a monofilament. With progressive wear and tear, the line tends to lose elasticity, not only because it is being used but also because, judging it to be indestructible, we are liable to neglect it. Simply leaving it in the sun may greatly reduce its strength. Obvious signs of change are discoloration, a dry appearance and the presence of a whitish dust due to intrinsic flaking. The line ought, therefore, to be replaced every year, especially if the fishing season is long and intensive.

Another type of line, used for fly fishing, is made of nylon or braided nylon. Anyone accustomed to freshwater fly fishing may be surprised to learn how it can be used, and with great versatility, at sea. Tarpon, marlin, snook, barracuda, and white thresher sharks are often caught with flies, and some anglers have even taken larger sharks by this method.

The lines used in saltwater are the classic fly line type, particularly those known as SWT, WF, and WFS. The SWT are heavy lines with an off-center or saltwater weight; the WF are more classic, off-center lines with the weight forward; and in the WFS the lines are off-center with a sinking tip. The last form a line in which the head is virtually considered a straight plummet.

As a rule, the fly line for sea fishing is connected to a main line of dacron (technically known as backing), averaging 650 ft (200 m) in length. Fly lines may be floating, sinking with variable speeds, or semi-submersible. The types used at sea have a numerical code from 6/7 to 12, corresponding to the weight in grams of the first 30 ft (9 m) of line, which varies from about 10 to 25 g.

When it comes to the greater challenge of big-game fishing, it is virtually obligatory to use lines of braided dacron, a polyester fiber which is already weakened in the course of manufacture, greatly reducing elasticity. This line is available both in a hollow or solid braid. The dacron hollow braid line is flat inasmuch as it lacks an inner core. Under traction, therefore, the line flattens and becomes elastic, enabling it to lengthen by 10–12 percent.

The dacron solid braid line, on the other hand, has an inner core made of straight fibers which give the line volume and shape, increasing its strength. The cross-section remains circular under traction and thus elasticity (lengthening by 6–12 percent) is restricted. This reduction of elasticity guarantees a better strike (the action exercised on the rod is rapidly transmitted to the hook), a quick retrieval and a more efficient tightening of the knots even though the line

---

METAL WIRE LINES

Metal wire lines, regarded almost as elongated plummets, are employed mainly for deep-water trolling, because they possess the following indisputable advantages:

—they offer less resistance to water movement;

—elasticity is greatly reduced so that every movement or vibration of the bait is transmitted to the angler. (It will lengthen by 10–15 percent before breaking);

—it is possible to maintain the desired depth with fewer weights.

The assumption that wire lines, which might be thought unrivalled for strength, automatically guarantee an easier catch is nevertheless unfounded. Indeed, big fish (for which such lines are designed) will often manage to escape, given that the strength of such lines is comparable in every way to that of synthetic fiber monofilament. It is also worth remembering that wire line is given a nylon or dacron backing which possesses a strength identical to that of the metallic fiber employed.

There are three basic types of wire line: solid stainless steel, stainless steel strands, and solid monel (a nickel- and copper-based alloy with small percentages of iron, manganese, silica, and carbon). The monel metal line is preferable because it has a broader cross-section due to the fact that it does not wear out like a braided line and does not kink or split like a solid line. Another considerable advantage, too, is that the monel line can be used with a limited range of reels, provided they are sufficiently strong, whereas steel lines require special reels.

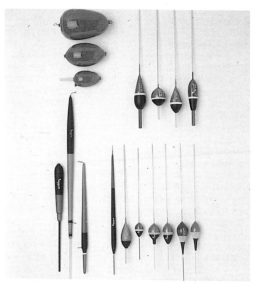

Left: A series of floats suitable for attachment to a line for coastal fishing. Opposite: An angler holding a broad-diameter line suitable for deep-sea fishing.

is much more sensitive to shock. One characteristic of dacron is that it comes in braids of mixed color: blue-white or blue-green.

A third type of dacron line has a lead core. The presence of lead makes the line sink and ensures little elasticity even though, when subjected to excessive traction, the line may lengthen by as much as 25 percent before breaking. The fact that this type of line will never recover its original length when stretched is something of an inconvenience and explains why it is seldom used.

The so-called terminal tackles or leaders are integral parts of fishing lines. These are strips of line of a different diameter from that of the main line, sometimes thinner, sometimes thicker, connected to the latter by swivels which bear the hook or hooks. Sometimes the leader may consist of several strands of different diameter, as in the case of the fly lines, but the majority comprise a single line connected to the main line by swivels.

The purpose of the swivels is to prevent the line, either because of the effects of current, drag or even the angler's handling action, from rotating and getting wound around itself. Composed of two linked rings which are capable of swiveling independently, they vary in measurement from 1–0 to 10–0, and are thus suitable for almost any contingency at sea, 6–0, 8–0 and 10–0 being appropriate for marlin, tuna, and swordfish. Swivels are of the barrel, wire or T type, and considering the conditions in which they are expected to function, they should be as strong as the leader itself. The best types are steel mounted on spherical pads (made by the Sampo company) which guarantee perfect rotation without any hitches.

Swivels may terminate in spring catches and have two or three attachments which can take two or three terminals at once. Spring catches are, in any event, to be preferred because they permit broken leaders to be replaced quickly (they are designed for this purpose and thus to give way before the main line breaks) or to be exchanged for others which may be more suitable. Leaders often come complete with hook and spring catch, so that replacing them is virtually child's play.

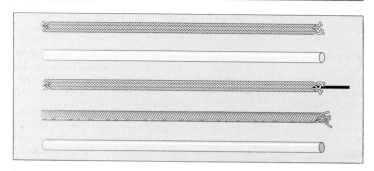

As for materials, leaders may be either of nylon or of steel wire. The former may be used conveniently for all kinds of still fishing or small and medium trolling (so long as one does not expect an encounter with a barracuda or other sharp-toothed species). The latter, commonly described as piano-wire because braided strands of wire, as used in pianos, were formerly employed for this purpose, are always recommended for fish with strong teeth such as sharks, or with mouth appendages capable of snapping the traces, like swordfish.

For shark fishing, some professionals advise against wire leaders covered with a layer of nylon. The shark's teeth will strip the covering away, thus exposing the wire, which is likely to break under the repeated strain. Even if this does not happen, however, the teeth are bound to cause damage, and the water that infiltrates the tiny, almost imperceptible cracks in the plastic coating will soon act on the metal, gradually reducing its strength.

Only continuous and scrupulous supervision of all tackle will yield guaranteed results. Very thick, strong nylon leaders, with breaking points much above 220 lb (100 kg), are normally used for giant tuna; but great care must be taken with the fittings of such leaders. They are too thick to ensure that knots will hold, so it is better to use lead links, preferably double ones. Terminal tackle is also regulated by the IGFA which permits a maximum leader length of about 16 ft (5 m) for classes up to 20 lb (9 kg) and about 30 ft (9 m) for classes above that.

Leaders with a larger diameter than that of the main line are also used for heavy surf-casting where, to counteract the recoil effect of casting a lead sinker of over 3 oz (100 g), it is necessary to use stronger terminal tackle, known as a shock leader.

Finally, reverting to the types of line used in sea fishing, it is possible to double the terminal part. Obviously there are limits to the length for doubling; according to the IGFA norms, these are 15 ft (4·57 m) for classes up to 20 lb (9 kg) and 30 ft (9·14 m) for classes above that. The reason why many anglers prefer a double line (and the fact that it is allowed for game fishing by the leading international organization indicates that there is nothing unethical about it) is that, when the fight is over, a line of double strength is almost indispensable, since in this situation the rod is virtually incapable of sustaining the shock and the rigidity of the rod-line combination, now very short, increases the likelihood of breakage.

HOOKS, KNOTS, AND LEADS

Catching a fish depends ultimately on the hook attached to the end of the line. For this reason, many consider the hook to be just as important as the rod, the line, and the reel. Some anglers, as fishing tales attest, are so superstitious that they will discard a hook after catching a fish with it, considering it no longer usable once it has fulfilled its purpose.

The realm of hooks is even more diversified than that of rods or lines; and here, too, technology has kept apace both as regards materials (steel remains sovereign, but hooks may be made of bronze, nickel, graphite, and even plated in precious metals), and manufacturing techniques. Nowadays one may even come across hooks that are sharpened chemically (Gamakatsu), hooks with

Opposite, top to bottom: Braided dacron line; nylon monofilament line; lead-core line; interwoven metallic wire line; solid metallic wire line.

Right: the various parts of the hook may be differently shaped.
A. Narrow-necked spade.
B. Flattened spade.
C. Pointed shank.
D. Toothed shank.
E. Split spade.
F. Grooved spade.
G. Needle-eye spade.
H. Ferruled eye.
I. Round eye.
L. Shortened eye.
M. Sharp point.
N. Dublin point.
O. Strengthened point.
P. Curved point.
Q. Straight point.

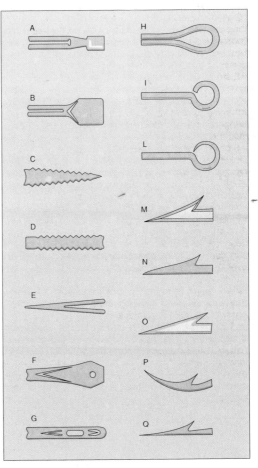

barbs that are branched by micrometry (Browning), and so on.

Hooks are made, quite simply, from steel wire of prearranged thickness. After cutting a section of the required length, the point is ground, the eye or spade is formed and the barb is cut. The eye of a large hook is welded to give additional strength. The hook is bent to shape, then hardened and tempered (in some cases entailing fourteen successive phases), scoured, and if need be colored, lacquered or plated (even in gold) to retard corrosion.

Although hooks are very common objects, equally familiar to those who take no interest in fishing, the individual parts of which they are composed are not so readily identified. Starting at the end which is to be connected to the line there is the eye or spade, the shank, the point, and the barb (the small projection which prevents the hook from slipping out). Other important parameters in the construction of the hook are the curvature, the neck (distance from the top of the curve to the point), and the aperture (distance between the shank and the point).

The sections of the hook may be round or rectangular. And the shapes assumed by the various parts are very diverse, as the following summary shows.

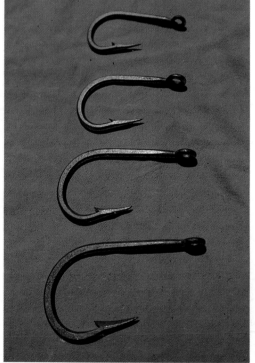

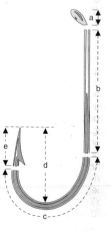

The hook is divided into the eye (A), shank (B), curvature (C), neck (D) and aperture (E). Left: Hooks for big game fishing.

SECTIONS OF THE HOOK

—*eye attachment: small, round, ferrule, external, internal, straight, tapered;*
—*spade attachment: needle-eye, pierced, split, flat, narrow;*
—*shank: serrated, clawed, short, medium, long, extra-long, pointed;*
—*point: straight, reversed, kirbed, tall, indented, reinforced, Dublin, sharp.*

All these features are variously combined according to the product that is required, so it is easy to understand why there are so many hooks to fill numerous catalog pages. On the basis of the definitions we have mentioned, there are straight hooks with long, spade shanks, hooks with an external eye, shaped and twisted, with an indented point, or twisted hooks with eye shank, short and round, with indented point and curve.

With a little patience, you will always be able to find the hook which has all the features you need. When choosing it, however, avoid hooks with too big a barb, too narrow an aperture or too long a point. Hooks with eyes must be properly closed to avoid the possibility of the line slipping out.

Fortunately, the choice of this or that hook is made easier by the fact that they are nowadays grouped in recognized "families" which are often named after their inventor or place of origin. So we have O'Shaughnessy hooks, which are straight, with eye or spade attachments; Limerick hooks with a more broadly bent barb, straight or twisted, with a long shank ending in an eye or spade; Crystal, which are straight, with spade attachment and an "Irish" curve; and Aberdeen with straight shank and perfectly semicircular bend.

Hooks, quite apart from their shape, are also cataloged according to an English numbered scale which takes account of the distance between point and shank, i.e. aperture. It is a decreasing scale, which means that the higher the number, the smaller the hook. The numerals of hooks used for sea angling start from number 20 (hooks with still higher numbers, although they exist, are considered too small for the purpose) and so on down to 1. After this, the numbers continue, this time increasing, but followed by a slash symbol and a zero: 1/0, 2/0, 3/0 etc. up to 10/0 and 13/0, suitable for quarry such as sharks and giant tuna. Obviously, these are hooks of considerable size with shanks over 4 in (10 cm) long and points of proportionate dimensions which, in the case of the bigger and more dangerous sharks, are more akin to meathooks.

The best commercial hooks are considered to be the Mustad and VMC types.

Having looked at the different categories of hook, the question is now one of choice. Naturally, this must depend ultimately on the kind of angling you have in mind. The most common hooks used at sea are the Crystal type numbered from 8 to 16 for reef fishing and the forged type numbers 1 to 8 for bottom fishing, these being suitable as well, provided they are long-shanked, for surf-casting.

For flatfish such as sole and flounder, it is best to choose hooks with a long shank and short aperture.

Where big-game fishing is concerned, hooks of sizes 3/0 or 4/0 are recommended for small tuna and species of similar dimensions. Larger sizes, from 5/0 to 7/0, will be needed for meager, dolphinfish or medium-sized tuna, while size 9/0 and upward are essential for even bigger prey.

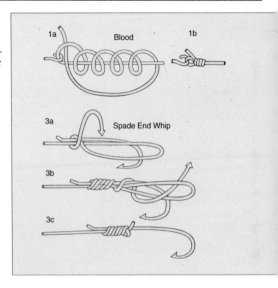

Another factor to be considered when choosing a hook is its shape or bend. For example, hooks with a short, straight shank, broad in diameter and with eye or needle-eye attachment, are best for large tuna. In the latest models, the eye is built into the shank in order to increase its strength.

For beaked fish, such as swordfish, sailfish or marlin, hooks should have a medium shank, wide bend, long barb, and eye attachment. And for sharks, the best hooks are the forged type, with a straight eye and curved point.

Round-eye are preferable to needle-eye attachments and swivel types are good, too, as they can be fitted with soft, natural-looking baits.

The choice of shape is not solely determined by the type of quarry but also by the predictable behavior of the hook once in the water. This is a very important consideration in trolling. As we have already mentioned in relation to swivels, a line in water will tend to wrap round itself. So a hook with a curved point, if not well concealed in the bait, is liable to rotate, and may cause the leader to snap and the bait to float free. Flat hooks are therefore used in trolling, with artificial baits such as the Kona Head (see chapter on Baits) or with natural baits.

The wide range of hooks available to anglers also includes double, triple, and quadruple types, better known as anchors, generally combined with artificial baits such as minnows, plugs, and spoons, but seldom used for sea fishing.

Types of attachment, too, are roughly subdivided for quick and easy reference. Spade types are suitable for tying to monofilament of maximum 0·35 diameter eye attachments are best for lines of greater diameter.

It may be helpful, at this point, to describe the hook's performance. Broadly speaking, at the moment the fish bites, the point is flush with the line; then it begins to rotate until, once the fish is caught, the dragging strain exercised by the quarry may be strong enough to flatten the hook's bend. This is important to bear in mind when considering points for a hook.

A good hook subjected to strain should not bend or, worse still, split. Nevertheless, prolonged use in sea water eventually alters the elasticity and resistance

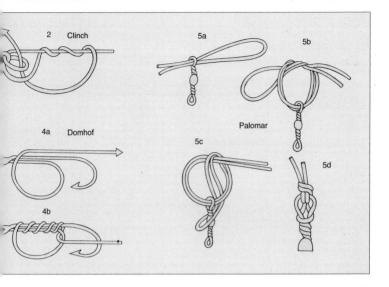

of even the best protected hooks. Discard rusty hooks immediately and pay particular attention to the attachments to terminal tackle and main line. One handy precaution in this respect is to rinse hooks in fresh water to get rid of any trace of bait before putting them back in the bag.

A final word of practical advice: always carry around a small file for sharpening hooks. Even the best hooks tend, with use, to become blunt and thus less effective, and it is frustrating to lose a catch because of a blunted point.

Knots play an important role in angling. Hooks, leaders, and lines are connected together by knots of various types, depending on their purpose. Remember that a knot, however strong, will reduce the overall resistance of a length of line by about 10 percent: the more knots, the greater the reduction. Soak the necessary section beforehand and tie the knots without tugging at the line. You can always get rid of a piece that is too long; otherwise you are likely to find yourself left with two short ends which prevent you tightening the knot properly, forcing you to start all over again.

Fishing knots, fortunately, bear a series of names which are in general use and mentioned in all books on the subject. Here we indicate their main uses:

—knots for fixing hooks, swivels, etc.: Uni-Knot System, Blood Knot, Spade End Whip, Domhol Knot (for hooks); Palomar Knot and Clinch Knot (for hooks and swivels); Spool Knot (for attaching the line to the spool); Needle Knot (for fly line);

—knots for joining two lines: Full Blood Knot, Water Knot or Surgeon's Knot, Shock Leader Knot, Loop to Loop, Bimini Twist (ideal for doubling the line);

—knots for forming loops: Double Overhand Loop, Blood Bight, Dropper Loop.

Having prepared the line, it has to be fitted, in varying measures, with leads. This will depend on whether the line is to be sunk deep or cast over a distance. Normal leads for weighing down light lines are normally used at sea for fish of average size.

For bottom fishing, it is possible to use drilled bullets of 3–10 g and boat leads.

Many surf-casters use pyramidal leads furnished with hooks designed to catch on to the bottom and hold the ballast firm without the risk of interference.

Equally effective are the spike-type, cylindrical or conical leads with four rear-facing fins. And the clock lead is also useful for bottom fishing, especially for flatfish.

Pear-shaped leads, available in a wide range of weights, from 1 oz to 2 lb (30 to 1,000 g), are suitable for many types of angling. The smaller ones are good for casting on sandy beds or even in rocky inlets while the bigger ones are used in fishing from a boat and often incorporate swivels.

For trolling, it is possible to use boat leads, drilled bullets or spiral leads of the Jardine type which will weigh down the line without need of a fixed attachment. In this way the weight can be inserted or removed at any point of the line. In any event, trolling leads are usually oblong in shape and have swivels welded at either end.

DOWNRIGGERS

A handy accessory for trolling is the downrigger. This is a small winch which supports a lead ball of 9–11 lb (4–5 kg), to which the line can be connected by means of an automatic release mechanism. The lead ball is lowered on a stout cable, together with the line, down to the depth desired for floating the bait. Thanks to this apparatus, leads are superfluous. In case of a bite, the line is released immediately to allow the normal fight with the quarry while the downrigger can be recovered quite simply by winch.

A particular type of downrigger is the so-called surfing or stim. This is a kind of shuttle with fixed fins to which the line is attached by means of a pulley. When the fish takes the bait, the line is released and the surfing re-emerges thanks to the inclined position of the fins.

A more modern type is the trolling pilot, which has a similar action, but is constructed differently, so that it can not only descend to a given depth but will also deviate to the right or left, enabling several lines to be trolled simultaneously, as if one were using submerged outriggers.

REELS

The reel is generally considered to be the most important part of fishing tackle. Many types of fish, particularly the larger species, would be practically impossible to catch were it not for the assistance of this item of equipment which saves untold time and effort.

Present-day reels are divided into two main categories: reels with fixed spools (spinning reels) and reels with rotating drums (baitcasting reels).

As we shall see, the two types have fairly well-defined uses, with little scope for overlapping, and their respective functions and limitations can thus be described quite precisely, much to the benefit of the angler.

Spinning reels

From the time it was invented, the spinning reel has brought about a veritable revolution in the fishing world, greatly facilitating the casting action for all concerned. The four external parts that make up the reel are the foot, the spool, the pick-up, and the handle or crank.

Both the foot and the crank should be strong enough to support the strain exercised on the line by the frightened fish and the corresponding action of retrieval. The foot should be perfectly adapted to the hand grip so as to form an integral part of the rod, while the crank should also be easily gripped by the fingers.

The function of the spool is to contain all the line necessary for playing the fish and should be full to the rim. From this point of view, it is similar to a reel of thread, the difference being that in fishing the line is alternately unwound and rewound. The spool of such reels, in fact, has a back and forth action along its

Spinning reels are made up of four main parts: the foot, the spool, the pick-up and the handle or crank.

own axis, parallel to the rod, thus making it easier for the full length of line to be rewound in neat spirals. This makes it possible for the line to unwind without any risk of entanglement as it is cast. Closely linked with the spool is the pick-up which, in its working position, prevents the nylon slipping out, facilitates casting and retrieval, and, when raised, permits the line to unwind freely with the thrust of the casting action.

These external parts are, in fact, common to all types of reel and not just the fixed-spool type. What really makes the difference between one model and another is the all-important internal mechanism, i.e. the gearing system which controls the movement of the spool, and the clutch.

The clutch is sufficiently important to merit a paragraph to itself. Despite the fact that in certain models the clutch is of the multiple-disk type, this part of the reel has nothing in common with the clutch of an automobile. In the present context it acts by friction and thus functions as a brake, so that it is virtually automatic. Its purpose is to pay out line to the fish at the very moment when it risks breakage under the combination of the quarry's resistance and the angler's physical efforts to bring it in. At this point the spool begins to revolve in a contrary direction to the rewinding, thus paying out the line before it can snap. At the same time, the connection with the crank is interrupted so that retrieval is impossible. When all the strain and effort is over, everything returns to normal and the fish, now near exhaustion, can be reeled in. This explains why it is never possible to catch a fish that weighs more than the breaking point of the line. The importance of the clutch should therefore be evident. When purchasing, you should make sure that it works perfectly and that you know how to use it. In some models it is fully automatic but in others it has to be regulated by hand, slackening or tightening the controls as necessary so that the line is only paid out when subjected to strong strain.

RATIO OF RETRIEVAL

Another important factor in choosing a reel is the ratio of retrieval, namely the number of turns of the spool for each turn of the crank. The lower this is, the less will be the quantity of line retrieved with each turn. To get an approximate idea of how much line will be recovered, it is worth bearing in mind that every turn of the spool will rewind about 4–6 in (10–15 cm) of line. A reel with a 3:1 ratio will therefore retrieve about 18 in (45 cm) of line for each turn of the crank; a 4:1 ratio will recover about 20 in (50 cm); and a 6:1 ratio approximately 30 in (75 cm). The gear ratio, moreover, will not only have a bearing on the amount of line rewound but also on the action of the fish. A spool with a high ratio is virtually useless for working a bait with a slow and constant movement. This should always be taken into consideration when planning to catch different species.

The spincasting reel is a variation of the spinny reel with a closed spool and no pick-up. The line runs through a hole at the front of the spool and is rewound by means of a rotating steel hinge. These reels are furnished with buttons for automatic regulation of the clutch and are mounted above the rod. They are very effective for fishing with light lines (0.10–0.15) but not recommended for stronger lines where there is a risk of damaging the delicate mechanism. Spincasting reels are more suited to freshwater fishing than saltwater.

Right: The famous Penn International 24-carat gold-plated reel. Below: A big-game reel, characterized by relatively low retrieval ratio.

The upper limit for spinning reels is about 30 lb (14 kg). They can also be used, therefore, for light trolling and with 0.50 lines. It is worth mentioning, however, although it may seem obvious, that a spool which normally accommodates 350–500 ft (100–150 m) of 0.20–0.30 nylon line cannot take the same amount of line of different thickness. For this reason it is advisable to have interchangeable spools (the operation is very simple). In better models, these are standard equipment, each accommodating a line of different diameter for coping with any type of angling.

The same holds true in the case of surf-casting, for which special reels with larger, conical spools are now on the market. These devices reduce the angle of friction between the monofilament and the upper rim, speeding up the existing velocity and allowing longer casts.

Baitcasting

These reels, designed for harder conditions ranging from surf-casting to big-game fishing, differ from the spinning reels in that the spool or drum rotates and is at a right angle to the rod axis. Outwardly it resembles a spool set between two disks and regulated by a handle, but appearance is in this instance deceptive. In fact, this is precision mechanism of the highest order, which in the most expensive and sophisticated models is made up of a hundred or so parts. The essential difference between this and the spinning reel is the presence of a brake.

Drum reels are generally made of plated steel (the Penn International, for example, is manufactured from a single piece of steel turned and plated with 24 carat gold), bronze, anodized aluminum or graphite to resist the corrosive action of sea water and the stresses to which they are subjected. Their retrieval ratio is usually quite low, between 2.5:1 and 4:1. This is why they are designed for the most laborious, albeit slow, retrievals. And in some models the retrieval ratio is automatically decreased as greater effort is expended.

The brake, which is the characteristic feature of these reels, and which cor-

Right: A fly-fishing reel. Opposite: A rotating drum reel for deep-sea fishing. These are reels with very precise types of mechanism.

responds in function to the clutch of the spinning reel, is, according to construction, either of the star or lever type.

Star-brake reels—Handbooks of deep-sea fishing generally describe the star-brake as being composed of a series of disks inserted into a rotating pinion attached to the drum handle. The disk action controls the braking, increasing or decreasing it as the angler turns the rudder-like wheel beneath the handle in one direction or the other. The famous Penn reels are the last to utilize this system, which allows for precise but jerky regulation. Yet many aficionados still consider them the most reliable overall, incredibly strong and capable of functioning after many years of use and maltreatment. The esteem in which they are held is demonstrated by the number of world records set up by sport fishermen with these reels.

Lever-brake reels—These reels are much simpler to use. All that is necessary is to push or pull a lever set close to the crank in order to increase or decrease, gradually and constantly, the braking force of the drum. The technique is similar, in the more streamlined models, to the disk brakes of a car. Another, smaller lever makes it possible to block the braking lever at the extreme breaking point applicable to the strength of line being used. The structure of lever-brake reels is nevertheless more complex, requiring great care in use, particularly in the retrieval stages, and for that reason they are best suited to experienced anglers.

Classification of reels

Having distinguished these reels on the basis of the type of brake fitted, it is important to note how the latter should be operated. Very often the line snaps because the angler forgets to regulate the brake while fishing, assuming that a preliminary calibration will be enough to overcome all problems. The fact is that, as the line is fed out, the ratio of forces between line, rod, and reel is altered

All rotating drum reels, like those used in this picture, are classified by conventional numbers that range from 1/0 to 16/0. For deep-sea angling the best models are 7/0 and above.

quite considerably. To avoid trouble, it is important to remember that the smaller the diameter of the line as it is paid out from the drum, the less the braking force necessary, but that this has to be increased when the line is retrieved.

All baitcasting reels are classified by conventional numbers ranging from 1/0 to 16/0. Those up to 3/0 are best used for surf-casting, while those from 4/0 to 6/0 are generally suited to trolling. For deep-sea trolling the 7/0 to 16/0 measurements should be used.

The most recent models for surf-casting are provided with a magnetic brake and devices to regulate the traction on the line while casting. This prevents the reel or, more properly, the drum continuing to rotate when the casting action is complete and feeding out more line which, in all likelihood, would become hopelessly entangled.

In the higher classes, the strength of the spool is of utmost importance since not only may it have to support a metal wire line, but the tension of a nylon line under traction, during the retrieval stage, causes it to behave like a length of elastic around a stiff support. To get some idea of the force exerted on the reel, just try winding a rubber band around your finger.

Make sure, too, that you do not drop or hit your rod against anything as this may unbalance the drum axis. Even the slightest knock can have serious consequences when, in the course of playing a large fish, you let out the line at a speed of 5,000 turns a minute.

Always take the greatest care in attaching the reels to the rod, fixing them tightly with the special steel braces supplied for models 9/0 and up; these reels are often furnished, too, with strong eyes that connect to the spring clips on the waist-lock to help take the strain.

BAITS

Of all aspects of fishing, few provide more opportunities for discussion and argument than baits. Every angler has his own infallible bait and is equally sure that his neighbor's bait has the unerring effect of attracting fish in the same way as the pied piper of Hamelin, with his magic instrument, attracted children. The truth is that in the complex world of angling, the only good bait is the one that catches fish.

It is probably fair to say that there has so far been no really painstaking, methodical, and scientific investigation into the relationship between bait and fish. We still know relatively little about fish and, although long angling experience has produced innumerable different baits, we do not really understand what attracts a particular fish and tempts it to bite. Nonetheless, some species will respond in a predictable way.

Some fish, such as barracuda and certain sharks, follow the bait in a straight line. Others, like dolphinfish, attack it sideways, surfacing so rapidly from the depths that they leap clean from the water. The beaked fish (swordfish, sailfish, and marlin) seize the bait from any position, but instead of biting on the spot, drag it along for short distances before swallowing it. Tuna attack almost exclusively from the front or the side. Whatever the method of approach, one thing is certain: baits only work because fish are fierce and greedy predators.

Baits are normally divided into two categories: natural and artificial.

Natural baits

The first rule for the use of natural baits (which also applies to artificial baits) is knowing what a fish eats, i.e. the nature and dimensions of its favorite prey. Although it may be amusing to catch a mackerel instead of a flounder, there is little satisfaction in hooking a shrimp when you are after marlin. These extreme examples are, of course, absurd but they make their point.

The sea is full of natural bait. Rocks and beaches or banks left exposed at low tide are excellent sources of live or fresh bait. Limpets, mussels, razor shells, crabs (including hermit crabs), and worms are all freely available to any angler prepared to collect and make use of them. Worms (especially lugworms and nereids), used whole or cut up, are baited on hooks of suitable size, with a long shank and barb that is wholly concealed, but with the point left to protrude. They are good for catching bass, gilthead, dentex, eels, mullet, mackerel, and flatfish (sole, plaice, and flounder). Such bait is best used live and fresh, but can also be used dead (and smelly), making an equally tasty tidbit.

The common earthworm may also be used for sea fishing, particularly in zones of brackish water where it is more likely that fish such as eels, flatfish, and occasionally mullet and gilthead, will identify it as possible prey. Never underestimate the reluctance of fish to approach unknown food. But be warned that the difference in salinity rapidly reduces an earthworm's vitality; the saltier the environment, the more quickly the worm loses water and swells up, transforming it into an unappetizing morsel.

Mollusks are another widespread form of bait. All reef fish appreciate them as food and lose few opportunities of nibbling the soft flesh of these normally inaccessible creatures. The solid body part of the limpet, in particular, makes an excellent bait. Perch and sea bream are fond of such bait, which will also tempt large gobies. Mussels, too, attract some species, including much-prized giltheads which feed on them regularly. Unlike limpets, the flesh of mussels is

very soft and watery, so it should be left to dry in the sun, preferably wrapped in gauze which acts as a kind of blotting paper, in order to make it firmer. Some anglers suggest inserting the hook into the valves after parting them slightly. The system guarantees a strong grip, but its efficacy seems doubtful in the case of giltheads which, although capable of munching the shell of a mussel, are not inclined to eat it shell and all.

The mollusks considered to be the classic forms of bait are the cephalopods: squid, octopus, and cuttlefish. These animals are normally a prey for many fish,

Right: Earthworms can also be used at sea.
Below: A hermit crab.
Opposite above: Octopus can be used as bait, even in pieces.
Opposite below: Typical limpet shells.

including big-game species, as indicated by the use of many artificial baits in the form of squid for marlin and sailfish.

These natural baits can be cut into pieces, attaching bits of tentacles or mantles to the hooks, fixing them close to the eye so that they do not slip out; or used whole, in which case their efficiency can be increased by inserting a chemical light "candle" under the mantle, which magnifies phosphorescence and the typical color variations of the cephalopods. The widespread use of freezing equipment also has the great advantage of making this form of bait, as well as

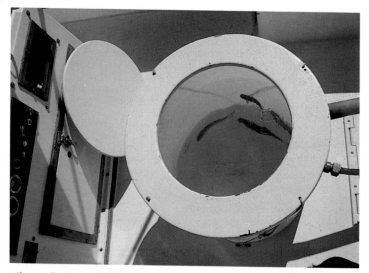

other mollusks, available whenever it is needed. It is even possible to use them live, fixing them to the hook by their tail.

As a rule it is preferable to reserve squid for surface trolling and cuttlefish for seabed trolling, whereas octopus, mostly used in pieces, is excellent for catching reef fish. There are, of course, exceptions to the rule, but this breakdown is based roughly on the actual biology of the bait and the fact that the fish to be caught are accustomed to their prey behaving in a very precise manner. It is common experience for a tuna or a marlin to encounter a squid swimming rapidly close to the surface, whereas a similar meeting with an octopus would be unlikely and bound to raise suspicion on their part. The same applies to fish of the seabed or the reef which are more accustomed to the presence of cuttlefish and ocotopus.

Crustaceans, especially crabs, hermit crabs, and shrimp, are ideal bait for medium-depth and bottom fishing and to catch white bream, eels, gilthead, bass, etc. Provided they are fixed by the tail or other non-vital body part, they can keep looking lively for some time so as to arouse the continual interest of the fish.

The old saying, "Big fish eat little fish," is perfectly valid when it comes to using fish as lures. Whether alive or dead, and particularly for trolling, they are, in fact, the ideal bait. Examination of the stomach contents of most large and medium-sized fish reveals that smaller species invariably form part of the diet. The most suitable species are those with oily, tasty flesh, such as sardines or herrings, or with firm flesh and a tapered shape, such as grouper, mackerel, horse mackerel, garfish, small skipjack, and bonito. The choice is quite large, which explains why these are the most commonly used natural baits.

On larger, better equipped boats, there are small tanks to accommodate live bait fished during the first few hours from setting out. Mackerel and small tuna are favorite live quarry and these are prepared and baited without too much loss of vitality. This technique, however, requires a good deal of skill in preparation. The bait has to be fixed to the hook securely yet in such a manner as not to damage any vital organs. For drifting, the fish are usually attached by the lip or close to the dorsal fin. For trolling the operation is more complicated and also more cruel, since a hook with thread has to be inserted above the eyes, stitched and attached to the fishing hook. This is not for the faint-hearted and frequently breaches legislation governing the protection of animals.

Great care is also needed in preparing dead fish to ensure that once in the water they do not assume unnatural positions as a result of rigor mortis. The baiting method most commonly used is to pierce the fish, through the belly and out from the nostrils or the tail, with a long darning needle. The terminal tackle, with hook connected, is then pulled inside the fish, leaving as much as necessary to protrude. Lacking such a needle, the point of the hook can simply be inserted through the gill, then manipulated in such a way that it slides further in, and the point eventually pulled out from the belly. The jaws are then closed around the terminal tackle with a strong length of line wrapped in regular spirals. This baiting technique may be adapted for the preparation of mackerel and garfish, where it is necessary to cut through the long snout. A similar procedure applies to grouper, in which a ball of lead is fixed to the head, this being connected to the bottom of the line so that the bait still remains submerged and, when pulled along, perfectly imitates the swimming motion of a live fish.

One trick often used to give a natural appearance to a dead fish is to split the spine in several places. This is done by means of a strong pair of scissors, so that the spine can be cut without causing too much damage to the fish, or with an instrument known as a deboner, which is simply a steel tube with a V-shaped opening and sharp edges. After this is inserted into the mouth of the fish, it is

Right: Various ways of baiting dead fish.
Opposite: A flask for keeping live bait.

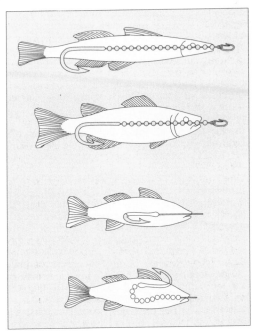

pushed toward the tail and gently rotated so that it gradually rips the flesh from the spine. When it almost reaches the area of the anal fin, a quick movement bends the rear part of the fish and cracks the spine, which can then be removed. If the operation is properly done, this remains inside the deboner. The deboner has to be complemented by the use of special hooks (the system is known as Pompanette, after the American firm holding the patent) mounted on steel cable with balls similar to the chains which are used at home as attachments to basin and bath plugs. These hooks are introduced into the body of the fish by means of a long pointed rod, itself fitted with a hook, and maneuvered into position. Then it is just a matter of fastening the end of the Pompanette rig to the terminal tackle, stitching the mouth of the fish and waiting for results. It is possible to prepare two or three hooks in this fashion inside the same fish, either separately or attached by the eye to one another.

A very much more complicated procedure, requiring considerable dexterity, is to slice the fish in half to remove the spine and then to restitch it after inserting the hook or hooks.

When dealing with beaked fish such as swordfish, sailfish, and marlin, it is essential to bait the hook upside-down in relation to the direction of the troll. The reason for this strange operation is that the above-mentioned fishes have the habit of turning the bait round before swallowing it, so that if it were mounted in the traditional way, it might slip off without taking hold.

It is possible to use multiple baits (e.g. the Newfoundland tandem system, named after the place where the method originated), in which case one of them bears the hook while the other tempts the fish to consume the apparently easy prey in its entirety. For drifting, smaller fish (notably sardines) may be used, attaching several to the same hook through the eye.

Yet another natural bait is what is called strip bait, whereby the fish is filleted. The advantage of this method is that everything can be prepared beforehand on land, and that the bait can be kept fresh in the boat's refrigerator or in a thermal container. To give them a more natural appearance, the strips are some-

Right and opposite: Various flies for that type of fishing. Designed originally for freshwater work, they can also be used at sea.

times placed on a special stiff metal frame which prevents them from curling up. Apart from fish, it is possible to use stout strips of pigskin, sometimes colored red, which are attached directly to the hook or together with artificial lures.

In certain circumstances, an alternative practice with natural bait is the scattering of so-called ground bait, or chum. This entails the use of tasty tidbits to entice fish from some distance away. As a rule, this bait consists of scraps of fish, mollusks, and crab, chopped up and mixed with bran or sawdust and fish oil so that it all makes a fairly solid and strong-smelling pulpy mass. The finished product is packed in jute bags or finely perforated receptacles which are submerged in the water or hung from the sides of the boat. Waves and currents will then carry the particles of odorous food over considerable distances, forming a path for hungry fish to follow until they reach the proper bait. Sharks are particularly tempted by such offerings if there is an additional sprinkling of blood. As for smaller fish, care must be taken to ensure that the food particles are not too large, otherwise they will merely provide a meal for the prey, distracting them from the bait.

To complement the chum, it is essential to drop sardines or pieces of fish into the sea, at regular intervals, to attract large species such as tuna, accustomed to following schools of bluefish, and to keep them hovering around the boat.

Artificial baits

Artificial baits or lures usually imitate a natural one, as is evident from their typical shape, which is designed to emphasize their likeness to living organisms. The world of artificial lures is just as varied as that of natural baits, and much more difficult to catalog. For example, dimensions alone can range from miniscule flies to Kona Heads measuring 15 in (40 cm), which is enough to give some

idea of the variety available. Fortunately, certain types tend to be used more than others; furthermore, it is possible to divide artificial baits into imitations and non-imitative originals.

Imitations

FLIES—Many of the flies devised for freshwater fishing are applicable as well to sea fishing, and many are created specifically for the latter purpose. Such artificial lures include streamers, surface poppers, and leaded flies for depth. Among the many models used (which often bear evocative and imaginative names) are the Glass Minnow, Dog Nobbler, Cockroach, Sally Micky, Bluetail, Pink Multiwing, Pink Shrimp, Marabu, Lefty's Deceiver, Caterpillar, Keel Hook, Blonde, Honey Blonde, and Rhodes Streamer (see also the chapter on Fly Fishing).

PLUGS—These very popular artificial baits are designed, often with extreme precision, to resemble small fishes. They come in various shapes and sizes, from 1¼ in (3–5 cm) to more than 8 in (20 cm), and may be floaters or sinkers. A common feature of virtually all plugs is the presence of a forward vane, adjustable in some models, so that during retrieval it is forced downward; thus the skillful angler can play the line in and out alternately to convey the wobbling movement of a fish that is hurt or in difficulties. To make them even more effective, many plugs have mobile eyes, and some are furnished with balls or other devices hidden inside which, as they move, produce vibrations to attract predators. And others have a hinged body, divided into two or three segments, so that they adopt a wriggling, darting movement which is very lifelike. Plugs are used both for trolling (at speeds of up to 8 knots) and for spinning.

MINNOWS—These look similar to plugs and also imitate small fishes. They are normally silver in color and made of one piece. They can be used for the same purpose as plugs.

SAND EELS—These artificial lures are made of plastic to imitate the slender, soft-finned, long-snouted fishes—in no way resembling the true eels—which are favorite prey of many large species. Some are perfect in shape and color-

Right: The "jig" bait, suitable for trolling. Opposite: Colored trolling baits. Colors are essential for attracting specific fish.

ation, while others, at least when not moving, bear little resemblance to cephalopods. Nevertheless they are effective for trolling, especially in the case of tuna and albacore, and particularly in conjunction with strip bait or pigskin.

SPINNERS—Shaped like fish, these artificial lures come in various colors (generally white combined with another color) and are dragged along at a distance of 30 ft (10 m) or more from the boat, acting by reflection to produce the effect of fish feeding at the surface, thus rousing and attracting predators from the depths. Spinners have no hooks and may be paid out in the sea, independently of other lines, and retrieved after the real bait has been taken, or they can be mounted on the fishing line together with other artificial or natural baits.

Originals

KONA HEADS—The most commonly used artificial lures for trolling are certainly those derived from the Hawaiian Kona Heads. This type of bait originally took the form of an object with a heavy wooden or metal head, to which various kinds of strips of material were attached. It was obviously a crude imitation of a squid, yet so effective that it has nowadays come to be imitated in innumerable more sophisticated versions.

Large or small, plain or brightly colored, the modern Kona Heads all behave in the same way, being dragged along to give the semblance of a swimming fish or squid. Despite their unanimity of function, the various models differ in shape of head (single, double or triple, with or without holes), which determines their performance in the water, and in construction material (nylon or steel). The colors, too, are important, many of them tending to be bluish for tuna, blue and white for skipjack, silver and white for grouper and green and yellow for pomfret.

JIGS—Smaller and lighter than the Kona Heads (some of which weigh almost 1 lb [400 g]), though not very different from them in conception, jigs, like streamers, are small furry or feathered lures under a variety of imaginative names, with a heavy head and tails or skirts of plastic which give them a soft, fluid movement. Jigs are used for trolling tuna, albacore, skipjack, bonito, pomfret, horse

mackerel, and bass, and for casting. These lures have given rise to a special form of angling known as jigging, whereby the up and down movement of the rod brings the bait rapidly up from the bottom to the surface, and vice versa.

SPOONS—Far removed from the aforementioned types of lure are the metallic baits in the form of rotating or undulating spoons. These are pieces of metal designed to be sunk and dragged jerkily through the water to produce vibrations that will attract fish. They differ in their action. The rotating types are so constructed that they revolve around themselves when dragged along, while the undulating types move in an irregular, rolling fashion. An important consideration when choosing a spoon is to make sure that they behave in the water as might be predicted. As a rule, spoons are made to be used with casting rods, but they can also be employed in light and medium trolling for cod and barracuda. For sea angling, preference should go to the heavier undulating types and to the revolving types with a brightly colored elongated vane completed by white feathers.

The latter are frequently used as baits in their own right and give good results. Typical of these are the streamers obtained by furnishing the hooks with a collar of feathers, which proves highly effective when fishing for mackerel. Also worthy of note are the so-called Japanese feathers, consisting of a head of colored lead, with or without eyes, and a tuft of feathers. Such lures are excellent for fishing tuna and skipjack, particularly when trolled at the right speed and distance. One method recommended by professionals is to troll with white feathers up to midday and after three o'clock, and to switch during the intervening hours to red, yellow, and black or greenish-yellow feathers.

Below: Various types of spoons. Opposite: Examples of spoons to sit on the bottom or to be trolled in fits and starts.

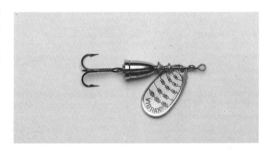

BOATS

We come now to the types of vessel suitable for fishing at sea, though not necessarily at any great distance from the shore.

Provided proper measures are taken, even a small boat or dinghy will serve for the basic purpose of reaching good, uncrowded fishing grounds. The boat must be properly equipped with everything required by law (life-jackets, flares, halyards, life-rafts, radio, etc.). If you own the boat, make sure you know the possibilities and limitations of the vessel, and avoid taking unnecessary risks. If you are not suitably equipped, do not go fishing at night. Always obtain detailed information about sea conditions and weather forecasts. As a general rule, remember that a large boat will perform every bit as well as a small boat, but not vice versa. With a vessel of 30 ft (10 m) or more, you can go trolling, drifting or bottom fishing, either along the coast or several hundred miles from shore—forms of angling that you cannot normally do from a smaller boat, albeit there are exceptions. Crossing the Atlantic by rubber dinghy has indeed been done but is not generally recommended!

Fishing vessels, in the broadest sense, can range from the most sophisticated craft to small dinghies fitting on to the roof rack of a car. Only two people are needed to launch such a boat and set off for the day's fishing, not necessarily a great distance but far enough from shore to reach any convenient rocks, headlands or sandbanks where fish abound.

Furnished with an outboard motor capable of generating a fair head of steam, a small craft is ideal for a quiet day's sport, casting, drifting or bottom fishing from the anchored boat. Although as a rule you will be navigating in full sight and in daylight, it is essential to pinpoint certain landmarks, particularly when the coastline is low and uniform, to avoid getting lost. Even when not venturing far from shore, do not forget to take adequate supplies. Outboard motors are reliable but can sometimes break down at inopportune moments. Take along at least two reserve sparking plugs and tools for changing them. Do not forget the oars. They are not optional items, and although your progress may be slow, in an emergency they make all the difference. Bear in mind that weather and sea conditions may change very quickly and that lightweight craft can be buffeted by wind and waves. If you are drift fishing, check your position in relation to the coast at regular intervals. Such advice may sound obvious, but many an angler has ended up much farther from shore than planned through not taking proper account of weather factors.

Keeled vessels with trimarans, of the *Dory* or *Boston Whaler* type, are very seaworthy and excellent for fishing. The larger models are in every way the equal of some medium-sized cabin craft as far as fittings, comfort, and price are concerned, but even the smaller ones of 16 ft (5 m) perform well. The main advantage of these boats is the amount of available space, their structure being such that virtually the entire craft can be fitted out for fishing. The central seat for the helmsman has good storage capacity and there is ample space, too, in the forepeak and afterpeak. The rod holders can be fixed easily to the stern and thus the lines can be trolled without having to be held all the time; the transom is sufficiently wide for two motors to be installed, one of them for slow trolling. What with the additional miniaturization of electronic equipment, it is very simple to incorporate radar and radio, which increase safety and make it possible to locate the best fishing grounds.

Similar observations apply to rubber craft, especially the larger ones with a

A typical fishing boat. Extremely stable, it is an excellent vessel for trolling.

rigid keel, which in many instances are fully equipped. Of course, they are basically rubber tubes filled with air, but provided you take care not to get hooks caught up in them and do not use them to go after sharks, they are very reliable.

Many owners of boats that can operate 6 miles or so from shore will sooner or later feel the inclination, if not the urge, to be more adventurous and attempt deep-sea fishing, whether it be trolling, drifting or still fishing.

A good boat for this purpose needs to be safe, stable, comfortable (everyone now and then needs a hot coffee, a cold drink or a shower), fast, and maneuverable. It is possible to troll under sail, but in most conditions it is very difficult, no matter how responsive the yacht, to follow all the twists and turns of the quarry.

As to speed, this should not be a prime consideration for purposes of trolling. It is obviously an advantage to be able to get to your destination as quickly as possible, but a marine counterpart of the Ferrari is not necessarily the answer, for it is not well suited to the very slow speeds that are sometimes required for hours on end in the course of trolling. This point should be kept in mind when choosing a boat in the first instance.

A deep-sea fishing craft should not measure less than 26 ft (8 m) and should have a very broad transom. This, in fact, is where most of the fishing activity takes place, where you expect to find the fighting chair, the rod holders, the gaff, and all the other items needed for the fishing exercise.

Speed may not be a determining factor here, but maneuverability most certainly is. Given the combined action of the motors (and it is always best to have two of them on such boats) and the rudder, the vessel should respond easily to

55

the skipper's controls. As we shall see in the chapter that deals specifically with deep-sea fishing, coordination of the angler's actions, after hooking the quarry, and the course of the boat as it follows the movements of the fish during retrieval of the line, is vital for the success of the whole operation. A miscalculated turn or a moment of indecision in applying a burst of speed or slowing down can result in a broken line.

In this context, it is useful to have a so-called flying bridge, a high position from which the boat controls can be operated. An advantage of the flying bridge is to afford a broader survey of the surroundings and a quicker sighting of the prey.

When you start going in seriously for deep-sea fishing, you will soon be aware of how much space is occupied by the rods, not to mention the reels and the lines. It will not always be possible to fix a rack for the neat arrangement of rods until they are needed, so the alternative is to use rod holders. These are tubes, pre-fixed to a suitable inclination, designed to accommodate the handle and to hold the rod in the right direction. So the choice of position is important (normally the edge of the well-deck), as is the correct inclination (60° is the optimum). The trade nowadays caters for every contingency, including holders that can be moved or orientated, and of proven convenience.

Mention should also be made of outriggers. These are very prominent fitments which arouse the curiosity of laymen and which, although often mounted, are seldom used. They are long spars with a rounded cross-section, wider at the base, which narrow toward the tip, placed at a height of 16–23 ft (5–7 m). The outriggers are mounted on mobile frames which serve to support supplementary lines, away from the boat, which can be combined with the lines normally trolled from the stern without any risk of them getting crossed and tangled in knots.

Left: Typical fishermen's superstructure.

As for the electronic gear, it should suffice to say that radio, radar, and sounders are nowadays normal equipment on any vessel of reasonable size and that the only problem is choosing the most suitable ones for maximum safety.

There are, in addition, numerous accessories that you will come to appreciate with time and experience. In this context, the only rule that you should really respect when fitting out a boat for fishing is to see that all is logically and neatly arranged. The old saying, "A place for everything and everything in its place," is especially apt for anglers, and its truth will be evident when, in the midst of playing a fish, you have to find a gaff, a new leader, another spool, the bait tin, a deboner or a knife.

Above: Rod-holding hooks on board a fishing boat.

*Above: A vessel adapted
for trolling. Note the rod-
holders directed
outward and the wake
that indicates the boat's
fairly slow speed.
Opposite: Fly-fishing
from a small boat.*

FLY FISHING AT SEA

Despite the fact that freshwater fly fishing is attracting new enthusiasts daily, this method of angling is still not extremely popular at sea, primarily because few fishermen are sufficiently aware of its possibilities in saltwater.

There is, nevertheless, a clear distinction to be made between fly fishing in lakes and rivers and at sea, based on a very simple biological truth. Freshwater flies are, in fact, usually similar to real insects. This is because the fish know exactly the types of insect that they are tempted to catch. Flies of strange shapes or colors, entirely different to those which normally occur at a particular season, will be ignored. Things are quite different at sea. Insects are very poorly represented in this environment and constitute an extremely small proportion of the diet of marine fishes, even those that live in brackish water, which contains many more insects. It is true that certain insects, propelled by the wind or during the course of migrations, may end up far from the coasts, and that some species (*Halobates*) live happily in the middle of the Sargasso Sea, but these are exceptions to the rule.

The function of the fly at sea is therefore to arouse the aggressive instincts of the fish, suggesting the notion of food without necessarily resembling a known prey. Seen in this light, fly fishing offers a wide range of opportunities and provides ample scope for the angler's ingenuity. But what applies here just as it does to freshwater fishing is the need to master the none too easy technique of casting.

As to equipment, experts usually recommend graphite rods at least 10 ft (3 m) long, capable of casting class 9–10 line, that is with the first 30 ft (9 m) weighing from 15·6 to 18·1 g. The reel should be strong and salt-resistant. The fixed spool needs to let out at least 660 ft (200 m) of nylon plus the typical fly line. The latter, especially when fishing in zones with natural obstacles, can be lengthened with a series of nylon tippets to prevent breakage, which is annoying and costly. For example, you can use a leader composed of three tippets,

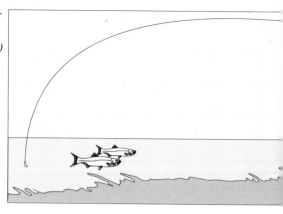

Diagram of casting in fly-fishing. For this type of angling the rod must be at least 10 feet (3 meters) in length. One of the best saltwater fish caught in this way is the tarpon.

each of 3 ft (1 m) and in decreasing diameters of 0.65, 0.50 and 0.40, or alternatively, one of five segments (four of 75 cm and one of 100 cm) in diameters of 0.60, 0.50, 0.45, 0.35 and 0.25.

Assuming you have mastered the skill of casting 65 ft (20 m) and more, the only remaining problems are those of choosing your fly and fly line. In shallow water, and for catching fish that tend to feed at the surface, you will need a floating fly line; in water over 6 ft (2 m) deep, the rapidly sinking form of fly line is preferable.

As for flies, these should be clearly visible, though not necessarily colored. A dark fly carefully trolled at dusk over the face of a calm lake is more likely to hook a gilthead than is a white or yellow fly. It may be deduced from this that skillful maneuvering of the bait is what will attract the fish, which means getting the fly to move in the appropriate manner, ideally by imitating its natural counterpart. Anyone who has seen a large insect falling into a lake or the sea will have noticed that it makes a series of short flights before dropping back to the surface. If you can get the bait to imitate this jerky action, the chances of success are good; and another ruse is to retrieve the fly in such a way that it looks like a small fish attempting to regain its burrow. Where types of fly are concerned, a general guideline is to use weighted flies for fish accustomed to feed on the bottom. For tarpon (*Megalops atlantica*), a typical quarry for fly fishermen, the bait should be mounted as a streamer so as to resemble a fish.

Examples of fishing

Anyone who has attempted to catch a tarpon with a fly can hardly wait to try again. Once hooked, the fish fights relentlessly, leaping clean out of the water, sometimes for distances of nearly 10 ft (3 m), in its struggle to get free.

Fly fishing for tarpon requires a 9-ft (2·7-m) fiberglass or graphite rod, capable of casting lines of classes 11 or 12. The reel should have a good brake and its spool should contain 650 ft (200 m) of dacron backing of 20–30 lb (9–13·5 kg), followed by a WFS type fly line of classes 11 or 12. The leader will therefore comprise 5 ft (1·5 m) of 0·60, 14 in (35 cm) of 0·40 and 12 in (30 cm) of 0·90 nylon fiber. Although this arrangement may seem a bit odd, the strength of the line will always depend on that of the weakest tippet, in whatever position it occurs. Some experts carry the breakage point to 12 lb (2·25 kg) but this seems to go

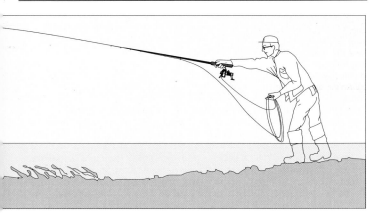

beyond purely sporting requirements.

Flies used for tarpon fishing are streamers made of yellow or black feathers with a red head mounted on 5/0 hooks. The line should be cast only when the prey is sighted, trying to land the fly close to the fish. The rod should be held low and parallel to the water. The tarpon's hit is fairly variable: sometimes it resembles that of a trout, sometimes it attacks the bait head-on.

The strike needs to be decisive, for the tarpon's mouth is leathery and not easily pierced by the point of the hook. As soon as it feels itself struck, the fish performs a series of upward leaps, followed by a rapid run out to sea. Lower the rod at every leap and give the fish plenty of line. This procedure, contrary to the norm, aims to prevent the tarpon hitting the line with its body, which is covered with large, strong scales. As soon as it begins its run, however, try to hold it back by setting the drag close to the breaking point. If possible, it is always better to play a tarpon from an unanchored boat, otherwise the line may tangle with the anchor rope. There are stories of anglers being dragged half a mile or more by a hooked tarpon. When the exhausted fish is close enough to the boat, it tends either to swim underneath or settle on the bottom. So it has to be encouraged to move by pulling the rod to the left or right or by repeatedly tapping it upward. Only when the tarpon is lying on its side near the boat can it be considered well and truly caught. If not in too bad shape, it can then be released, since its flesh is tough and not very tasty.

Another ideal species for fly fishing is the bonefish (*Albula vulpes*). The recommended tackle consists of a graphite rod just over 6 ft (2 m) long, a reel with 650 ft (200 m) of 8 lb (3·6 kg) nylon backing line and a class 6–7 fly line. The small hooks (1/0–2/0) should be mounted with streamers or shrimp. The best time for fishing is when the tide is on the turn. Given its behavior (bonefish swim in small schools and feed on the bottom with tails out of water), it is quite easy to land the bait close by. The whole operation is further simplified by the fact that the bonefish frequents the clear waters of tropical lagoons.

The fish does not always use the same approach. Sometimes it nibbles at the bait, sometimes it grabs it greedily. Either way, it pays not to apply too much pressure. Let it run, as it will the moment it takes the hook, and check, though not too hard, when it gets to the end of the run. Do not underestimate its fairly small size (4–10 lb [1·5–4·5 kg]), for it is capable of sudden and repeated bursts

INTERNATIONAL IGFA REGULATIONS FOR FLY FISHING

The International Game Fish Association (IGFA) has established a code of practice for fly fishing which has to be adhered to by anyone wishing to have their catch recognized for record purposes.

LINE

Any type of fly line and backing may be used. The breaking strength of the fly line and backing are not restricted.

LEADER

Leaders must conform to generally accepted fly fishing customs.

A leader includes a class tippet and, optionally, a shock tippet. A butt or taper section between the fly line and the class tippet shall also be considered part of the leader, and there are no limits on its length, material or strength. A class tippet must be made of nonmetallic material and either attached directly to the fly or to the shock tippet if one is used. The class tippet must be at least 15 in (38·10 cm) long (measured inside connecting knots). With respect to knotless, tapered leaders, the terminal 15 in (38·10 cm) will also determine tippet class. There is no maximum length limitation. The breaking strength determines the class of the tippet.

A shock tippet, not to exceed 12 in (30·48 cm) in length, may be added to the class tippet and tied to the lure. It can be made of any type of material, and there is no limit on its breaking strength. The shock tippet is measured from the eye of the hook to the single strand of class tippet and includes any knots used to connect the shock tippet to the class tippet.

In the case of a tandem hook fly, the shock tippet shall be measured from the eye of the leading hook.

ROD

A rod shall not measure less than 6 ft (1·82 m) in overall length. Any rod that gives the angler an unsporting advantage will be disqualified.

REEL

The reel must be designed expressly for fly fishing and cannot be used in casting the fly other than as a storage spool for the line. There are no restrictions on gear ratio or type of drag employed except where the angler would gain an unfair advantage. Electric or electronically operated reels are prohibited.

HOOKS

A conventional fly may be dressed on a single or double hook or two single hooks in tandem. The second hook in any tandem fly must not extend beyond the wing material. The eyes of the hooks shall be no farther than 6 in (15·24 cm) apart. Treble hooks are prohibited.

LURES

The lure must be a recognized type of artificial fly, which includes streamer, bucktail, tube fly, wet fly, dry fly, nymph, popper, and bug. The use of any other type of lure or natural bait, either singularly or attached to the fly, is expressly prohibited. The fact that a lure can be cast with a fly rod is not evidence in itself that it fits the definition of a fly. The use of any lure designed to entangle or foul-hook a fish is prohibited.

GAFFS AND NETS

Gaffs and nets used to land a fish must not exceed 8 ft (2·48 m) in overall length. (When fishing from a bridge, pier or other high stationary structure, this length limitation does not apply.) The use of a flying gaff is not permitted. Only a single hook is permitted on any gaff. Harpoon or lance attachments are prohibited.

An angler fly-fishing in a stream. Although this is a technique originally intended for freshwater, it is highly effective, too, for sea angling.

of speed which have earned it the nickname "dynamite fish." Within a few seconds, it can use up 600 ft (180 m) of line, and if the tension is too great, one of these runs can break it.

An unlikely candidate for fly fishing is the sailfish (*Istiophorus platypterus*). Not only is it a very satisfactory quarry for normal trolling with light and medium tackle, but it also provides plenty of excitement for anglers prepared to resort to a more unorthodox method.

Obviously a heavier rod will be needed than for bonefish, ideally a fiberglass model of about 9 ft (2·7–2·9 m). The reel has to be of large capacity with an easily controllable clutch. The spool will be mounted with a backing of 800–1,000 ft (250–300 m) followed by a class 12 SWT type fly line with a nylon leader of 20 lb (9 kg) and 2/0 hook. In this case, too, bait can be a streamer, considering that these fish are hearty feeders.

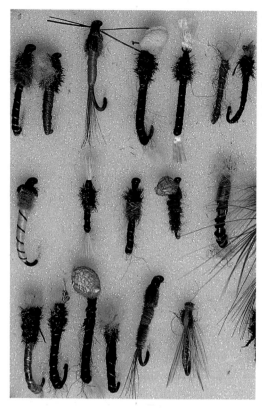

Flies should be clearly visible but not necessarily colored. The fly is drifted along the water surface in such a way that it imitates the movement of an insect that has tumbled into the sea. Opposite: Diagram to illustrate surf-casting.

As a rule, sailfish, once they take the bite, perform series of acrobatic leaps, offering the fierce resistance which makes them such an exciting prey for sporting anglers. If the fish comes very close, it is best to hold the rod parallel to the water surface, gradually slackening the tension but always endeavoring to retrieve as much line as possible. Obviously, with such a light line, the struggle may continue for some time, but fortunately sailfish are somewhat lacking in stamina and sooner or later will come floating alongside the boat, defeated at last. A fly for a sailfish would seem to be a fair exchange and worth all the trouble.

SURF-CASTING

For some anglers surf-casting is virtually a philosophy of life. Here the contact with nature is both physical and mental, for the surf-casting fisherman needs to understand the sea in all its changing moods, to interpret the movement of the waves, the course of the currents, the development and composition of the depths, and finally to synthesize all this information in order to decide how and where to cast the bait. Add to this the fact that, more often than not, this is done in rough sea conditions, under a gray and rain-threatening sky, or at night amid the solitude of sand and shingle, and it will be evident that successful surf-casting depends essentially on acceptance of natural laws.

This type of fishing originates, and is mainly practiced, along the vast stretches of shoreline fronting the Atlantic and the Pacific where angling conditions are ideal.

Bays enclosing long stretches of sandy coastline constitute ideal areas for surf-casting, and the points where the fish congregate are the hollows and canyons scooped out, at varying distances from the shore, by the constant advance and retreat of the waves. For this reason, understanding what goes on in the sea is much enhanced by some familiarity with the local coastline and offshore waters. In summer, such information is not difficult to obtain with the aid of mask and flippers. Knowledge of what lies below the surface enables the keen angler to interpret correctly the signals that are continually relayed by the sea. It is also important to have information on the tides. The currents which form when the tide turns often indicate to the fish that the time has come to go hunting, with particularly favorable conditions to be found in the turbulent waters at the mouths of rivers.

This, of course, is all theory, so what in practice justifies the need for all this patient waiting and study? In rough sea conditions, the beds, especially when composed of mobile sand or mud, are disturbed, all the more when they are near the surface and subjected to powerful wave action. This means that buried mollusks, worms, crustaceans, and other animals are uncovered and made available for a vast range of fishes, including large predators. Obviously the at-

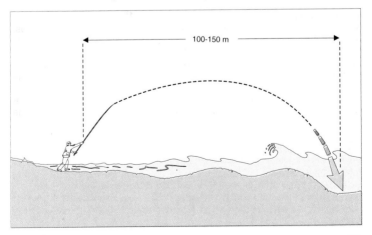

100-150 m

tention span of many fish is diminished by the poor visibility and the unaccustomed sounds of the waves. The abundance of food is an open invitation, and a well-prepared bait will be treated as just another morsel, to every angler's delight.

In addition to the signals derived from the sea, much can be learned, too, from those transmitted by the marine creatures themselves. The insistent flight of gulls above a restricted zone is a clear sign that schools of small fish are present, pursued by predators. A noise similar to the pelting of rain is frequently caused by such fish making sudden leaps out of the water to escape the attacks of a large bass.

Technique

From the viewpoint of technique, surf-casting is regarded by some anglers as a normal form of deep-sea fishing, at least when using lines with natural bait; but the existence of specialized material and instruction is sufficient to justify the claim that surf-casting is a technique in its own right.

Moreover, this method of angling is nowadays codified so as to warrant it being divided into four categories: super-light, light, semi-heavy, and heavy surf-casting.

Each category requires increasingly complex tackle. In heavy surf-casting, for example, rods up to 16 ft (5 m) long require the use of both hands and are capable of casting weights of 3½–7 oz (100–200 g) a distance of up to 650 ft (200 m) from shore. Obviously, this is a form of sport that requires considerable strength and entails special training.

As regards the characteristics of rods for the individual classes, the reader is referred to the chapters that deal with these accessories. This is the place for observations of a more general nature.

Surf-casting rods, no matter the category concerned, must possess certain basic characteristics, i.e. they must be lightweight and balanced. These are fundamental requirements, for the sport involves numerous casts during a day's fishing and several hours will be spent with rod actually in hand.

The action, i.e. the shape assumed by the rod under stress, is of vital importance. In this case it should be an almost perfect and uniform parabola so as to allow the lure, under the action of the splice, to accelerate gradually, gently at the start, then more strongly and eventually with maximum power. All this must happen without any jerking, to avoid any whiplash effect at the end of the line which might cause it to break or at least for the bait to be lost as it is brought up short.

In this context, too, the guide rings must be of good quality, not only made of materials with low friction but also of adequate diameter for the line to unwind without interruption. The tip ring must therefore be of a diameter equal to that of the spool. It is obvious that the other rings (in a surf-casting rod there are four in addition to the one at the tip) should be proportionately wide, tending to increase progressively, from tip to butt, by an inch or so (2–3 cm) every time, e.g. 3, 4, 5, 6 in (7, 9, 12, 15 cm) or 2, 3, 4, 5 in (5, 7, 9, 12 cm).

The reel is a necessary complement to the surf-casting rod. Fixed-spool reels may be used for light classes while rotating-drum reels are virtually obligatory for the heavy classes. In either case the reel must be capable of holding 500–650 ft (150–200 m) of monofilament, the diameter of which will vary according to the size of the rod. On average, 0.20 lines are suitable for the super-light class, 0.35 lines for the light class and lines of 0.50 and above for heavy casting.

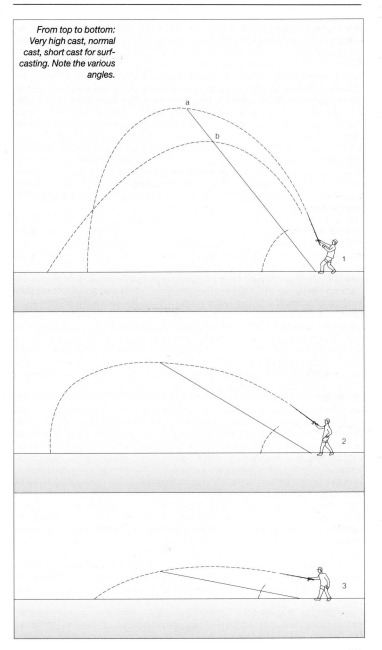

From top to bottom: Very high cast, normal cast, short cast for surf-casting. Note the various angles.

This type of fishing often entails the use of a shock leader at the end of the line, namely a leader of greater diameter designed to absorb the thrust of the casting action.

Hooks should be selected in relation to the fish to be caught but preferably of a long-shanked type for better tenure of the bait.

Leads for surf-casting, as a rule mobile or positioned beneath the line, must always be heavy, flat or pyramidal in shape, and often furnished with grapnels for fixing to the bottom and holding the lure steady.

The typical surf-casting line has a leader fixed by swivel to the main line, with the lead underneath, surmounted by two or three drops about 12 in (30 cm) long and 20–24 in (50–60 cm) apart. The choice of bait depends on the kind of fish to be caught. Generally speaking, flatfish and small sea bass are fond of worms and crabs, as well as strips of squid and mollusks; larger bass and rays appreciate fishes and squid, either in large pieces or whole. Surface or semisinking poppers and plugs can also be used, in which case the retrieval operation is very important.

Examples of fishing

The sea bass is one of the traditional game fish of continental seas. For surf-casting it is possible to use undulating spoons of 2–2¾ in (5–7 cm) with a light sinker just as successfully as more ambitious baits such as eels and live grouper. The leader should be 0.35–0.40 mounted with forged 5 or 7 hooks. A medium-heavy rod 11½ ft (3·5 m) long should be fitted with a reel either of the fixed spool or rotating drum type, provided it is capable of holding at least 500 ft (150 m) of 0.30–0.35 nylon monofilament (bearing in mind that a bass can weigh as much as 22 lb [10 kg]). The shock leader should be composed of a single 0.50 tippet of 5–6½ ft (1·5–2 m). The mounting can be of the sliding type or a paternoster with a lead of 1–3 oz (30–90 g). The hook will be of the type mentioned above, measuring at most 1/0–4/0.

The best time for fishing sea bass is at the turn of the tide, particularly at night and in coastal canyons or near the spots where the waves break in rough sea conditions.

Another fascinating exercise is to go surf-casting for rays, even though this is not the most suitable method. Obviously, success depends on knowing the behavior of these creatures which usually approach the shore in winter and spring. Although they may not attain any great size, their flat shape and fighting qualities require some stamina on the angler's part together with reliable tackle. Above all, heavy surf-casting rods are essential for casting as far as possible from the shore. For this reason it is best to use bait-casting reels with 0.45–0.60 nylon and 4/0 hooks baited with pieces of mackerel or squid.

Surf-fishing for flatfish such as sole, plaice, flounder, and turbot, typical inhabitants of sandy bottoms, can be rewarding. These species can be caught by casting lures a distance of 100 ft (30 m) or so from shore, aiming at a spot where breakers are just appearing. Use a 10–11½- ft (3–3·5-m) surf-casting rod with a fixed-spool reel and 0.30 line. The end of the line should be fixed to the lure with a swivel; the leader will be just over 6 ft (2 m) long, terminating in a long-shanked 10 hook of modest aperture, so that it can be easily swallowed by the small mouths of these fish. Above this hook, fix an 0.3 g sinker and above that attach a short drop of a lesser diameter and a hook of the same size as the head. Position another drop some 4 in (10 cm) from this, and then another just underneath and so on, to a maximum of ten. As bait use pieces of crab, hermit crab, crayfish, limpets, strips of squid, etc. You can also get good results with spoons,

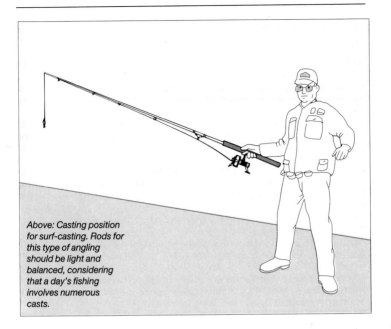

Above: Casting position for surf-casting. Rods for this type of angling should be light and balanced, considering that a day's fishing involves numerous casts.

especially if a worm is fixed to the hook.

After casting, it is best to wait until the lure has reached the bottom before retrieving it slowly in fits and jerks. This method raises clouds of sediment which are bound to get the attention of the flatfish and persuade them to take the dragging bait. The flexible rod tip will record the first touches, but it is best to ignore these and wait until the rod bends decisively as the fish swallows the bait.

In the course of surf-casting, it is also possible to catch other fish such as striped bream, greater weever, salpa, and even gilthead and meager, especially if there are plenty of rocks in the vicinity.

BOTTOM FISHING AND CASTING

If it were possible to count the sporting anglers practicing various angling techniques, by far the greatest number would undoubtedly be engaged in bottom fishing. The explanation for this is that this form of angling can be done almost anywhere and with very simple tackle.

This category includes both float fishing, which is done from piers and jetties, and fishing from an anchored boat. The range is immense and the potential prey embraces all types of fish which do not figure specifically in other categories.

Fixed-rod angling

This method of angling requires the least elaborate tackle. All it needs is a fixed rod, without rings or reels, and a line equipped with a float. The most suitable spots are off piers and rocks where the water is fairly deep. In any event, scope for action is somewhat limited, since the line, for all practical purposes, is only the same length as the rod. But because a fixed rod can be of considerable length, results are often better than might be thought possible.

Somewhat more scope, though still restricted, is afforded by using the float not to fish on the bottom but in midwater. More line is thus available between the float and the tip, so that the bait can be worked at a distance roughly one and a half times the length of the rod. But lengthening the line to any greater extent is inadvisable because it becomes almost impossible to cast it.

Rods that can be used are the same as for freshwater angling in rivers and lakes, provided they are sturdy and have a slightly stiffened tip.

The lines are thin (0.10–0.12), in blue or a darker color, taking account of the fact that the waters close to shore are often murky.

The hooks are obviously adapted to the fish likely to be caught; so they will be 14 (for any small species such as ox-eye bream, rainbow wrasse, perch, and mullet) or 10 (should an eel be tempted to bite, especially near ports). As for bait, the fishing ground itself, if not overrun by other anglers or tourists, will usually furnish enough material for the line, but if not, scraps of bread or cheese, with a few sardines thrown in, will suffice.

Casting and bottom fishing

Casting is a natural development of fixed-rod angling, culminating in surf-casting, which has already been dealt with in a separate chapter. Casting with a fixed rod offers greatly increased opportunities and hence more satisfaction in the long run. With a casting rod it becomes possible to cast the bait 65–100 ft (20–30 m) from shore, virtually picking the spot where you want to fish.

Nor do you need special rods for this type of angling. A stout fiberglass or graphite rod 8½–11 ft (2·5–3·5 m) long, furnished with rings, will be quite sufficient for the purpose, and there are plenty of commercial outlets to cater to every need. But if you are choosing a rod for sea angling, make sure that all the metal parts are rust-proof.

An indispensable accessory is a strong, reliable reel with a good retrieval ratio. This becomes important when you are fishing on a rocky bottom and have to reel in the bait quickly, allowing it to skim over the surface to prevent it snagging. The same technique can be used for fishing from rocky promontories, using a spoon. Given the weight, you can make reasonably long casts which, if retrieved rapidly, will credibly imitate the silvery flanks of a small fish in flight, awakening the interest of predators, always plentiful in transitional zones of rock, algae, and sand. Better results will be achieved by regulating the action of the lure, retrieving the spoon by fits and starts in alternate up and down movements that simulate the uncertain behavior of a fish attempting to get back to its hiding place. The occasional wrasse, or perhaps a striped, saddled or white bream, may well be found hanging from your line after one of these casts.

Examples of fishing

One of the most interesting species likely to be caught on the bottom by this method is the grouper. Its flesh is often disdained, and can indeed be disagreeable if the fish is taken in or near harbors, but it can be also excellent when caught in cleaner water. Yet this is not the only reason for going after it. The grouper's habit of sucking the bait off the hook and its reluctance to take the lure if it does not feel so inclined offer a constant challenge to the angler. Because of its diffidence, it is best fished with a very thin line (0.20), a leader of 0.15–0.18 and a single 8–10 Crystal hook. The lead may be fixed or sliding, if the bed is sandy. There is a choice of innumerable lures, depending on the surroundings. A little finely minced chum helps to attract grouper which have the interesting habit of swimming in schools. A bread roll attached to a line anchored on the bottom may also be useful for tempting grouper and keeping them gathered together around the spot where you intend to cast the lure.

River mouths are ideal places for casting. Brackish waters, by reason both of tidal influence and the continuous mingling of river and sea water, have always been regarded as extremely rich fishing zones and, in fact, many big fish congregate there. In addition to grouper, there may be sea bass, gilthead, flounder, and sole; and this list may sometimes be extended to include small sharks, cod, and turbot. A small boat will often be enough to increase the scope of action immeasurably. There are places along many coasts, not more than a few hundred yards offshore, where the sea suddenly deepens, providing marvelous opportunities for catching a vast range of fish. A nautical chart and hints from local people will frequently guide you to the ideal site, as, for example, the spot where sand gives way to prairies of *Posidonia*. Among the many species in these parts are large wrasse and white bream. Use an 0.30 line with an 0.25 leader and 10–14 Crystal hooks. The lead should be terminal, preceded, a few feet up the line, by the first of several drops bearing hooks baited with worms, mollusks or pieces of squid or octopus. Lower the line until you feel it touching the bottom and then raise it a few inches to retain sensitivity. Then it needs to be kept still. Some anglers can tell simply from the type of touch what species has taken the bait, but this is the fruit of long experience with the sea and its inhabitants.

A little farther on, close to rock walls, you may find and hook a conger eel or even a rockling. Eels are difficult fish because they tend to find their way into crevices and hide there almost motionless. You can easily get your line stuck without knowing what has happened. The rockling, related to cod, can be caught more easily on the bottom with mollusks or worms baited on 7–8 hooks preceded by the splice. In any case, mountings for this type of fish should be as simple as possible, normally on one or two hooks, seldom more. But it is always useful to have a terminal sinker of 6½–10½ oz (180–300 g) so as to keep the line taut and give warning when it touches bottom.

With a slightly larger and faster boat such as a rubber dinghy of 13–17 ft (4–5 m), on a fine day you can venture out 3 miles (5 km), as far as the law allows. This is quite far enough to cast for mackerel, a species which can be

Left: Anglers on a pier. Below: Fishing from a boat. Opposite: Fishing from rocks. Prey vary according to the chosen area of fishing. River mouths, for example, are ideal places for casting for mullet, gilthead, and bass.

caught just as successfully by trolling, and which comes near to shore in spring when ready to spawn. To catch mackerel you need a casting rod with an 0.30 line and a leader with a bottom lead. Mount a series of drops on the leader, each with a streamer. This is nothing more than a hook baited with a feather and very easy to prepare. Use 12 hooks, with eyes, the shank designed to take two joined feathers, together extending more than ¼ in or so (4–6 mm) beyond the hook point. Take strong thread of a bright color and make a tight knot to link the feathers, preferably white, to the shank so that you finish up with a large feathery fly with a colored head.

Six to twelve streamers of this type will appear to predators as an alluring and appetizing school of small fish. If you cast them carefully into the midst of a school of mackerel, along with a small bag of tasty and tempting chum of chopped fish and fish oil, the streamers will soon reach the required level of the terminal leader and start to have their effect. Rapid flicks of the rod will keep the lure moving and they can then be reeled in calmly.

For fishing mackerel, you can also use metallic streamers by wrapping silver paper around the hook shank to give the impression of a gleaming fly. And yet another, ridiculously simple, lure for mackerel is the colored insulation of an electric wire wound around the hook.

With somewhat larger boats, though not of the game-fishing class, you can go looking for schools and wrecks. Your equipment will now be that much more sophisticated, probably including an echo-sounder, indispensable for successful bottom fishing. With such facilities, there will be many surprises in store, and if place and time are right, you may even liven up your day by unexpectedly hooking a shark.

More likely catches will be hake, cod, and related species. These are fish of quite reasonable dimensions—4½–6½ lb (2–3 kg) or more according to species—which put up a fierce fight when reeling in and thus need strong tackle. Use an 0.30–0.50 line with 3/0–4/0 hooks.

A bait-casting reel will be required for fishing at greater depths. The choice of

73

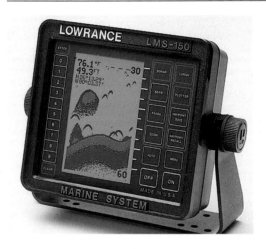

splice will depend not only on the depth but also on the currents. After casting check the descent of the lead to the bottom with your finger on the line and then raise the rod at regular intervals. In this way the line can be moved by the action of the current (if it exists) or by yourself.

In fishing for cod, it is worth using a pilker, a marvelous lure from Newfoundland. The pilker is extremely easy to dress, for it is simply a piece of chrome-plated metal with a treble hook which can be made very effectively from piping filled with iron filings and closed by hammering flat the tip. Certainly you can buy pilkers that look much more handsome, but since fish do not appreciate beauty for its own sake, your home-made versions will do the trick just as well, particularly if baited with tasty strips of squid.

Above: An echo-sounder, useful for bottom fishing.
Opposite: Drift fishing.

DRIFTING

If you were in a poetic vein, you might describe drifting as an attempt to merge with the sea, yielding yourself up to all its moods and movements. More prosaically, it is a method of fishing designed for catching sharks but which also provides the opportunity for catching other pelagic fish such as dolphinfish, meager, swordfish, and other large species. It is practiced, without exception, from the deck of a motor vessel with the engine switched off so that the boat drifts with the action of the current or the wind, trolling lines that float free in the water with the reel in neutral.

This type of fishing, therefore, needs little in the way of special equipment, but obviously the type of prey caught depends, luck permitting, on the kind of boat you use and the distance operated from shore. Hence, as in trolling, there is a distinction made between light, medium, and heavy drifting. To all intents and purposes, however, this is theoretical. Drifting is drifting, which is all that matters!

Do not assume, though, that the entire drifting operation can proceed without the help of the engine. When a big tuna is hovering around the hook, the skipper will need to start up the motors and follow with absolute precision every maneuver both of angler and fish.

Whereas with a moving motor vessel you can always follow the fish, or in the case of bottom fishing you can be sure of what is below, drifting requires a good deal more skill. Not only must you be familiar with the routes and behavior of various fish but you must also know how to attract them and bring them alongside the boat.

Because of this, the use of chum is essential (see chapter on Baits). In fish, the senses of smell and hearing are exceptionally well developed, and the fisherman will take fullest advantage of this fact. Any angler who has prepared chum

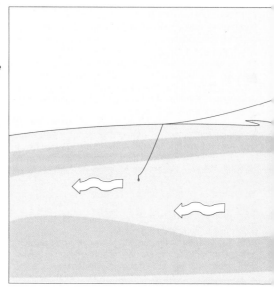

Diagram for strewing ground bait or chum. The odorous substance is dispersed by the current to form a wake that attracts the fish. The wake can be distributed on the surface or at depth depending on its relative position to the current.

and been exposed to the odor in all its glory will appreciate why few fish can resist it. There is a wide choice of likely ingredients. Bits and pieces of fish, crustaceans, and mollusks can be ground or chopped up and mixed with oil, bran or bread to form a concoction designed to excite the interest of hungry predators. But the consistency of the feed must be such that it is dispersed gradually in the water by action of wave and current, creating a strong-smelling swathe of food particles so minute as to attract insatiable fish from far and wide.

A rather more elaborate chum is required for sharks, calculated to appeal to their specialized predatory tastes. This may consist of oily fat fish (sardines, mackerel or tuna) mixed with bran or sawdust, fish oil, and blood. The whole lot is then dangled overboard in a sack which is dipped rhythmically into the water with the roll of the boat. It is a simple matter to distribute the bait evenly through the water by hanging it over the side alternately in the direction of the current, which will disperse it over the surface, and against the current, which carries the tiny food particles down into the depths.

Examples of fishing

Someone planning a drifting expedition for big fish should prepare for every possible contingency. Thus the best combination of suitable equipment will be a pair of heavy rods for tuna with rotating-drum reels containing 650–1,000 ft (200–300 m) of line with a breaking strain of 80–130 lb (35–60 kg), a pair of medium rods for sharks with rotating-drum reels containing the same length of line with a breaking strain of 55 lb (25 kg) and steel leaders, optional for tuna. In addition, there will be a light rod for mackerel, designed to serve as bait.

Having reached your destination, hang the lines overboard, dropping baited lines at different levels. Needless to say, knowledge of the habits of the local sharks will determine the best depths for positioning the bait. Begin to distribute the chum immediately and at the same time get busy fishing for mack-

erel. This will relieve the monotony of the first few hours and also provide useful indications as to the likely presence of large predators, which will probably station themselves at the same depths as their prey. Having caught a sufficient quantity of mackerel, bait them while still alive, fixing them under the dorsal fin to the hook. If you suspect that the sharks are swimming near the surface, resort to the balloon technique. After baiting the fish as described, lower it to the desired depth by attaching a balloon or a plastic bottle 30–65 ft (10–20 m) from the bait, fixing it in a very simple way. Some anglers tie a knot around a match or use adhesive tape. In any event, the join must conform to one requirement: it must break as soon as the fight begins.

Other baits that can be used to catch sharks are bundles of sardines, dead mackerel (the roll of the boat is generally sufficient to impart fairly realistic movement even to a dead bait) or skipjack. The last are particularly suitable for fishing hammerhead sharks which approach their prey by swimming on the surface; but they must be baited carefully, with at least a couple of hooks, one of which should protrude from the gill, because the mouth of this shark is of surgical precision and can slice your bait in two, leaving only the bit containing the hook attached to the line.

When the shark decides to attack, it does so from beneath and swallows the prey decisively, although there may always be the exception to the rule. For example, sharks may sometimes be seen encircling the bait cautiously, or they may vanish into deeper water and never reappear. But even if one shark vanishes, the chances are that another will appear, so it is essential to wait. Remember, in this respect, that in big-game fishing nobody abandons the hunt until a certain time has elapsed. At the first sign of a bite, grasp the rod, turn it in the direction of the bait and release the reel, just checking the rotation of the drum with your thumb. In this way you will feel the line feeding out while the shark swims quietly away. If you feel it stop, get ready. This is the moment when

Bait ready for scattering in the sea. As a rule pieces of fish and minced crustaceans and mollusks are mixed with oil, bran, and bread.

the prey is swallowed and as soon as you feel the line continuing to be paid out, strike decisively—and enjoy the sport. Despite its fame, nevertheless, a shark on the hook seldom defends itself fiercely, nor does the struggle it puts up depend on size. A small blue shark is liable to fight with more determination than many of its larger relatives. The prize for sporting prowess, by unanimous consent, goes to the mako shark which swims on the surface and indulges in spectacular leaps above the waves.

The major problems in catching sharks occur as it is being brought up. No matter what may have happened under the water, the shark displays unexpected resistance when it senses that it is about to be dragged on board, and it is not unusual for it to break free. So it is necessary to use both the gaff and the tail noose. Some experience is needed to secure a struggling shark, especially a large one, by the tail. It is by no means easy and has to be done at exactly the right moment. Shark fishing, at least the first time, needs careful planning, and it must always be kept in mind that not only do these animals possess a mouth with powerful teeth but that they are also endowed by nature with a rough skin, similar to sandpaper and capable of inflicting painful abrasions on delicate human skin.

A far more interesting exercise is drift fishing for tuna. In this case, chum, always useful, serves only to attract mackerel which tuna are accustomed to attack in the mass. Once the latter have been sighted and kept close by throwing sardines at random into the sea, it is easier and less painstaking to collect the mackerel as bait. Heavy tackle is required: 80-lb (35-kg) rods, bait-casting reels accommodating 800–1,000 ft (250–300 m) of 0.80 line, hooks with eye attachment and metal leaders of at least 13 ft (4 m) or of 200 nylon, because drifting is the traditional method of fishing giant tuna.

In drifting, it is possible to use three or four lines simultaneously which should be paid out 100–135 ft (30–40 m) apart, resorting to an outrigger, if need be, to extend the range of action. The bait, very fresh or preferably alive, is lowered a little way below the surface, at a maximum depth of 30–50 ft (10–15 m) by means of the float described above. It is essential to have a fighting chair on board because to hook a giant tuna is akin to the force of a locomotive hitting the rod. This sensation, moreover, accords with the calculations made by various students who have reckoned that a tuna of about 650 lb (300 kg) generates something like 90 hp.

Night fishing

At dusk or at night, drifting is a good way to try catching a swordfish, a species likewise fished by trolling. It is largely a matter of knowing the routes normally traveled by the fish and hoping they will lead to your bait. This must be a live one since the swordfish is only interested in natural baits. The most suitable are small tuna, bonito, large mullet or mackerel which must be attached very precisely and almost exclusively upside-down, because the predator, like other beaked fish, has the habit of circling the bait before swallowing it. Another excellent bait for swordfish is squid; whether alive or dead, it is irresistible if you carry out the simple operation of inserting a fluorescent chemical light candle beneath the mantle, which gives the squid a very attractive color. Use heavy tackle, consisting of 80–130-lb (36–60-kg) rods and an equally strong line with 12/0–14/0 bait-casting reels. The leader must also be very strong, either metallic or of 400–600-lb (180–250-kg) nylon, to withstand the blows of the sword which the fish will certainly deliver as it struggles to get free. A 12/0 hook will be suitable for this tackle. The mouth of the swordfish is fairly weak, so the strike will not be immediate. It is best to wait and offer no resistance until the fish has dragged off several dozen yards of line, and only when you are quite sure the bait is fixed firmly in its mouth should you tug to set the hook. The swordfish will put up a fierce struggle and you will need a sturdy fighting chair to play it successfully.

Meager can also be caught by the drifting method. These fish are extremely popular, mainly for the exciting battles they wage with the angler from the moment they are hooked. Light tackle of 20–30 lb (9–14 kg) is required, suitable for use as well on average-size boats.

The best baits are garfish, grouper or similar fish, depending on the locality. Careful baiting is essential, so as to preserve as much vitality as possible.

In this case use 20–30-lb (9–14-kg) rods with nylon or, better still, dacron monofilament of suitable diameter, and 4/0 rotating-drum reels. The leader, of metal or nylon, is attached to a spherical sinker of 17¾ oz (500 g) with swivels fixed to the line and bears 5/0–6/0 long-shanked, eyed hooks. The touch of the meager is light but decisive, as is the case with other carangids. Only a few seconds need elapse between touch and strike. The hooked fish defends itself by diving to the bottom and bending the rod sharply. In the first stage it is wise not to resist the fish, but to apply the brake and reel in only when the meager heads upward again. The pumping action will gradually become more insistent, but then ebbs off, particularly toward the end when the fish, by now exhausted, floats on the surface and can either be brought aboard with the gaff or released.

LIGHT AND MEDIUM TROLLING

Trolling for fish consists quite simply of dragging a bait behind a boat. But our customary passion for classifying everything has led to this activity being divided into categories according to the type of tackle used, regardless of the distance from shore. This means, for example, that to practice big-game fishing and go after giant tuna, it is not always essential to operate at a great distance from the coast, whereas this is indispensable for catching mackerel.

Light and medium trolling is done with tackle of 6, 12, 20, 30 and up to a maximum of 50 lb (IGFA or analogous classifications) when it starts to enter the higher classes. But as an indication of how little value this classification has for all practical purposes of angling, as against the possibility of recognizing a record or the need for a minimum of fair play (which, truth to tell, is generally observed by big-game fishermen), there are the so-called light tackle anglers who like to take on fish of 220–440 lb (100–200 kg) with 30-lb (14-kg) rods, 4/0–6/0 reels and 30–45-lb (14–20-kg) lines.

Trolling is done at the surface, in midwater or on the bottom, depending on the fish to be attempted. Given the scope of such activities, the angler has at his disposal an almost unlimited range of potential prey from grouper and sea bream to mackerel, skipjack, and marlin.

Examples of fishing

Used continuously as bait for larger prey, the gar (*Belone acus*) is itself commonly regarded by anglers as a satisfying prey, suitable for light trolling. To enjoy to the full the opportunities offered by this species, it is best to use a light 6-lb (2·7-kg) rod with at most 0.15–0.20 monofilament and a good fixed-spool reel.

The line terminates in a 10–12 or even 6 hook to which is attached a feather of a gull, chicken or any other bird, provided only that it is white and of uniform consistency. The feather, in fact, should be soft rather than stiff. It is fixed to the leader so that it just covers the hook (4–5 mm) and tied firmly with a brightly colored thread. The respective positions of hook and feather are important, for if the latter protrudes unduly, the fish will merely nibble it without taking the hook, while if the hook itself is too prominent, the fish will remain undecided. Another suitable bait for trolling gar is a spoon, which should be small, long, and very shiny, terminating in a gang hook to fit the mouth of the fish.

The speed of trolling should be slow (2–3 knots), so that suitable vessels can include small boats and rubber dinghies with outboard motors, all the more since gar do not venture too far from the shore. Pay out the line some 65 ft (20 m) from the boat and trail it along the surface without letting it sink too deep. If a school is sighted, you can try to keep it near the vessel by scattering a little chum from the stern. When you sense the fish beginning to take an interest in the bait, it is worth letting out a few more yards of line. This will slow down the bait so that it resembles an injured fish. The gar will bite decisively, particularly when it forms part of a large school (competition among individuals of the same species plays a primary role here) and this makes for a certain strike. Once on the hook, the gar is transformed into a miniature marlin, performing twists and leaps up to several feet out of the water in its efforts to break free. The fight is never long, but considering that one bite will follow another for some considerable time, there is never any shortage of entertainment.

One of the most interesting fish for trolling is the Atlantic bonito (*Sarda sarda*), a small predator which much resembles a tuna, although it belongs to another family. For full appreciation of its fighting qualities, fish it with a rod of not more than 12 lb (5·5-kg), with a 2/0 bait-casting reel or a reliable spinning reel with nylon monofilament. Considering the bonito's sharp teeth, the leader should preferably be of wire and very long, mounted with a 2/0 hook. There is a wide choice of bait. You can either use artificial lures (chrome spoons with or without a feather and with a gang hook, plugs or jigs), live bait or pieces of mackerel or sardine. The bonito is particularly fond of chum which includes sardines. While trolling (at 4–5 knots), you can strew this on the sea surface through a pipe connected to a pump or with a bailer so as to simulate the seething water activity created by a fleeing school of sardines or herrings and to conceal the outline of the boat.

Let out the line at least 165 ft (50 m) from the stern and see that the bait remains almost constantly at the surface. After the strike, the fish will head for the bottom, defending itself with strength and tenacity, characterized by sharp jolts on the line which are likely to cause aches in your arms long after the fight is over.

Having used up all their energy in their struggle to throw off the hook, these fish can be easily boated with a gaff or noose. The best catches are often made in the winter months with natural or live bait.

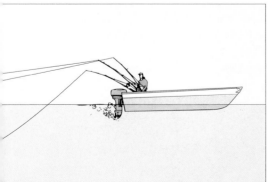

Trolling can be done on the surface, in midwater or along the bottom, according to the species being fished. The speed of trolling should be slow, not more than 2–3 knots.

The dolphinfish (*Coryphaena hippurus*) is a splendid creature and an excellent quarry for light and medium trolling, whose capture provides moments of spectacular beauty. In the water, individuals of this species are distinguished by their gleaming blue-green back, golden-bronze flanks, and white belly. The fins are bluish, but the tail is gold with blue and reddish tints. Mere description, however, can only give an approximate idea of the superb coloration, but this only applies to the fish when alive. Once out of the water, in its last spasms of life, the dolphinfish changes color: the blue becomes green, the gold fades, and eventually the whole body turns gray, with not a hint of its original beauty.

Tackle comprises 20–30-lb (9–14-kg) rods with 4/0 bait-casting reels, 20-lb (9-kg) nylon monofilament, with or without a leader, and a 4/0 hook. Natural or artificial baits may be used. A dead fish is preferable to a live one because of the fast trolling speed involved. The best baits are species normally eaten by the dolphinfish (mackerel, horse mackerel or gar), baited with a hook that projects from the ventral fins. Strips of fish, provided they are firmly attached, are a satisfactory alternative.

Since trolling is fairly fast, excellent results are possible, too, with small yellow, blue or white feathers, in that order of preference, which function best when combined with strips of filleted mackerel.

The bait is trolled at 6–7 knots just beneath the surface and about 65–165 ft (20–50 m) astern. If the vessel is mounted with outriggers, it may not be a bad idea to use them, as bait trolled from these long spars takes on a jumping movement which attracts the prey. The strike is sudden and the ensuing fight will be notable for its speed, for the dolphinfish is likely to swim rapidly toward the boat without giving the angler a chance to reel in the line, and then, just as unexpectedly, to reverse course, diving and surfacing with spectacular leaps.

Oddly enough, one of the most effective baits is another dolphinfish, and for that reason many anglers troll their first catch behind the boat, confident that other dolphinfish will follow, particularly if more bait is thrown from the stern in its wake. But the intelligence of the fish must never be underestimated, for sooner or later it will begin to associate certain baits with the notion of danger and shy away.

Right: A crew busy landing a meager. Opposite: An angler's rod bent by the weight of the fish. For this type of trolling, the most suitable rods have a strength of 20–30 lb (9–13 kg).

As for the most likely fishing grounds, dolphinfish tend to stick close to the surface, often in the shadow of floating objects. A wreck is therefore always worth inspecting as a possible refuge.

Medium trolling (which simply means trolling with tackle of medium strength, regardless of distance from shore or type of vessel) is an ideal way of fishing for members of the Carangidae, a family of marine species which might have been created for sporting anglers, including as it does the amberjacks, leerfish (*Lichia amia*), pompano (*Trachinotus ovatus*), and crevalles (species of the genus *Caranx*). These are fish of the coral reef, weighing 45–65 lb (20–30 kg), which take trolled bait with great enthusiasm. Tackle should consist of a 30-lb (14-kg) rod with a very stout fixed-spool reel or a more ductile and safer rotating-drum reel. The 20-lb (9-kg) nylon line should have a steel leader mounted with 4/0–6/0 hooks and torpedo-shaped leads. Baits may be artificial (plugs) or natural (squid, shrimp or strips of fish).

Species that test medium trolling to the limit include the white marlin (*Tetrapturus albidus*), the striped marlin (*Tetrapturus audax*) and the sailfish (*Istiophorus platypterus*). They are not the giants of the beaked fish realm, yet their very names are enough to excite the interest of a sporting fisherman, and to catch

83

one is a thrilling experience.

Trolling for marlin entails a line speed of 6–7 knots, not too fast considering how rapidly these species swim in pursuit of prey. Tackle consists of 30–50-lb (14–23-kg) rods with 4/0–6/0 rotating-drum reels. The most important thing is that they can accommodate a fair length of line, for marlin can drag off 650 ft (200 m) of line in a matter of seconds. It can be of 50 lb (23 kg) nylon or dacron, with a steel leader of at least 33 ft (10 m) to avoid the sword breaking the line, especially a dacron one. Hooks should be 10/0–14/0. Baits can either be artificial, of the Kona Head type, or natural (bonito or mackerel).

If you take advantage of an outrigger when playing marlin, you can troll two baits, some distance apart, at the same time. Artificial lures should be kept quite close to the boat, if possible in the wake created by the propeller, though as a rule marlin, like all beaked species, normally shy clear of such lures and will suddenly leave go even after biting. So jig or Kona Head types of lure need to be skimmed over the surface and submerged at intervals so that they leave behind a trace of bubbles that are more likely to tempt the prey. The fact that everything goes on at the surface and only a short distance from the boat gives you every chance to spot the marlin as it approaches and makes a decision to take the bait.

If the fish displays interest, it will bite immediately, but if it hesitates, there is little hope. Should all go well, the marlin, after slashing at the bait, will hold it at the front of its mouth for a while, and it is during this interval that the artificial lure, obviously not tasty or appetizing, may fail its purpose. So in such circumstances, everything depends on the angler's experience and dexterity. If he strikes too soon, he may pull the lure out of the prey's mouth; if he waits too long, there is a greater chance of the trick being discovered. But when the strike succeeds, the marlin explodes into action with all its power, performing the spectacular leaps for which it is rightly famed. Each time it will appear at a different place, in turns close at hand and at a distance, testing to the full the capacity of the tackle, the angler's arm muscles and the skipper's maneuvering skill.

Slow and steady pumping, with constant control of the line strain, are the only answer. Eventually—and time is of no consequence—the marlin will be hoisted on board as the centerpiece for the obligatory photographs.

Other species that lend themselves to light and medium trolling are the barracuda (*Sphyraena barracuda*), the striped bass (*Morone saxatilis*), the bluefish (*Pomatomus saltatrix*), the cobia (*Rachycentron canadus*), the red drum (*Sciaenops ocellatus*), the king mackerel (*Scomberomorus cavalla*), the rainbow runner (*Elegatis bipinnulata*), the snook or robalo (*Centropomus undecimalis*), the blackfin tuna (*Thunnus atlanticus*), and the wahoo (*Acanthocybium solanderi*).

Right: Catching a dentex, one of the most satisfying fish to be trolled. Opposite: Landing a small shark.

BIG-GAME FISHING

This technique of angling is exclusively concerned with catching the giants of the sea, as clearly shown by the type of tackle used, ranging from 80 lb (35 kg) to 130 lb (60 kg) and above, i.e. the heavy and unlimited categories. The fish in question weigh 440–660 lb (200–300 kg) and more, and the equipment used must therefore be suitable for coping with such quarry, while remaining, as ever, within the bounds of sport.

Everything about big-game fishing is on a large scale, starting with the boats which have to be comfortable, perfectly seaworthy, absolutely safe and capable not only of fast maneuvering but also of trolling for many hours at low speeds. An absolute essential for this kind of activity is a fighting chair, because it is impossible otherwise to withstand the power exercised by a giant tuna or a blue marlin, both capable of putting up fierce resistance for hours on end. Indeed, so violent are the demands imposed by the sport that it requires specialized equipment of the highest quality. Big-game fishing is an expensive pastime. Except for those who happen to own their own craft, the principal expense is the hire and maintenance of the boat, and on top of that comes the cost of the tackle. Moreover, since the accent is on quality, there are no limits. Broadly speaking, you get what you pay for. Rods will conform to IGFA standards, reels will be exclusively of the rotating drum type, furnished with either star or lever brakes, and the lines will be of nylon or dacron with 300–500-lb (135–230-kg) steel or nylon leaders.

Big-game angling requires more preparation and less improvisation than any other form of fishing. A fisherman at this level of the sport does not set out as if on a pleasure cruise. Knowing precisely the prey he is after, and exactly how and where to find it, he is ready for instant action. Of course, the unexpected often happens: a shark may be lurking while he is trolling for tuna or marlin, or a speedy wahoo may shear through the leader and make off with the bait intended for a much larger quarry. But this is all part of the game, as is returning to

Right: A flying gaff, useful for the final stages of retrieving a prey. Opposite: A fighting chair.

harbor at the end of the day with nothing to show for it save a little extra experience.

The most convenient method of big-game fishing is to troll several baits simultaneously not so much for the purpose of catching more fish (anglers, as a rule, use two at the same time so as to avoid problems with lines) as to increase the likelihood of catching just one. With the aid of the outriggers which all big-game fishing vessels possess, it is easy to troll at least four baits which are played out into the sea at varying distances from the stern, for example, 50, 100, 200 and 250 ft (15, 30, 60 and 75 m) respectively. The reason for this is that it has not been established with certainty that these lures tempt the fish. The marlin is attracted by the turbulence of the propellers whereas this actually disturbs tuna and sharks which rely more on uninterrupted vision.

Both the angler and the skipper (who as a rule is familiar with the habitats and behavior of the local fish) need an equally clear view of the surroundings to read the signs of the sea. Flocks of gulls bent on fishing are a sure indication that schools of fish are present and hence that predators will be in pursuit. In the Bahamas, one of the many so-called hot spots of big-game fishing, anglers pay particular attention to the flight of frigate birds, which they nickname marlin birds, to signal the presence of quarry. A check on the water temperature can also provide a clue as to the best zones for trolling. Fish are cold-blooded animals and since their body temperature depends on the outside temperature, they tend to seek out the water that suits them best. Marlin, for instance, prefer temperatures of 75°–80°F (24°–27°C), tuna go for water of 61°–66°F (16°–19°C) and mako sharks for temperatures of 64°–71°F (18°–22°C).

Echo-sounders are useful accessories for big-game fishing, and the more sophisticated models will locate schools and reveal, second by second, what is going on beneath the surface.

The traditional big-game fish are the giant tuna (*Thunnus thynnus*), the black marlin (*Makaira indica*) and the blue marlin (*Makaira nigricans*). In addition, there are the swordfish (*Xiphias gladius*) and a series of sharks, notably the white shark (*Carcharodon carcharias*), the tiger shark (*Galeocerdo cuvieri*), and the mako shark (*Isurus oxyrhynchus*).

Examples of fishing

We will begin with the giant tuna. This is a species that has long been known to professional anglers the world over. It constitutes an important economic and food resource, and since it embarks on regular migrations year after year, it is possible to go fishing for it virtually "by appointment."

Since you know that tuna are in the vicinity, either having been caught or at least sighted, and because blind trolling (as all anglers agree) is useless, you can set out for an expedition with at least two 130-lb (63-kg) rods. In theory you could equally well use 80-lb (36-kg) rods, but this depends on what risks you are prepared to take and on your sporting expectations. The rod should permit about an equal chance of success for yourself and the fish. If the tuna were to enjoy a marked advantage, there would be no point in trying to catch it, and if your own tackle were so powerful as to ensure you landed your quarry in five minutes or so, there would be no enjoyment in the exercise.

Back to technical details. Reels can only be of the 14/0–16/0 type with a rotating drum, the drag being accurately calibrated beforehand with a dynamometer. The line will be of nylon or dacron and at least 1,650 ft (500 m) in length. A tuna at full speed, you should be warned, can unwind the entire reel in a few seconds. Leaders should be of steel or nylon, of 400–600 lb (185–275 kg). The hooks (10/0–12/0) will be chosen from those specified for giant tuna (Mustad, Gamakatsu). As for bait, there is nothing better than skipjack or mackerel, properly mounted, but just as effective are dead fish (prepared with a deboner), artificial Kona Head lures, and white or red feathers (which seem to guarantee the best results). All require special splicing so that they are maintained just below the surface.

A marlin is hoisted on board. The maneuver will be completed by tying a rope around its tail.

Lines should be trolled 50–230 ft (15–70 m) astern at a speed of 6–7 knots. When all the preparations are done, do not be tempted to take a nap. Several hours of tedium may ensue traveling to and fro before the tuna decides to bite. If the fish is sighted close to the bait, you can try to whet its appetite by giving brief tugs to the line, playing with the tuna as you might with a cat.

We will now assume that you have hooked your giant tuna and are firmly settled in your fighting chair. After making an initial escape bid with a run of a few hundred yards, the fish will pause for a moment, giving you a chance to reel in a little line, thanks as well to the movement of the boat which will be following every twist and turn of the prey, taking care not to get the line crossed. As soon as the tuna feels the new strain on the line, it will take off in any direction. If it heads for the bottom, hope that this is nearby because a tuna suspended 1,000–1,300 ft (300–400 m) beneath you may become very awkward to handle.

It is impossible to predict how long the battle may last—half an hour, an hour or more—but eventually the exhausted tuna will come floating to the surface on its flank, alongside the boat. One blow of the gaff, a noose around the tail and your fish is in the hoist and on board, unless, of course, you decided to let it go.

Fishing marlin

The technique for catching blue and black marlin has been described in the chapter dealing with light and medium trolling. The only real difference when it comes to big-game fishing is the comparative size of the prey.

Heavy rods are required, of 80–130 lb (36–63 kg), preferably the former. All the remaining tackle, as already described, will be adequate: a 1,650-ft (500-m) line with steel leaders, obligatory for these fish, baited with live bonito, colored jigs or Kona Head lures. You can also try offering different baits at the same time, letting out more lines and making sure that they travel through the zone of water turbulence.

At this stage it is essential that you or someone else keep an eye on the bait, so as to be ready for the marlin when it appears, which does not necessarily happen right away. As soon as the fish gets close, as is its habit, it will slash at the bait to stun and swallow it. But before doing so, it is content to sample it, carrying off some line, which you must let it have. The suspense grows while you assess the line inch by inch as it unwinds from the reel and try to determine the best moment to strike. Then, in an instant, everything happens at once. You have to strike, apply the brake and rely on the boat to increase speed and help you to sink the hook firmly in the hard mouth of the marlin. And then the duel begins.

Anyone along with you for the ride will surely thrill to the sight of the hooked marlin and its acrobatics; but you, the angler, being directly involved, have other things to worry about. You have to follow the huge fish in all its frantic maneuvers, anticipating its runs, leaps, and dives, exerting your full strength even when your muscles are aching and begging you to relent. Grit your teeth and carry on.

The shape of the marlin's body and fins have the effect of increasing its resistance to traction. In practice, the harder you tug, the more the fish is difficult to pull in. So you have to tire it out by keeping a little extra length of line available. In this way you can keep the fish under control (15-lb [7-kg] traction), allowing it to leap and swim up and down at will. When the marlin is calmer, get the boat to turn a wide circle and prepare to retrieve the line. As the fish pulls, increase the traction to 30 lb (14 kg) and start reeling in. The skipper, meanwhile, should aim to keep the boat alongside and parallel to the marlin so that the fish is compelled to fight off balance. All these maneuvers may of course need to be repeated and for that reason it is important to conserve your energy. A fight with a big marlin can last as much as five hours but is well worth the effort.

Sharks, by reason of their size and reputation, naturally belong to the ranks of big-game fish. Yet although they are always lurking in the vicinity, ready to snatch your bait, sharks are not a favorite quarry of sporting anglers and much of the pride in catching them stems from their fame as fearsome predators. The fact that they are so often victims of drift fishing is proof of their innate laziness. Indeed, it is not that they are unable to bite at a trolled lure, simply that they have no inclination for it and prefer a quiet meal. Obviously, this is a side to their nature that is not normally emphasized by those who write about sharks, but it is worth bearing in mind if you come across them on a fishing expedition. One exception to the rule, however, is the mako, the first shark, along with the thresher shark (*Alopias vulpinus*), to have been included since inception (1939)

Now the fight is over, the crews of the two vessels stop to recover the prey. A fight with a big marlin may last as much as five hours but is well worth the effort.

on the IGFA list of sporting fish.

This powerful and aggressive shark is reputed to be the only natural enemy of the swordfish and the large marlins, pursuing and overtaking them thanks to its speed, estimated by some to be in the region of 45–50 mph (70–80 kmh). This was the evil shark which ate the gigantic marlin hunted by Santiago, the fisherman of Hemingway's *The Old Man and the Sea*.

The tackle generally used for this shark is a 130-lb (60-kg) rod with strong steel leaders and forged 10/0–14/0 hooks baited with live tuna or skipjack. The baits are trolled some 150 ft (50 m) astern at a speed of 5 knots, and work even better if chum, always used for fishing sharks, is scattered in conjunction.

No great perception is required for the strike. After several prods, the mako hurls itself so ferociously at the prey that the fight begins then and there. At first the shark makes off, quite untroubled by the hook. Only when aware of the line traction does it become agitated, rearing up and performing a series of leaps

The fighting chair is essential equipment for deep-sea trolling. Without the anchorage provided by the chair, the angler cannot withstand the strain imposed by a prey that may weigh 450–650 lb (200–300 kg).

above the waves. For the angler it is no easy fight. Such is the strength of the shark's resistance that every inch of the line has to be won back with a slow, steady pumping action, and all efforts may be frustrated in an instant by a few swipes of the animal's fin.

Even when you manage to bring it alongside, it may be too soon to claim victory. Sharks are noted for their vitality, struggling to the last, and your quarry can still surprise you by turning tail and making off with a few hundred feet of line in a final desperate fling. At this point you will need to start virtually from scratch to get it alongside again. This time the flying gaff and the noose around the tail will bring the battle to an end once and for all. Remember, nevertheless, that a shark may reserve its last ounce of strength for the moment it is lifted from the water and that in addition to its powerful jaws it has terribly abrasive skin. The use of thick gloves and the decision, if necessary, to leave the shark in the water, particularly if it is a large individual, will avoid serious injury.

IGFA RULES

Several times in the preceding chapters we have mentioned the classifications laid down by the International Game Fishing Association (IGFA), the organization which establishes the official rules for world-wide angling, including saltwater game fishing.

The IGFA was founded on 7 June 1939 when, at a conference held at the Science Museum of New York it was decided to set up this association for the benefit of angling enthusiasts and scientists alike, as testimony to the fact that catching fish was as important as knowing about them.

The aims of the IGFA, as then set out, have remained virtually unchanged and may be summarized as follows:

—to promote the study of game fishing, mainly for scientific purposes;
—to lay down strict rules for angling and to ensure that these rules are accepted by most fishermen;
—to encourage the spread of this sport both for recreational and scientific purposes; to make the scientific data available to institutions and interested individuals;
—to recognize all world records for game fishing and to keep relative documentation.

From the start, matters were handled earnestly and with extreme fastidiousness, so much so that the novelist Zane Grey, an aficionado of big-game fishing in the twenties and thirties, and one of the co-founders of the IGFA, did not obtain recognition for his own record catch (a marlin of 1,000 lb [470 kg]) because the fish had been bitten by a man-eater shark prior to capture, which had probably reduced its powers of resistance. This story answers the allegation that angling has nothing to do with sport. Another famous name associated with big-game fishing is Ernest Hemingway, who was vice-president of the IGFA uninterruptedly from 1944 to 1962, the year of his death.

Remember that the Association's rules and regulations are simply suggestions and only to be observed by those who intend to have their catch recognized as a record. They constitute, therefore, more of a suggested code of practice; and it is nice to think that every angler who captures or attempts to catch a fish with rod, reel, line, and hook (IGFA definition) should adhere to it in a sporting way.

The rules for saltwater species are as follows:

EQUIPMENT REGULATIONS
LINE
1. Monofilament, multifilament, and lead core multifilament lines may be used. For line classes, see *World Record Requirements*.
2. Wire lines are prohibited.

LINE BACKING
1. Backing not attached to the fishing line is permissible with no restrictions as to size or material.
2. If the fishing line is attached to the backing, the catch shall be classified under the heavier of the two lines. The backing may not exceed the 130-lb (60-kg) line class and must be of a type approved for use in these angling rules.

DOUBLE LINE

The use of a double line is not required. If one is used, it must meet the following specifications:

1. A double line must consist of the actual line used to catch the fish.
2. Double lines are measured from the start of the knot, braid, roll or splice making the double to the farthermost end of the knot, splice, snap, swivel or other device used for securing the trace, leader, lure or hook to the double line.

In all line classes up to and including 20 lb (10 kg), the double line shall be limited to 15 ft (4·57 m). The combined length of the double line and leader shall not exceed 20 ft (6·1 m).

The double line on all classes of tackle over 20 lb (10 kg) shall be limited to 30 ft (9·14 m). The combined length of the double line and leader shall not exceed 40 ft (12·19 m).

LEADER

The use of a leader is not required. If one is used, it must meet the following specifications:

1. The length of the leader is the overall length including any lure, hook arrangement or other device.
2. The leader must be connected to the line with a snap, knot, splice, swivel or other device. There are no regulations regarding the material or strength of the leader.

In all classes up to and including 20 lb (10 kg), the leader shall be limited to 15 ft (4·57 m). The combined length of the double line and leader shall not exceed 20 ft (6·1 m).

The leader on all classes of tackle over 20 lb (10 kg) shall be limited to 30 ft (9·14 m). The combined length of the double line and leader shall be limited to 40 ft (12·19 m).

ROD

1. Rods must comply with sporting ethics and customs. Considerable latitude is allowed in the choice of a rod, but rods giving the angler an unfair advantage will be disqualified. This rule is intended to eliminate the use of unconventional rods.
2. The rod tip must be a minimum of 40 in (101 cm) in length. The rod butt cannot exceed 27 in (68·58 cm) in length. These measurements must be made from a point directly beneath the center of the reel. A curved butt is measured in a straight line. (The above measurements do not apply to surf-casting rods.)

REEL

1. Reels must comply with sporting ethics and customs.
2. Power-driven reels of any kind are prohibited. This includes motor, hydraulic or electrically driven reels, and any device which gives the angler an unfair advantage.
3. Ratchet handle reels are prohibited.
4. Reels designed to be cranked with both hands at the same time are prohibited.

HOOKS FOR BAIT FISHING

1. For live or dead bait fishing no more than two single hooks may be used.

. Both must be firmly embedded in or securely attached to the bait. The eyes of the hooks must be no less than a hook's length (the length of the largest hook used) apart and no more than 18 in (45·72 cm) apart. The only exception is that the point of one hook may be passed through the eye of the other hook.

2. The use of a dangling or swinging hook is prohibited. Double or treble hooks are prohibited.

3. A two-hook rig for bottom fishing is acceptable if it consists of two single hooks on separate leaders or drops. Both hooks must be embedded in the respective baits and separated sufficiently so that a fish caught on one hook cannot be foul-hooked by the other.

4. All record applications made for fish caught on two-hook tackle must be accompanied by a photograph or sketch of the hook arrangement.

HOOKS AND LURES

1. When using an artificial lure with a skirt or trailing material, no more than two single hooks may be attached to the line, leader or trace. The hooks need not be attached separately. The eyes of the hooks must be no less than an overall hook's length (the overall length of the largest hook used) apart and no more than 12 in (30·48 cm) apart. The only exception is that the point of one hook may be passed through the eye of the other hook. The trailing hook may not extend more than a hook's length beyond the skirt of the lure. A photograph or sketch showing the hook arrangement must accompany a record application.

2. Gang hooks are permitted when attached to plugs and other artificial lures that are specifically designed for this use. Gang hooks must be free swinging and shall be limited to a maximum of three hooks (either single, double or treble, or a combination of any three). Baits may not be used with gang hooks. A photograph or sketch of the plug or lure must be submitted with record applications.

OTHER EQUIPMENT

1. Fighting chairs may not have any mechanically propelled devices which aid the angler in fighting a fish.

2. Gimbals must be free swinging, which includes gimbals that swing in a vertical plane only. Any gimbal that allows the angler to reduce strain or to rest while fighting the fish is prohibited.

3. Gaffs and nets used to boat or land a fish must not exceed 8 ft (2·43 m) in overall length. (When fishing from a bridge, pier or other high platform or structure, this length limitation does not apply.) In using a flying or detachable gaff, the rope may not exceed 30 ft (9·14 m). The gaff rope must be measured from the point where it is secured to the detachable head to the other end. Only the effective length will be considered. If a fixed head gaff is used, the same limitations shall apply and the gaff rope shall be measured from the same location on the gaff hook. Only a single hook is permitted on any gaff. Harpoon or lance attachments are prohibited.

4. Floats are prohibited with the exception of any small flotation device attached to the line or leader for the sole purpose of regulating the depth of the bait. The flotation device must not in any way hamper the fighting ability of the fish.

5. Entangling devices, either with or without a hook, are prohibited and may not be used for any purpose including baiting, hooking, fighting or landing the fish.

6. Outriggers, downriggers, and kites are permitted to be used provided that the actual fishing line is attached to the snap or other release device, either directly or with some other material. The leader or double line may not be connected to the release mechanism either directly or with the use of a connecting device.
7. A safety line may be attached to the rod provided that it does not in any way assist the angler in fighting the fish.

ANGLING REGULATIONS

1. From the time that a fish strikes or takes a bait or lure, the angler must hook, fight, and land or boat the fish without the aid of any other person, except as provided in these regulations.
2. If a rod holder is used and a fish strikes or takes the bait or lure, the angler must remove the rod from the holder as quickly as possible. The intent of this rule is that the angler shall strike and hook the fish with the rod in hand.
3. In the event of a multiple strike on separate lines being fished by a single angler, only the first fish fought by the angler will be considered for a world record.
4. If a double line is used, the intent of the regulations is that the fish will be fought on the single line most of the time that it takes to land the fish.
5. A harness may be attached to the reel or rod, but not to the fighting chair. The harness may be replaced or adjusted by a person other than the angler.
6. Use of a rod belt or waist gimbal is permitted.
7. When angling from a boat, once the leader is brought within the grasp of the mate, or the end of the leader is wound to the rod tip, more than one person is permitted to hold the leader.
8. One or more gaffers may be used in addition to persons holding the leader. The gaff handle must be in hand when the fish is gaffed.
9. The angling and equipment regulations shall apply until the fish is weighed.

THE FOLLOWING ACTS WILL DISQUALIFY A CATCH

1. Failure to comply with equipment or angling regulations.
2. The act of persons other than the angler in touching any part of the rod, reel or line (including the double line) either bodily or with any device during the playing of the fish, or in giving any aid other than that allowed in the rules and regulations. If an obstacle to the passage of the line through the rod guides has to be removed from the line, then the obstacle (whether chum, floatline, rubber band or other material) shall be held and cut free. Under no circumstances should the line be held or touched by anyone other than the angler during this process.
3. Resting the rod in a rod holder, on the gunwhale of the boat, or any other object while playing the fish.
4. Handlining or using a handline or rope attached in any manner to the angler's line or leader for the purpose of holding or lifting the fish.
5. Shooting, harpooning or lancing the fish being played (including sharks) prior to landing or boating the catch.
6. Chumming with or using as bait the flesh, blood, skin or any part of mammals other than hair or pork rind used in lures designed for trolling or casting.
7. Using a boat or device to beach or drive a fish into shallow water in order

. to deprive the fish of its normal ability to swim.
8. Changing the rod or reel while the fish is being played.
9. Splicing, removing or adding to the line while the fish is being played.
10. Intentionally foul-hooking a fish.
11. Catching a fish in a manner that the double line never leaves the rod tip.
12. Using a size or kind of bait that is illegal to possess.
13. Attaching the angler's line or leader to part of a boat or other object for the purpose of holding or lifting the fish.
14. If a fish escapes before gaffing or netting and is recaptured by any method other than as outlined in the angling rules.

THE FOLLOWING SITUATIONS WILL DISQUALIFY A CATCH
1. When the rod breaks (while the fish is being played) in a manner that reduces the length of the tip below minimum dimensions or severely impairs its angling characteristics.
2. Mutilation to the fish, prior to landing or boating the catch, caused by sharks, other fish, mammals or propellers that remove or penetrate the flesh. (Injuries caused by leader or line, scratches, old healed scars or regeneration deformities are not considered to be disqualifying injuries.) Any mutilation on the fish must be shown in a photograph and fully explained in a separate report accompanying the record application.
3. When a fish is hooked or entangled on more than one line.

If you have adhered to all these rules and suspect you may have landed a record catch, and if in addition:
1. The fish caught is a species and not a subspecies or variety.
2. The fish is commonly fished with rod and reel in the zone where the catch has been made.
3. The fish is clearly identified by a photograph.
4. The fish has record measurements.
. . . all that remains is to obtain the relevant form from
The International Game Fish Association,
3000 East La Solas Blvd.,
Fort Lauderdale,
Florida 33316-1616, USA.

Common name
Wahoo

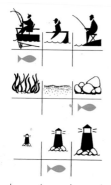

Description Very elongated, fusiform body, slightly compressed on the flanks. The long head terminates in a pointed snout and the mouth is full of sharp, pointed teeth. The first of the two dorsal fins is very long and can be folded into an appropriate longitudinal groove in the back. The second dorsal and anal fins are small and followed respectively by 7–10 and 7–9 finlets. The caudal fin is similar to that of tuna and the caudal peduncle bears three keels, a central one and two laterals. Coloration is blue-green, iridescent on the back. The flanks and belly are silver. Numerous vertical blue stripes extend along the flanks, often joining together on the belly.

Average dimensions 40–52 in (100–130 cm), max. 72 in (180 cm).

Distribution Indo-Pacific and Atlantic.

Habitat Surface and pelagic waters of tropical and temperate warm seas.

Behavior Tends to be solitary but may form groups of 3–6 individuals. Seasonally, in the above-mentioned places, and in the spawning period (spring-summer), it comes together in large numbers. Migratory species which gathers in summer off the coasts of California, Panama, and Costa Rica. In the Atlantic it approaches the coasts of Cuba in winter and those of the Bahamas in the spring and fall.

Feeding Voracious predator which feeds on squid, mackerel, small tuna, flying fish, and whatever other species catch its attention.

Fishing methods Trolling with natural or artificial bait.

Common name
Bonefish

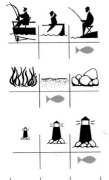

Description   Body long and fusiform, ventrally compressed. The head terminates in a conical snout, which has been compared to the muzzle of a fox. The lower jaw is small so that the mouth is directed downward. The single dorsal fin and large caudal fin combine to give the fish a good turn of speed. The ventral fins are on the same level as the last rays of the dorsal fin. In the early stages of development the species undergoes a curious metamorphosis; before taking on its definitive form it goes through an eel-like phase and then takes on the appearance of a leptocephalus (eel larva). Coloration is olive with silvery tints on the back, and silvery on flanks and belly. The young are distinguished by 8–9 dark dorsal stripes which become paler in the adults.

Average dimensions   16–20 in   (40–50 cm),   max.   40 in (100 cm).

Distribution   Indo-Pacific and American Atlantic coasts.

Habitat   Tropical and subtropical coastal waters. Has a preference for sandy, muddy seabeds.

Behavior   Schools of young are larger than those of adults. This species has the habit of searching for food on the bottom, assuming a vertical position, the tail directed upward and emerging above the water surface in shallows.

Feeding   The diet is varied and includes shrimp, crabs, mollusks, worms, sea-urchins, and small fish.

Fishing methods   Surf-casting, fly fishing or casting from a boat. Recommended natural baits are shrimp, crabs, bivalve mollusks, small cephalopods and sand-worms.

3   ALECTIS CILIARIS

Common name
African pompano

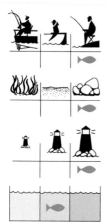

Description Body much compressed and high, almost rhomboid; front of snout rounded off like that of most Carangiformes. The first rays of the dorsal fin, very high at the front, are long and filamentous. This feature, which applies as well to the anal fin, is particularly evident in the young, with their typical diamond shape; in their case, the first rays of the dorsal and anal fins are bent backward beyond the caudal fin, being up to four times the length of the body. The pectoral fins are long, falciform and pointed. The caudal fin is distinctly bilobate. Close to the caudal peduncle, the scales of the lateral line are transformed into raised and very prominent bony plates. Coloration is silver-blue or bluish on the back, silver on the flanks and belly. There may be dark spots on the opercula, the caudal peduncle, and the front part of the dorsal and anal fins.

Average dimensions 12–20 in (30–50 cm), max. 36 in (90 cm).

Distribution Tropical waters on both sides of the Atlantic Ocean.

Habitat The adults inhabit coastal waters, the young are pelagic.

Behavior Tends to be solitary. Younger individuals are caught in the open sea between July and September while adults prefer to frequent the more distant waters around rocks and reefs.

Feeding Small fish, crustaceans, and mollusks.

Fishing methods Casting, bottom fishing and, occasionally, trolling. Use natural baits of small dimensions, live or dead, or artificial lures (spoons and feathers).

Common name
Thresher shark

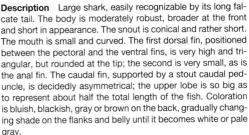

Description Large shark, easily recognizable by its long falcate tail. The body is moderately robust, broader at the front and short in appearance. The snout is conical and rather short. The mouth is small and curved. The first dorsal fin, positioned between the pectoral and the ventral fins, is very high and triangular, but rounded at the tip; the second is very small, as is the anal fin. The caudal fin, supported by a stout caudal peduncle, is decidedly asymmetrical; the upper lobe is so big as to represent about half the total length of the fish. Coloration is bluish, blackish, gray or brown on the back, gradually changing shade on the flanks and belly until it becomes white or pale gray.

Average dimensions 80–120 in (200–300 cm), max. 240 in (600 cm).

Distribution All waters between roughly latitudes 45°N and 45°S.

Habitat Pelagic in warm and temperate coastal and oceanic waters.

Behavior Tends to be solitary although several individuals may group together close to large schools of fish. They have also been seen hunting in pairs. The shark uses its long tail to stun and catch the fish which it normally eats.

Feeding Squid and various species of pelagic fish.

Fishing methods Surface or deep trolling and drifting. It will follow natural bait (preferably whole fish), dead or live, as well as artificial lures of the type used for fishing tuna and marlin (e.g. Kona Head).

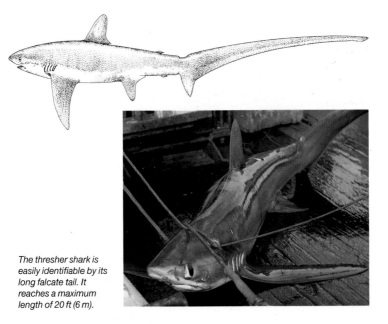

The thresher shark is easily identifiable by its long falcate tail. It reaches a maximum length of 20 ft (6 m).

Common name
White sea bass

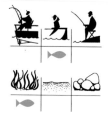

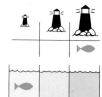

Description Fairly robust, elongated, moderately compressed body. Large, broad mouth. The dorsal fin is divided by a deep notch which separates the spiny part from that with soft rays. Along the center of the belly runs a characteristic keel of scales which extends to the anal opening at the base of the ventral fins. Coloration is silvery, darker on the back. At the base of the pectorals there is a black spot. Young measuring up to 18 in (45 cm) in length may have 3–6 vertical, broad black bands on the flanks.

Average dimensions 20–28 in (50–70 cm), max. 40 in (100 cm).

Distribution Along all American coastlines of the Pacific, from Alaska to Chile. It is most abundant in the zone bounded by the Bay of California and Baja California, Mexico.

Habitat Coastal waters where the bottom consists of dense forests of kelp or other types of giant brown seaweed.

Behavior Lives isolated or in small groups. At night it tends to move closer to the bottom. It spawns in spring and summer. In Californian waters the species becomes more frequent between May and September, perhaps in response to reproductive behavior.

Feeding This fairly voracious predator feeds on sardines, anchovies, mackerel, squid, and small crustaceans.

Fishing methods It may be caught anywhere from the surface to the bottom, and therefore by different methods: casting, drifting, bottom fishing from an anchored boat or from shore or slow trolling. Use live baits or spoons and feathers.

Common names
Crevalle jack
Pacific crevalle jack
Horse-eye jack

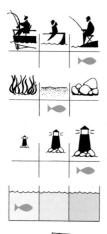

Description Elongated body, high and slightly compressed. The front of the snout is angled and blunt. The eyes are fairly large and characterized by an adipose lid. The mouth is wide and the teeth of the upper jaw are arranged in a double row. The dorsal fin has 8 spiny rays linked by a membrane, followed by a single spine which precedes the soft rays. The anal fin is preceded by 2 isolated spines. The caudal fin, deeply notched and bilobate, bears a double keel. Unlike the two other related species, *Caranx caninus* and *Caranx latus* the crevalle jack has no scales on its throat and displays an oval spot on the pectoral fins. Coloration is dark blue or blue-gray on the back, silver-white with golden tints on the lower part of the flanks and belly.

Average dimensions *Caranx hippos* and *C. caninus* 24 in (60 cm), max. 40 in (100 cm); *C. latus* 20 in (50 cm), max. 32 in (80 cm).

Distribution *Caranx hippos:* Mediterranean, eastern Atlantic from Portugal to Angola, western Atlantic from Nova Scotia to Uruguay; *C. latus:* eastern Atlantic along the African coasts, western Atlantic from New Jersey to Brazil; *C. caninus:* eastern Pacific.

Habitat Tropical and warm temperate coastal waters on sandy bottoms, also brackish water and fresh water.

Behavior They form schools of varying size which move rapidly along the shore. Larger individuals tend to become solitary.

Feeding Fish, shrimp, and other invertebrates.

Fishing methods Surf-casting, casting, fly fishing, trolling. Use live bait for preference (small mullet and other small fish).

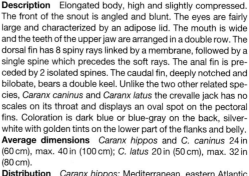

Common name
Giant kingfish

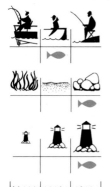

Description Carangid with fairly tall body that terminates in front with a convex head and at the rear in a narrow caudal peduncle furnished with two keels situated on either side of the terminal part of the lateral line, composed of raised bony plates. An oval zone, provided with scales and located below the mouth and slightly in front of the ventral fins, in an area otherwise wholly without scales, makes it possible to distinguish this species easily from other Carangidae. Coloration is variable, but in general gray-blue with brownish tints on the back, graduating to iridescent silver on the flanks and belly. There are no spots on the flanks and opercula, in contrast to the species *Caranx sexfasciatus* (see plate 54).

Average dimensions 28–32 in (70–80 cm), max. 56–60 in (140–150 cm).

Distribution Indo-Pacific from coasts of Kenya to Hawaii and the Marquesas.

Habitat Tropical coastal waters close to rocks and coral reefs where the seabed slopes rapidly.

Behavior Sedentary and quiet, it tends to live on its own as an adult and to form small groups when young. There is more activity at night, particularly among the adults.

Feeding Fish and crustaceans.

Fishing methods Surf-casting, drifting or bottom fishing from anchored boat. Both natural baits (mullet, herring, sardines, garfish, squid) and artificial lures (feathers, spoons, plugs, Kona Heads, and jigs) may be used. Fishing at night proves particularly effective, the darker the better.

Common name
Great trevally

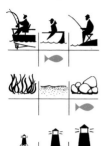

Description Long, compressed body with rounded back. The head is compact and notable for the eyes which in diameter measure up to one-fifth of its length. The lower jaw projects. The mouth is equipped with conical, well-spaced teeth. There are two dorsal fins, very close together, the second being taller than the first. The pectoral fins are typically long and falciform. The caudal fin is deeply notched and its peduncle bears two keels on either side of the terminal part of the lateral line, composed of raised bony plates. Coloration is variable. The back is as a rule dark gray-blue or bluish-green, but in certain specimens it appears golden, yellow, red or completely black. The flanks are yellow-green or silvery. The belly is silver or white. The upper lobe of the caudal fin is black while the lower one is yellow like the ventral fins. A dark spot adorns the opercula. The young are golden yellow with 4–7 broad, vertical dark bands on the body.
Average dimensions 16–20 in (40–50 cm), max. 30–32 in (75–80 cm).
Distribution Indian Ocean and Pacific to Hawaii.
Habitat Tropical coastal waters close to reefs or rocky shores, especially where they slope rapidly.
Behavior Adults live more on their own than the young who tend to form groups in shallow water close to sandy beds.
Feeding Fish and crustaceans.
Fishing methods Trolling and casting from boat, either anchored or left to drift. Use either natural baits (mullet, herring, sardines, garfish, squid) or artificial lures (feathers, spoons, plugs, Kona Heads, and jigs).

Common name
White shark

Description Large, albeit fusiform body. The head is pointed and terminates in a short snout. The mouth is ventral, wide, and decidedly rounded. Although quite numerous, the teeth are of a good size, those of the lower jaw being more pointed than the upper ones, triangular and finely serrated. The first dorsal fin is very large and broad. The anal fin is under-developed in comparison with the second dorsal fin. The much compressed caudal peduncle is furnished with two keels that extend almost to the caudal fin, which is shaped like a half-moon, with two very similar lobes. Coloration of the back is variable, gray-brown, gray-blue, blue or pale gray. The belly is white. There is a black spot at the base of each dark-pointed pectoral fin.

Average dimensions 120–240 in (300–600 cm), max. 26–33 ft (8–10 m).

Distribution Cosmopolitan. More frequent in temperate waters of the southern hemisphere.

Habitat Pelagic species of cold, temperate, and tropical coastal and oceanic waters.

Behavior Solitary and extremely aggressive species. It is judged to be particularly dangerous to humans because it will attack even if unprovoked.

Feeding Feeds on a wide variety of marine organisms including other sharks, cetacians, seals, turtles, and gulls.

Fishing methods Trolling from anchored boat. Strewing ground bait is essential, as is the use of natural baits, especially fish with oily flesh such as mackerel, skipjack, etc. It is regarded as the biggest game fish capable of being caught by the rod.

Common name
Snook

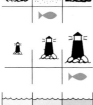

Description   Elongated body, higher in the middle and almost flattened below. The outline of the snout is slightly concave. The mouth is large and the lower jaw is longer than the upper jaw. The margin of the opercula is smooth and sharp. The first dorsal fin, characterized by spiny rays, is triangular in shape. The second spiny ray of the anal fin is particularly large and strong. The tail appears bifurcate. On the flanks is a clear black lateral line that extends to the rear edge of the caudal fin. Coloration is quite variable, according to place. As a rule it is brownish-yellow or olive on the back, silvery on the flanks and belly.

Average dimensions   20–27 in (50–67 cm), max. 52 in (130 cm).

Distribution   Western Atlantic from coasts of southern Florida to the Rio di Janeiro region of Brazil. It is also found in the West Indies and the Caribbean.

Habitat   Tropical coastal waters. It prefers shallow water, on average not more than 65 ft (20 m), lagoons, and estuaries from which it ventures into fresh water. It is highly sensitive to temperature and is never present in waters below 59°F (15°C).

Behavior   Lives in schools of varying numbers. It moves about with some regularity, gathering near river mouths during the spawning season (May to September). As a rule it approaches the shore at high tide.

Feeding   Fish and crustaceans.

Fishing methods   Trolling or casting with artificial lures (plugs and spoons), fly fishing or casting from anchored boat with live bait (small fish, shrimp or crabs).

Common name
Black sea bass

Description Medium-sized fish with an elongated and slightly compressed body. The head is sturdy and during the spawning phase terminates in a bulge. The mouth is large and oblique, partly as a result of the protruding lower jaw. There is a single dorsal fin. The first 10 rays are spiny and may inflict painful wounds if the fish is handled clumsily. The caudal fin is rounded or trilobate, and in adults the first ray of the upper lobe is typically elongated. Coloration is normally brown or blackish. The dorsal fin displays rows of oblique stripes and white spots. All the other fins are dark and spotted. During the spawning season a blue mark appears between the eyes of the males.

Average dimensions 12–14 in (30–35 cm), max. 18 in (45 cm).

Distribution North-west Atlantic Ocean from Massachusetts to Florida and Gulf of Mexico. Most abundant from Long Island to South Carolina.

Habitat Offshore waters: quite common on rocky bottoms and in the vicinity of quays, jetties, and wrecks.

Behavior Tends to form groups, numerous in certain zones. The species seems to be hermaphroditic: female in youth, male in adulthood. In May-June and November-December it tends to gather at depths of about 35 ft (10 m) to 120–130 ft (35–40 m).

Feeding Varied, including fish, shrimp, squid, and worms.

Fishing methods Drifting and bottom fishing from anchored boat or piers. Use artificial lures (plugs) and natural baits of habitual prey such as mollusks, shrimp, crabs, and squid. It is fished with light tackle.

Common name
Conger eel

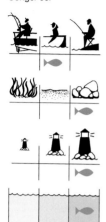

Description Elongated, subcylindrical, snake-like body, compressed at the rear. The head is flattened at eye level. The upper jaw is prominent. Both jaws contain an external row of flat, sharp-edged teeth. The dorsal, anal, and caudal fins are fused together as in the freshwater eel. Pectoral fins are present, but no ventral fins. The coloration of the back varies from black to a darkish slate-gray, while the belly is lighter. The pores of the lateral line are whitish.

Average dimensions 24–60 in (60–150 cm), max. 120 in (300 cm).

Distribution Mediterranean and eastern Atlantic from Norway to Senegal.

Habitat Lives near the bottom, hidden in rock clefts and caves and around wrecks.

Behavior Solitary. During the day it stays hidden in its burrow or in a rock cleft, with only the head protruding. With the approach of sexual maturity, adult individuals migrate toward much deeper waters, around 6,500–10,000 ft (2,000–3,000 m), to spawn in the summer.

Feeding Fish, crustaceans, and cephalopods.

Fishing methods Bottom fishing either from shore or from an anchored boat. Use natural bait such as squid, octopus or pieces of fish. Once hooked, the conger eel can offer fierce resistance, especially if it has time to retreat to its burrow, where it may protect itself so effectively that it is almost impossible to dislodge. An added problem is the power of its bite, capable of snapping a line of reasonable thickness.

Common name
Dolphinfish

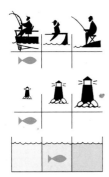

Description   Elongated, compressed fish, tapering considerably toward the tail. The head is bulky and very high, changing in the course of growth. Adult males actually develop a bony frontal crest which makes the snout look very squat and squarish. In females, the snout is more rounded. The mouth is large and contains many thin teeth. The very long dorsal and anal fins are joined almost to the caudal fin which is strongly curved and supported by a proportionately thin peduncle. The coloration is conspicuous. The back has metallic blue-green reflections, the flanks are speckled silver-gold with many small black spots. These vivid colors rapidly disappear as soon as the fish is removed from the water.

Average dimensions   20–40 in (50–100 cm), max. 80 in (200 cm).

Distribution   In all tropical and temperate warm seas. Widespread in the Pacific and Atlantic, but rare in the Mediterranean. A similar but rather smaller species is *Coryphaena equisetis*.

Habitat   Pelagic species of warm or tropical surface waters.

Behavior   The dolphinfish lives in large schools, although it is sometimes sighted alone. It shows a marked tendency to collect underneath floating wreckage, tufts of seaweed, etc.

Feeding   Mainly fish but also crustaceans and squid.

Fishing methods   Trolling with natural and artificial baits. The trolling speed should be quite fast, around 6 knots. Yellow-colored artificial lures appear to give the best results. When hooked, dolphinfish can exhibit a remarkable turn of speed.

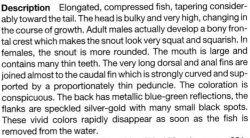

Above: The dorsal surface of the tongue of the dolphinfish. The dorsal and anal fins are linked almost as far as the strongly falcate caudal fin.

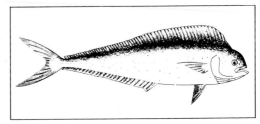

Common name
Spotted sea trout

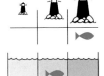

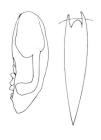

Description   Sturdy fish with elongated and moderately compressed body. The mouth is large and oblique. The lower jaw is larger than the upper jaw, which is provided with two prominent canine teeth. The dorsal fin is divided into two parts by a deep notch. The scales, rough to the touch on the body, are smooth on the head. Coloration is silvery with olive-green tints on the back. On the upper part of the flanks, above the lateral line, there are numerous small black marks which extend over the second half of the dorsal fin.

Average dimensions   16–20 in   (40–50 cm),   max.   36 in (90 cm).

Distribution   Western Atlantic coasts from New York to the Gulf of Mexico.

Habitat   Shallow coastal waters near bottoms of sand or mixed mud and sand. Most abundant in bays or along estuaries.

Behavior   Gregarious species which forms groups that may become larger during the reproductive season. During the summer months it tends to gather at the mouth of rivers to spawn and find food. In winter it partly abandons enclosed bays.

Feeding   Principally crustaceans and fish, also mollusks and worms.

Fishing methods   Drifting, bottom fishing from anchored boat, slow trolling, and surf-casting. The best bait consists of shrimp. Silver, gleaming artificial lures such as metal spoons are also excellent. The mouth is very delicate and can easily be torn by the hook, enabling the fish to get away.

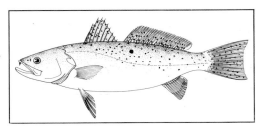

Above left: Inner surface of the otolith of the spotted sea trout's hearing organ. Above right: The swim bladder.

Common name
Weakfish

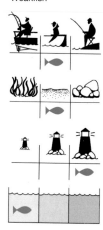

Description Average-sized fish with elongated and slightly compressed body. The flattened snout terminates in a mouth full of small, conical teeth, except for a pair of large, curved canines positioned at the ends of the upper jaw. The dorsal fin appears to be divided in two by a deep notch. The broad caudal fin is truncate or slightly concave. The body is entirely covered by scales that extend even to the base of the part of the dorsal with soft rays. Coloration is greenish on the back and silver on the flanks and belly. Small black spots tend to form oblique lines on the back and upper part of the flanks. The ventral and anal fins are bright yellow.

Average dimensions 36–40 in (90–100 cm), max. 62 in (155 cm).

Distribution American coasts of the western Atlantic from the Gulf of Mexico to southern Florida and north to New York.

Habitat Coastal waters, estuaries, and mouths of rivers, although it does not venture upriver. Seeks beds of sand and mixed mud and sand, and favors zones of breakers.

Behavior Gregarious, forming schools. Spawns from May to October. Approaches coasts during summer months and returns to deeper water of 165–300 ft (50–90 m) in winter.

Feeding Crabs, shrimp, mollusks, and small fish.

Fishing methods Trolling, surf-casting, casting, bottom fishing from shore or from anchored or drifting boat. Use either natural baits (crabs, shrimp, worms, mollusks, strips of squid) or artificial lures (spoons, surface or sinking plugs, minnows, etc.).

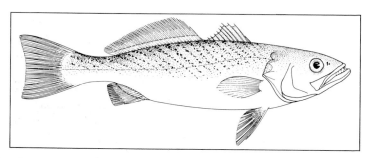

From left to right: Swim bladder, internal and lateral view of the otolith of the weakfish. The dorsal fin is divided into two parts by a deep notch.

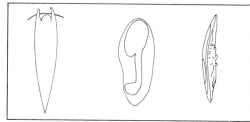

Common name
Sea bass

Description Body long and fusiform, slightly compressed, with a fairly high caudal peduncle. The head is sturdy and the mouth large. The eyes are particularly large. There are two distinct dorsal fins on the back, the first exclusively composed of spiny rays. Two spines are also present on the opercula, the borders of which are very sharp. Coloration is silvery gray with bluish tints on the back, and silvery on the flanks and belly, the latter sometimes displaying variably clear yellowish tones.

Average dimensions 12–20 in (30–50 cm), max. 40–48 in (100–120 cm).

Distribution Eastern Atlantic (from Norway to Senegal) and Mediterranean.

Habitat Temperate coastal waters down to a depth of about 350 ft (100 m). It frequents all types of shoreline, rocky, pebbly, and sandy, as well as prairies of eelgrass. It is often found, too, in brackish lagoon waters and even in fresh water.

Behavior Gregarious when young, tending to become gradually more solitary in adulthood. Forms groups when spawning from January to March, when it moves from brackish to typical sea waters. The young carry out the reverse journey in spring.

Feeding Voracious predator which feeds on small fish, shrimp, mollusks, and worms, hunted mainly at night.

Fishing methods Typical surf-casting quarry, but may also be caught by bottom fishing or light trolling from an anchored boat. It is attracted by shining artificial lures (spoons, feathers) and live or dead natural bait.

Common name
Rainbow runner

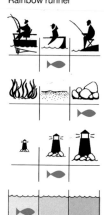

Description Markedly elongated, fusiform body. Pointed mouth and snout, small mouth but well provided with tiny teeth. There are two dorsal fins which, like the anal fin, are followed by a biradial finlet. The caudal fin is deeply notched. The caudal peduncle has two grooves, one dorsal, the other ventral. The color of the back is olive-blue or green, white on the belly. The flanks are yellow, with two light blue stripes running along either side, making a vivid contrast. The caudal fin is yellow while the other fins are dark, either greenish or olive-yellow.

Average dimensions 28–32 in (70–80 cm), max. 52 in (130 cm).

Distribution Tropical belts of the Pacific and Atlantic.

Habitat Warm tropical pelagic waters, near the surface or among reefs far from shore.

Behavior May form schools, sometimes large, especially when composed of young individuals, which are also given to swimming around floating wreckage and other objects, or accompanying big sharks, mingling with pilot fish. The adults tend to become solitary.

Feeding Invertebrates and small fish.

Fishing methods Principally casting, preferably with light tackle which allows a flexible response to the fish. This does not always happen because the rainbow runner has the habit of attacking any type of bait presented. If possible, use natural baits, particularly live small fish, or artificial lures. It may also be fished for use as bait for marlin, sharks, and tuna.

Common name
Jewfish

Description   This is the largest of all the groupers. The very sturdy body appears almost circular in cross-section. The head is long, extremely broad, and flattened on top. The mouth is very wide and oblique. There are three flat spines on the operculum, the middle one being the largest. The single dorsal fin has no notches. The spiny rays are shorter than the soft rays. The rear edge of the powerful caudal fin is rounded. The body is covered with small, rough, overlapping scales. Coloration is generally greenish or gray with small black spots and larger brown patches.

Average dimensions   24–32 in (60–80 cm), max. 100 in (250 cm).

Distribution   Western Atlantic from Florida to Brazil. It is also found in the eastern Pacific from Costa Rica to Peru.

Habitat   Coastal species which lives in shallow tropical waters with mangrove swamps and clefts where it can shelter.

Behavior   A sedentary, indolent fish despite its agility in moving among the caves and crevices of its territory.

Feeding   Principally crustaceans, but also fish which it literally sucks in with its huge mouth.

Fishing methods   Bottom fishing and sometimes slow trolling. Only natural bait should be used, preferably from among the crustaceans on which it feeds (crabs, shrimp, and small crayfish). When hooked, it offers no self defense but makes for the nearest cavity, literally wedging itself inside by bending its fins so that it is very difficult to remove.

Common name
Kawakawa

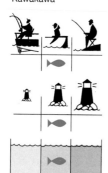

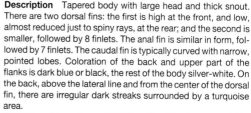

Description Tapered body with large head and thick snout. There are two dorsal fins: the first is high at the front, and low, almost reduced just to spiny rays, at the rear; and the second is smaller, followed by 8 finlets. The anal fin is similar in form, followed by 7 finlets. The caudal fin is typically curved with narrow, pointed lobes. Coloration of the back and upper part of the flanks is dark blue or black, the rest of the body silver-white. On the back, above the lateral line and from the center of the dorsal fin, there are irregular dark streaks surrounded by a turquoise area.

Average dimensions 16–24 in (40–60 cm), max. 40 in (100 cm).

Distribution Typical Indo-Pacific species. It is widely distributed from the Red Sea to South Africa and eastward to Japan, Australia, and Hawaii. Practically absent outside these zones, it appears to be replaced there by the related *Euthynnus lineatus* (see plate 21).

Habitat Pelagic species of warm and temperate waters which tends frequently to approach coasts near coral reefs.

Behavior Gregarious species which moves about in large schools. It undertakes regular migrations associated both with food and reproduction.

Feeding The diet seems to consist principally of various crustacean species and also pelagic fish and squid.

Fishing methods Mainly trolling. Use live or dead natural baits (squid, herring, mackerel, anchovy, and garfish).

Above: one of the two appendages situated between the ventral fins of the little tuna, which is notable for its two dorsal fins separated by a very brief gap.

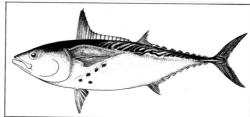

Common name
Little tuna

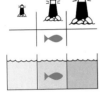

Description   Robust, fusiform body. The two dorsal fins are separated by a very brief gap. The first dorsal fin is relatively high and, by reason of the elongated first ray, has a concave rear margin. The second dorsal fin is followed by 8 finlets, and the anal fin by 7 finlets. The narrow caudal peduncle bears three keels, a large central one and two laterals at the base of the tail. The body possesses no scales, except on the corselet and lateral line. Coloration is dark blue on the back, which is characterized as well by wavy bands that extend from around the middle of the first dorsal to the tail, but not beyond the lateral line. The lower part of the flanks and the belly are silver-white. There is a series of dark spots between the pectoral and ventral fins.

Average dimensions   23–32 in (50–80 cm), max. 40–48 in (100–120 cm).

Distribution   Atlantic and Mediterranean.

Habitat   Pelagic in coastal waters above the continental platform.

Behavior   Markedly gregarious species that gathers very near the coasts in schools made up of several thousand individuals. Its migrations are short and its populations tend to remain in the same waters almost all the year round.

Feeding   Mainly pelagic fish, such as sardines and anchovies, as well as crustaceans and cephalopods.

Fishing methods   Trolling or casting with natural or artificial bait. Utilize chum based on sardines and anchovies and to resort to the ruse of spraying the sea with a pump so as to imitate the effect of schools of small fish swimming at the surface.

Common name
Black skipjack

Description Rounded, fusiform body which terminates at the front in a pointed snout and at the rear in a very slender caudal peduncle. The two dorsal fins are separated by a brief gap. The second is very small while the first is fairly high at the front, a feature that makes it easy to identify the species. Both the dorsal and the anal fins are followed by 7–9 finlets. The caudal peduncle bears a keel on either side, and there are two smaller ones as well on the lobes of the caudal fin. The body is not covered by scales, except at the front of the head and along the lateral line. Coloration is dark blue-gray on the back and almost white on the belly. The black skipjack is distinguished from similar species by the 4–5 broad black stripes that run horizontally along the back and by a series of dark spots between the pectoral and ventral fins.

Average dimensions 16–24 in (40–60 cm), max. 32 in (80 cm).

Distribution Eastern Pacific from California to Peru. It is sometimes sighted in the central Pacific.

Habitat Pelagic tropical and temperate warm waters.

Behavior Typically gregarious species which lives in large schools. It spawns in late spring and early summer.

Feeding Small pelagic fish, squid, and crustaceans.

Fishing methods Trolling or casting. Use small natural bait, whole or filleted, and artificial lures such as spoons, plugs, jigs, and feathers. The skipjack seems particularly attracted by the speed of the lure and, according to experts, will bite any object trolled at 8–10 mph (13–16 kmh).

The first dorsal fin of the black skipjack, which has a pointed snout that is fairly high at the front, thus distinguishing the species from the bonito.

Common name
Skipjack

Description Fusiform, elongated and rounded body that terminates in a short and rather pointed snout. The two dorsal fins (of which the first is higher) are separated by a short gap. The second dorsal and anal fins are followed respectively by 7–9 and 7–8 finlets. The pectoral and ventral fins are short. The caudal peduncle bears three keels: one in the center and one to each lobe. The body is not covered by scales, except on the lateral line and corselet. Coloration of the back is dark blue. The flanks and belly are silver, with 4–6 dark longitudinal stripes, typical of the species, extending from the corselet toward the tail and terminating at the lateral line.

Average dimensions 20–28 in (50–70 cm), max. 40 in (100 cm).

Distribution Cosmopolitan in tropical and subtropical waters. Western Atlantic from Cape Cod to Argentina, Indian and Pacific Oceans.

Habitat Pelagic and coastal tropical and subtropical waters.

Behavior Migratory and markedly gregarious species which forms large schools that may number as many as 50,000 individuals, often mingling with other tuna species such as *Thunnus atlanticus* and *T. albacares*. In the summer months it makes for more northerly and southern parts of its range.

Feeding Pelagic fish such as herring, sardines, and small mackerel, as well as squid and crustaceans.

Fishing methods Trolling or casting from anchored boat with natural or artificial bait. An ideal quarry for angling with light tackle given that the fish weigh on average 4–13 lb (2–6 kg).

Common names
Atlantic cod
Pacific cod

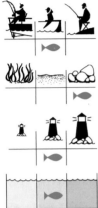

Description Long, sturdy, and somewhat corpulent body. There are three distinct dorsal fins, of decreasing height. The anal fin is double. The rear edge of the caudal fin is almost straight. The mouth is turned downward and has a single barbel under the chin. The lateral line is curved. Coloration is rather variable, depending mainly on the surroundings in which the fish lives. The back and flanks may be brown or green, yellow or red, or even a combination of these colors with a series of lighter markings. The belly is white. A long light band runs along the flanks to coincide with the lateral line. The fins are dark.

Average dimensions 32–40 in (80–100 cm), max. 64–72 in (170–180 cm).

Distribution American and European North Atlantic coasts above 45°N. In the Pacific the species is replaced by *Gadus macrocephalus*, which is smaller. The Pacific cod is found along the American coasts from California to Alaska and from Siberia to the Yellow Sea.

Habitat Cold coastal waters up to a depth of 1,650–2,000 ft (500–600 m), among rocks or mixed rock and sand.

Behavior Typically gregarious fish forming dense shoals. The Atlantic cod embarks on regular migrations during the spring spawning season, seeking waters with a temperature of 39°–43°F (4°–6°C).

Feeding Fish, crustaceans, mollusks, and worms.

Fishing methods Mainly bottom fishing from an anchored boat, or drifting. The best forms of bait are bivalve mollusks, pieces of squid or mackerel or small whole fish.

Common name
Tiger shark

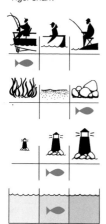

Description   Large, strong body. The head is obtuse, almost square, and the snout is short and rounded. The teeth are the same in both jaws, large with the point turned obliquely outward and the edge finely serrated. The caudal peduncle is keeled. The caudal fin has pointed lobes, particularly the upper one which displays a deep notch. Coloration is gray-brown or near ocher on the back, paler on the flanks and white on the belly. There are characteristic stripes on the back and upper part of the flanks, more accentuated in the young, this feature giving rise to the common name of the species.

Average dimensions   80–120 in (200–300 cm); max. 240 in (600 cm).

Distribution   Cosmopolitan. Found in all tropical and subtropical seas. In the summer it heads farther north and has been sighted in temperate waters, as in the western Atlantic as far as Iceland.

Habitat   Tropical and temperate warm waters. Frequently found close to shore, even in very shallow water.

Behavior   Lives solitary or in small groups. Very dangerous to humans. Moves toward more northerly zones of its range during the summer months.

Feeding   Extremely varied: it feeds on practically everything (fish, turtles, birds, cetaceans, and organic or inorganic waste).

Fishing methods   Trolling or drifting with natural bait, live or dead, and ample chum. Playing the shark often involves many hours of strenuous effort.

Common name
Tope

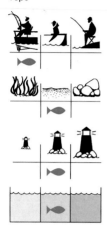

Description A medium-sized shark with a moderately tapered body. The head is depressed so that the snout is rather long and obtuse. The eyes are markedly oval and have well-developed nictitating membranes (which can be raised to protect the eyes). The teeth are triangular and pointed, with 3–4 notches at the base of the outer edge. The two dorsal fins, well separated, have no spines. The caudal fin has large lobes: apical (divided by a notch) and inferior. Coloration is dark gray or brown on the back and white on the belly. The rear margins of the pectorals and dorsals are white.

Average dimensions 32–48 in (80–120 cm), max. 80 in (200 cm).

Distribution Mediterranean and eastern Atlantic from Scandinavia to South Africa, southwestern Atlantic, eastern and southwestern Pacific.

Habitat Coastal and temperate pelagic waters at depths of 65–1,300 ft (20–400 m) close to beds of mud and mixed mud and sand, where it seeks its food.

Behavior Gregarious, tending to form schools of varying numbers.

Feeding Feeds abundantly on pelagic and demersal school fish (sardines, anchovies, cod) and also catches crustaceans and echinoderms.

Fishing methods Drifting and surf-casting in some areas. It has recently become a popular game fish. Natural baits are used, such as sardines, mullet, small hake, and crustaceans.

The caudal fin of the tope has large apical, inferior lobes, divided by an evident notch. The rear edges of the pectoral and dorsal fins are white.

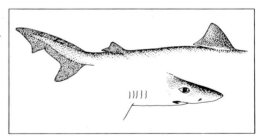

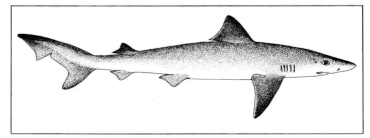

Common name
Dogtooth tuna

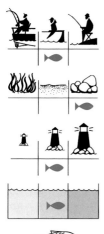

Description The shape of the body is proportionately longer than in other tuna although it remains fusiform and rounded in cross-section. The wide mouth is furnished with large, conical teeth which constitute one of the typical features of this species. The other distinctive characteristic is the absence of scales, except on the front part of the body and the lateral line. The two dorsal fins are very close together, the first low and the second higher, followed by 6–7 finlets. The anal fin is followed by 6 finlets. The caudal peduncle bears three keels, a central one at the end of the lateral line and two on either lobe. Coloration of the back is dark steel blue, perhaps with purple reflections, or blue-green, while flanks and belly shade to a lighter silvery tone. The second dorsal and anal fins have a white spot, the other fins are yellowish or gray.

Average dimensions 24–32 in (60–80 cm), max. 72 in (180 cm).

Distribution Western Pacific, Indian Ocean, and Red Sea. Sometimes it is caught off New Guinea and in the stretch of ocean between East Africa and Australia.

Habitat Pelagic and coastal tropical and subtropical waters.

Behavior Gregarious species which forms schools.

Feeding Squid, small mackerel, and other pelagic fish.

Fishing methods Deep trolling or bottom fishing close to reefs and channels that connect coral reefs to the open sea. It is seldom caught and then usually when angling for other species. As a rule it goes for natural bait (squid, mackerel, mullet) but can also be attracted by spoons, plugs, and feathers.

The dogtooth tuna is notable for a wavy lateral line. The two dorsal fins are very close together, the second being higher than the first.

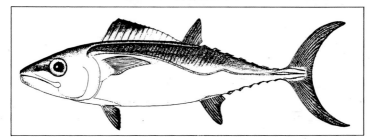

Common names
Atlantic halibut
Pacific halibut

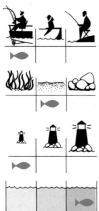

Description   Fairly long, thick body. The eyes are normally positioned on the right side, but there are exceptions. It is the largest of all the Pleuronectiformes. Coloration is variable: the upper side is greenish or olive-brown, while the blind side is generally white, although in some individuals it may take on a reddish tone.

Average dimensions   16–28 up to 60 in (40–70 up to 150 cm), max. 120–160 in (300–400 cm).

Distribution   North Atlantic from Bering Sea to the Bay of Biscay in Europe, and from Greenland to Virginia along the coasts of America. In the northeastern Pacific, from the Sea of Japan and the Bering Strait to California, the related Pacific halibut is likewise known to migrate considerable distances, as shown by marked specimens recovered after traveling some 2,000 miles.

Habitat   Coastal waters that are fairly cold, 37°–48°F (3°–9°C), and deep, 165–6,500 ft (50–2,000 m), on muddy bottoms.

Behavior   Lives in large schools. From December to April the Atlantic halibut moves toward waters with a temperature of 41°–45°F (5°–7°C) and a depth of 1,000–3,300 ft (300–1,000 m) to spawn at sea off Newfoundland and between Scotland and the Faroe Islands. After spawning, the adults seek calmer and shallower waters.

Feeding   Fish, cephalopods, and large crustaceans.

Fishing methods   Drifting with heavy tackle. Use natural baits such as cod, mackerel, hake, herring, squid, and crabs.

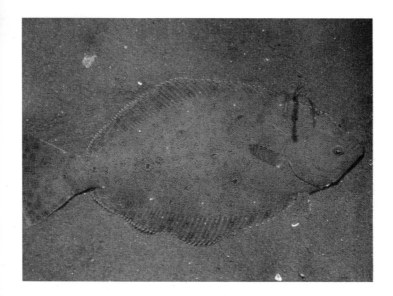

Common name
Atlantic sailfish

Description Body elongated and compressed, narrowing progressively toward the tail. Like the marlin, the sailfish has an elongated upper jaw transformed into a rostrum. Unlike the marlin, however, it has an exceptionally large dorsal fin that is twice as high as the fish itself, making it immediately identifiable. The body is steel blue with silvery flanks and belly. The dorsal fin is cobalt blue with a scattering of small black spots.

Average dimensions 100 in (250 cm), max 120 in (300 cm). The maximum measurements apply more frequently to individuals from the Pacific.

Distribution Indo-Pacific and Atlantic to southern shores of the Mediterranean.

Habitat Coastal and pelagic tropical and subtropical waters, sometimes temperate seas as well. As a rule the fish remain above the thermocline and seldom rise beyond 35–50 ft (10–15 m) from the surface.

Behavior Tends to be solitary and only occasionally forms small groups. Migrates seasonally.

Feeding A wide variety of fish, crustaceans, and cephalopods.

Fishing methods The best quarry for trolling with light tackle. Its leaps, which constitute the most spectacular aspect of its defensive maneuvers, are familiar to all anglers. Natural or artificial baits are cast as soon as the sailfish is sighted, usually by a swirling of the water near the surface as small fish flee from this swift predator, capable of reaching 60 mph (100 kmh) over short distances.

Common name
Mako shark

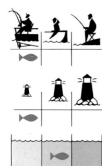

Description Neat, elegantly shaped body. Conical snout, terminating in a point. The jaws bear long, straight teeth, lacking cusps at the base and directed backward. The first dorsal fin, originating behind the pectorals, is large and triangular, while the second is fairly small and similar to the anal fin. The caudal peduncle has a flattened, prominent keel on either side. The caudal fin is large and falcate, like that of the best ocean swimmers such as tuna and marlin. Coloration of the back is bright blue-gray or cobalt blue, turning lighter on the flanks. The belly is pure white.

Average dimensions 72–96 in (180–240 cm), max. 160 in (400 cm).

Distribution Cosmopolitan.

Habitat Mainly pelagic in tropical and temperate warm waters. It approaches coasts in search of food.

Behavior Tends to be solitary. It may be dangerous to humans. It usually remains close to the shore in summer and ventures farther out in winter.

Feeding Principally fish that live in schools, e.g. mackerel.

Fishing methods Classic shark for trolling, capable of putting up fierce resistance, as exhibited mainly by repeated leaps which may be as high as 20–35 ft (6–10 m). Ideal baits are whole tuna, mackerel, squid, and mullet. It is regarded by anglers as potentially dangerous, and there have been instances of mako sharks which, after being reeled in, have made a final bid for freedom, jumping over the boat and doing considerable damage to anglers and equipment.

Common name
Porbeagle shark

Description   Powerful body even though apparently stocky and rather high at the front. The head is conical and the mouth, markedly rounded, has averagely large teeth, although not very many, with cusps at the base. There are a few large pores on the snout which exude a lot of mucus. The first dorsal fin, with a well-rounded tip, is large, whereas the second is much smaller, similar to and opposite the anal fin. The caudal peduncle is depressed and provided with lateral keels which extend to the caudal fin and are flanked by another, smaller one, in the terminal portion. The tail is lunate and nearly symmetrical. The scales are so tiny that the skin of this shark appears to be almost velvety. Coloration is gray-blue on the back, white on the flanks and belly. The rear tip of the first dorsal fin is white.

Average dimensions   36–104 in (260 cm), max. 140 in (350 cm).

Distribution   Cosmopolitan except for the North Pacific.

Habitat   Pelagic species which dives down to a depth of about 1,350 ft (400 m). It lives in coastal and oceanic waters of cold or temperate warm seas, generally to the north and south of an average annual isotherm of 68°F (20°C).

Behavior   Tends to be solitary. Considered potentially dangerous to humans. It becomes more frequent in coastal waters during summer.

Feeding   Mackerel, herring, sardines, cod, and squid.

Fishing methods   Trolling or drifting with plenty of chum. Use only natural baits, preferably selected from habitual prey (mackerel, herring, skipjack, squid).

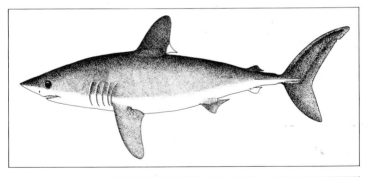

Right: Diagram of the head seen from below and the teeth of the left side, from front to back.

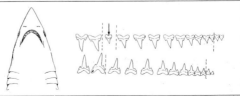

Common names
Cubera snapper
Pacific snapper
Mutton snapper

Similar species
Lutjanus analis
Lutjanus sebae

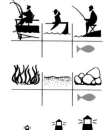

Description The Cubera snapper (*Lutjanus cyanopterus*) is the largest of the group of fish (Lutianidae) commonly known as snappers, so called because of their aggressive nature. The body is quite long, yet sturdy, and thus appears streamlined. The head is large, terminating in a wide mouth furnished with thick lips and big canine teeth which are partly visible even when the jaws are locked. The single dorsal fin bears 10 spiny rays followed by 14 soft rays. The rear margin of the anal fin is rounded while the caudal fin appears to be truncated. Coloration of the back and flanks, above the lateral line, is gray with reddish tints that are more abundant on the front part of the body. The belly is white. The rather similar mutton snapper (*L. analis*) may be distinguished fundamentally from the above by having a well-defined dark spot on the flanks beneath the dorsal fin. The Pacific snapper (*L. sebae*), comparable in overall shape, has smaller teeth and bigger pectoral fins. Its coloration is much more vivid: orange-brown on the back and bright orange on the belly. Young individuals have a series of scarlet bands that disappear with time. Specimens from deep waters are more brilliantly colored.

Average dimensions *L. cyanopterus*, 28–36 in (70–90 cm), max. 64 in (160 cm); *L. analis*, 16–20 in (40–50 cm), max. 30 in (75 cm); *L. sebae*, 16–24 in (40–60 cm), max. 32 in (80 cm).

Distribution *L. cyanopterus* and *L. analis* are found in the western Atlantic from Florida to Brazil. *L. sebae* is typical of Australian coasts along the Great Barrier Reef.

Habitat Tropical and temperate warm coastal waters on rocky or coral bottoms at depths of not more than 135 ft (40 m). *L. analis*, however, prefers sandy bottoms with plenty of vegetation.

Behavior Tend to be solitary as adults, more gregarious when young. *L. analis* is liable to form groups by day. There seems to be no well-pronounced seasonal activity for the individual species. The young are known to live in shallower and even brackish water.

Feeding The Lutianidae are voracious predators of fish although they also eat crustaceans and mollusks.

Fishing methods Bottom fishing with artificial lures (plugs) or natural baits (shrimp and small fish).

The single dorsal fin bears 10 spiny rays and 14 soft rays. The body is quite long and the large head terminates in a broad mouth furnished with thick lips and well-developed teeth.

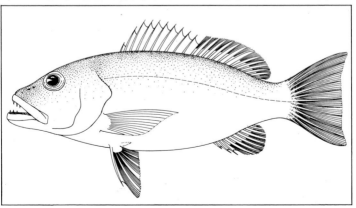

Common name
Black marlin

The black marlin's first dorsal fin is the lowest among all marlins.

Description   Body long, powerful and slightly compressed, rising rapidly to top of head. The upper jaw is typically elongated to form a slender lance-shaped rostrum. There are two dorsal fins: the first is long and initially high, although proportionately the lowest among all marlins; the second is smaller and composed of 6–7 rays. There are likewise two anal fins. The pectoral fins are very stiff and cannot be bent toward the animal without breaking them. This is a distinctive feature of the species. The ventral fins are very short; based on measurements carried out on many specimens, these never appear to exceed a length of 14–16 in (35–40 cm), no matter how large the fish. Coloration is blue on the back, becoming silver-white on the flanks beneath the lateral line. Vertical light blue stripes form typically on the marlin's flanks when it pursues prey or leaps out of the water.

Average dimensions   120 in (300 cm), max. 160 in (400 cm).

Distribution   Indo-Pacific, although specimens which have rounded the Cape of Good Hope and been carried as far north as the Ivory Coast have been sighted occasionally in the Atlantic. Other sightings have been reported from around Rio de Janeiro and in the West Indies.

Habitat   Pelagic tropical waters, in general above the thermocline. It appears more frequently along coasts and near islands.

Behavior   Lives in small groups.

Feeding   Small tuna and mackerel.

Fishing methods   Classic big game quarry. The best baits are natural (squid, skipjack, and mackerel), but artificial lures of the Kona Head type also prove quite satisfactory.

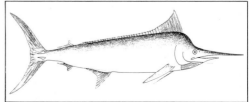

33 MAKAIRA NIGRICANS

Common name
Blue marlin

Description Body elongated but not too compressed, and high at front. The profile of the head from the preorbital region to the attachment of the first dorsal fin is sharply outlined. The upper jaw is extended into a typical rostrum, rounded in cross-section. The first dorsal fin is high in front and then suddenly slopes down. The anal fin is double. The body is thickly covered with scales that terminate in 1–2 long spines. Coloration is dark blue or brownish on the back and silver-white on the flanks and belly. The first dorsal fin is blue-black and generally without spots. On the flanks, some 15 vertical light blue bands are formed by spots that more or less come together.

Average dimensions Pacific populations reach an average length of over 140 in (350 cm) while those of the Atlantic measure about 100 in (250 cm). The maximum length for the species is around 160 in (400 cm).

Distribution Atlantic Ocean (45°N–35°S) and Pacific Ocean (48°S–48°N).

Habitat Tropical and subtropical waters.

Behavior It forms small schools. In the Atlantic, blue marlin tend to concentrate between latitudes 5° and 30°S from January to April, moving to latitudes 10° and 35°N from June to October.

Feeding Pelagic fish that live in schools (particularly mackerel and small tuna), cephalopods, and crustaceans.

Fishing methods Trolling. Use whole natural baits (skipjack, mackerel, mullet, pomfret, and squid) and artificial lures.

Common name
Tarpon

Similar species
Megalops cyprinoides

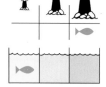

Description Averagely high and compressed body. Huge head and snout characterized by the big, upward-turned lower jaw. The fins lack spiny rays. The last ray of the single dorsal is very long and faces backward. The body is covered with typically broad, thick scales. Coloration of the back is metallic gray, either light or dark, with green and blue reflections. The flanks and belly are silvery. Individuals caught in freshwater are often brown or golden in color due to the different environment in which they live.

Average dimensions 48–52 in (120–130 cm), max. 100 in (250 cm).

Distribution Western Atlantic from Nova Scotia to Brazil. A small population has also been sighted in the eastern Pacific close to the entrance of the Panama Canal, evidently the progeny of a few pairs of tarpon.

Habitat Tropical and warm coastal waters, especially in estuaries, lagoons, mangrove swamps, and rivers.

Behavior Forms small schools which become more numerous at time of reproduction. Migrates to open sea from April to August in order to spawn, or heads northward. The larvae, similar to those of eels, return to shallower waters, lagoons or even coastal ponds where conditions are right for growth. In these surroundings, sometimes poor in oxygen, these fish manage to live without problems thanks to their ability to breathe atmospheric air and to utilize, in the normal manner, oxygen dissolved in the water.

Feeding Principally school fish (sardines, anchovies, mullet) and crustaceans.

Fishing methods Slow trolling, casting from anchored boat and fly fishing. Using live bait (mullet, crabs, shrimp), the best results are achieved at night, when tarpon prefer to hunt. The strike should be firm and repeated several times because the tarpon's mouth is very tough. Once hooked, it proves worthy of its fierce fighting reputation, performing acrobatic leaps up to 10 ft (3 m) above the surface in its efforts to break free.

The tarpon, a fish that puts up a strong fight, has a snout with a large, upward-turned lower jaw.

Common name
Striped bass

Description   Its overall shape is fairly similar to that of the sea bass. The body is long and fusiform, slightly compressed, with an averagely high caudal peduncle. The head is sturdy, with a smooth profile. The lower jaw is slightly prominent. There are two distinct dorsal fins on the back, the first with spiny rays. Coloration is silvery gray with bluish tints on the back, silvery on the flanks and belly. On the flanks there are 7–8 clear black stripes, one of which overlaps the lateral line while the others are evenly divided above and beneath it.

Average dimensions   24–36 in (60–90 cm), max. 68 in (170 cm).

Distribution   Originally restricted to the American coasts of the Atlantic, from the Gulf of St Lawrence to Florida. Between 1879 and 1882 it was introduced to the Pacific where it acclimatized perfectly, so that nowadays it is found from California to Washington.

Habitat   Lives in coastal waters close to sandy and rocky bottoms. It ventures into brackish and fresh water, and may in certain cases form populations isolated from the sea which spawn in inland waters.

Behavior   Similar to that of the sea bass. It tends to move north in spring and early summer, and south in the fall.

Feeding   An opportunistic predator with an extremely varied diet that consists mainly of fish.

Fishing methods   Medium trolling, casting, bottom fishing, surf-casting and fly fishing. An equally wide range of artificial lures and natural baits can be used.

Common name
Roosterfish

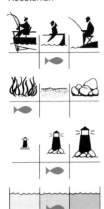

Description Elongated, very slightly compressed body. The head is broad with a projecting lower jaw. The dorsal fin is double, the first being characteristic inasmuch as the rays are mostly free and elongated, resembling the crest of a cock. When the fish is swimming, the dorsal fins are conveniently folded into a fairly deep dorsal groove. The anal fin has a concave margin. The pectorals are long and falciform. The caudal fin, too, is falciform and deeply notched. Coloration is lead-gray with bluish reflections on the back, but some individuals are green or black; the flanks are golden and the belly whitish. Two transverse blue or black bands run diagonally along the flanks from head to tail. The spines of the dorsal fin are distinguished by light and dark stripes. The base of the pectorals is black.

Average dimensions 16–24 in (40–60 cm), max. 48 in (120 cm).

Distribution Eastern Pacific from Gulf of California to Peru. Appears to be abundant in the sea off Ecuador.

Habitat Subtropical and temperate coastal waters, on sandy bottoms and at moderate depth.

Behavior Lives alone or in small groups which tend to remain close to zone of breakers.

Feeding An active and voracious predator of small fish.

Fishing methods Trolling or casting from a boat or shore. Use natural baits, either live (especially when fishing from a boat) or dead, or artificial lures. When hooked, the fish offers some resistance, arching its back and making repeated leaps above the surface.

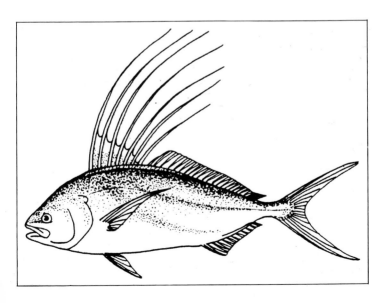

Common name
Lingcod

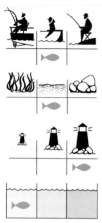

Description Elongated body which terminates in a huge conical-shaped head. The mouth is large and turned upward because the lower jaw is bigger than the upper jaw. Characteristic features are the canine teeth, hooked like those of a snake. The single dorsal fin is fairly long and divided in two by a deep notch. The very large pectoral fins are fan-shaped. The front part of the anal fin displays three small spines which in adults are covered by epidermis and perceptible only to touch. The head and body are covered by small, smooth scales. Coloration is highly variable (from brown or black to bluish or greenish with black spots), depending essentially on the surroundings in which the fish lives.

Average dimensions 12–20 in (30–50 cm), max. 60 in (150 cm).

Distribution Exclusive to eastern Pacific from Baia California in Mexico to Kodiak Island, Alaska.

Habitat Temperate or cold coastal waters on bottoms rich in large species of seaweed.

Behavior Tends to assemble in large numbers which makes the species very popular among professional anglers. From December to March adults make for shallower waters, the females laying their eggs on rocky seabeds. The young remain in these areas and then gradually descend to a depth of around 330 ft (100 m).

Feeding Various fish, crustaceans, and octopus.

Fishing methods Bottom fishing with heavy artificial lures (metal jigs) suspended at 30–650 ft (10–200 m).

Common name
California halibut

Description   Body oblong with a rather large mouth. Each jaw bears a single row of thin teeth. The dorsal fin is very long and begins in front of the eyes. The caudal fin has elongated lobes. Although the California halibut belongs to the family Botidae, the representatives of which usually have eyes on the left side, about half the population has eyes on the right side. Coloration of the upper side of the body is brownish while the blind side is white, but in some individuals both flanks may be colored.

Average dimensions   28–36 in   (70–90 cm),   max.   80 in (200 cm).

Distribution   American Pacific states from San Francisco Bay to Baia California in Mexico. It is sometimes sighted farther north but its presence there is considered accidental.

Habitat   Shallow coastal waters of 65–135 ft (20–40 m) on sandy bottoms.

Behavior   Potentially gregarious. It undertakes seasonal migrations, frequenting surface waters in the summer months.

Feeding   Anchovies and other small fish in addition to crustaceans, squid, and various mollusks. When anchovy schools are in the vicinity the California halibut becomes particularly active, abandons the sedentary habits of a benthic fish and comes to the surface to pursue the small fish.

Fishing methods   Drifting with live bait (anchovy or shrimp). Results can also be obtained by slow trolling, especially during the passage of anchovy schools.

Common name
Summer flounder

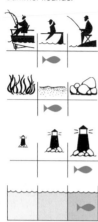

Description   Typical representative of Pleuronectiformes with eyes positioned on the left side. The body is oblong, the mouth is large and the lower jaw projects beyond the upper jaw. The dorsal fin is very long, extending from the area of the right eye to the tail. Coloration is variable, given from the notable ability of the fish to blend with the bottom. There are 10–14 scattered eye spots. The blind side is whitish.

Average   dimensions   12–14 in   (30–60 cm),   max.   38 in (95 cm).

Distribution   Western Atlantic from Maine to South Carolina.

Habitat   Coastal waters, at no great depth, on beds of sand or mud and sand.

Behavior   They collect in large numbers on the bottom, wherever suitable. During summer they ascend to the surface and may even be found in 6 in (15 cm) of water, venturing into bays, canals, estuaries, and harbors in search of warm and sheltered spots. In winter populations of summer flounder inhabit deeper water, at 130–500 ft (40–150 m).

Feeding   Fish, caught on the bottom and in midwater, as well as squid, worms, and crustaceans.

Fishing methods   The ideal technique is drifting, which keeps the bait constantly on the move, exciting the flounder's curiosity. The most popular baits consist of strips of fish or squid, accompanied by shiny metal spoons, shaped so as to mimic the rolling action of a fish. The best times for catching summer flounder would seem to be periods of flood tide and during the fall. The fish habitually samples the bait before swallowing it.

Common name
Sea drum

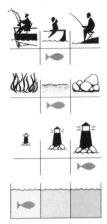

Description Elongated but high body, laterally compressed. The forehead is slightly sunken above the eyes. A number of small barbels beneath the throat make the species easy to recognize. At the back of the mouth are platelike teeth designed for chewing mollusks. The single dorsal fin has a deep notch which separates the parts bearing spiny and soft rays. The anal fin has two quite large and pointed spiny rays. The margin of the caudal fin is straight or slightly concave. Coloration is grayish with reddish or coppery tones. The young have 4–5 prominent dark vertical bands against a silver-gray background.

Average dimensions 16–24 in (40–60 cm), max. 80 in (200 cm).

Distribution Western Atlantic from Massachusetts to the Gulf of Mexico and the coasts of Argentina.

Habitat Coastal waters and estuaries above sandy beds where the waves are strong.

Behavior A fairly indolent fish that lives in schools. The social tendency is also enhanced by its capacity to utter sounds, louder among males, which probably help to facilitate meeting and recognition of the sexes.

Feeding Chiefly mollusks and crustaceans which the fish locates under the sand with its sensitive barbels. The species is considered a scourge among mussel and oyster farmers along the coasts of the United States.

Fishing methods Bottom fishing, casting from a boat or slow offshore trolling. The ideal baits are shrimp, crabs, bivalve mollusks or squid.

Common name
Pollack

Description Representative of the family Gadidae, with an elongated, fusiform, sturdy body. However, features that distinguish it from other species of the family are the lower jaw, better developed than the upper jaw, the absence of barbels on the chin, and the bifurcate tail. The three dorsal fins are clearly distinct, and each is of decreasing height. There are two anal fins. The ventral fins are positioned far forward, just beyond the opercula. Coloration of the back varies from olive-green to brownish-green. The flanks are lighter, yellowish or gray, and the belly is white. The ventral fins are pink while the others are black. The upper part of the flanks often exhibits dark yellow or orange spots.

Average dimensions 20–24 in (50–60 cm), max. 48 in (120 cm).

Distribution North Sea and northern European Atlantic coasts from Norway to Spain.

Habitat Cold temperate surface waters, to a depth of 650 ft (200 m), close to coasts and rocky bottoms.

Behavior They form large schools which move between the bottom and the intermediate layers of water. The species reproduces from January to April.

Feeding Small pelagic or benthic fish (sand launces, small cod, herring, blennies, and labrids), cephalopods, and crustaceans.

Fishing methods Bottom fishing or slow trolling. Use either natural baits (shrimp, squid, and small fish) or artificial lures (spoons, pirks, spinners, and plugs).

Common name
Bluefish

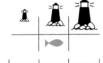

Description Large fish with elongated, compressed body, sturdy head, and keeled dorsal profile. Terminal mouth with conspicuous pointed teeth. There are two dorsal fins, the first low, the second long with a spiny first ray, a feature that distinguishes the bluefin from the apparently similar amberjack. The caudal fin is slightly notched. Small scales cover the entire body, head and base of fins. Coloration is gray-green on the back and silvery on flanks and belly. The dorsal, caudal, and anal fins are light green with yellow tints. The pectoral fins have a bluish spot at the base, more evident in the young.

Average dimensions 16–24 in (40–60 cm), max. 44 in (120 cm).

Distribution American Atlantic coasts from Nova Scotia to Argentina, eastern Atlantic, Mediterranean, and Indo-Pacific.

Habitat Pelagic species typical of tropical and temperate warm waters.

Behavior Individuals in juvenile stages congregate in large schools, but these tend to become more rare with age. Tends to approach coasts in late spring and summer when it spawns.

Feeding Mainly fish.

Fishing methods Trolling, surf-casting or drifting. Natural baits, alive or dead, yield better results than artificial lures, the best of the latter being jointed fish and imitation squid. Wire leaders are recommended because the teeth of bluefish can easily snap weak lines. Trolling should be carried out near promontories, islands, and reefs.

Common name
Blue shark

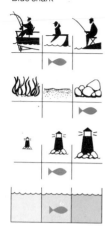

Description Long, tapering body which terminates in a pointed snout, blunt at the tip. The upper jaw of the mouth contains serrated triangular teeth with one concave and one convex edge. The teeth in the lower jaw are straighter and pointed. The first dorsal fin is situated almost in the center of the body; the second is symmetrical to the anal fin. The falciform pectoral fins are long and narrow. The caudal fin is large, with a notched upper lobe about twice the length of the lower lobe. The typical coloration is uniformly dark blue on the back, becoming gradually lighter on the flanks. The belly is white.

Average dimensions 72–120 in (180–300 cm), max. 160 in (400 cm).

Distribution Found virtually in all the world's seas and oceans.

Habitat Pelagic temperate waters with a temperature range of 50°–68°F (10°–20°C). As a rule it lives close to the surface but it may dive to around 500 ft (150 m) and more, particularly in the tropics, so as to avoid water that is too hot. It often approaches the shore.

Behavior Lives isolated or in schools, often following in the wake of ships to feed on refuse thrown overboard.

Feeding Mainly fish, including benthic species, of small or medium dimensions, squid and sometimes even sea birds, taken by surprise as they float on the surface.

Fishing methods Drifting and trolling. Natural baits, live or dead. As is the case with all sharks, a scattering of chum beforehand is indispensable.

Common name
Cobia

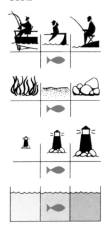

Description Elongated body thinning in front to terminate in a broad, depressed head. The characteristic first dorsal fin is composed of a series of 8–10 isolated spiny rays which can be folded back into a dorsal cavity. Both the second dorsal and the anal fin are very high at the front. The caudal fin is large and powerful. In appearance the cobia resembles a sucker-fish, and it has the same habit of keeping company with sharks and other large fish. The back is chocolate-brown, the flanks are lighter with alternating brown and silvery stripes; the belly is white with orange spots between the ventral and anal fins.

Average dimensions 20–40 in (50–100 cm), max. 80 in (200 cm).

Distribution Cosmopolitan and widespread in all tropical and temperate warm waters. It has recently entered the Mediterranean from the Red Sea.

Habitat Tropical and subtropical waters, preferably those above the continental platform.

Behavior It moves about in small schools, often accompanying large sharks and rays. When following the latter, the cobia takes advantage of catching crustaceans which the rays dislodge while swimming. It finds shelter near floating objects such as buoys, wrecks, and anchored ships.

Feeding Small fish and especially crustaceans.

Fishing methods Trolling, bottom fishing, and casting. It is best to use natural baits (crabs, squid, and fish), particularly live ones. Curiously, when this fish is hooked and boated, the rest of the school follows closely, brushing its sides.

The cobia looks like a suckerfish. The elongated body narrows at the front into a broad, flat head.

Common names
Atlantic bonito
Pacific bonito

Similar species
Sarda australis
Sarda chilensis
Sarda orientalis

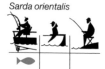

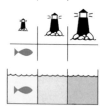

Description Body relatively thin, resembling a miniature tuna. The mouth is quite large and the upper jaw extends vertically to the rear edge of the eye. The two dorsal fins are situated close together, the first very long, straight or slightly concave, usually with 20–23 spiny rays, the second succeeded by 7–9 finlets, and the anal fin, too, by 6–8 finlets. The caudal fin is bilobate and strongly notched with three keels at the base. Coloration is steely blue on the back and upper part of the flanks where 5–11 oblique dark stripes appear. The rest of the body is silvery.

Average dimensions 16–24 in (40–60 cm), max. 40 in (100 cm).

Distribution Atlantic and Mediterranean. Its distribution is discontinuous, however, as it is not found everywhere in the same abundance. In the Pacific it is replaced by the related *Sarda chilensis*, *S. orientalis*, and *S. australis*, all similar in appearance to *S. sarda*.

Habitat Pelagic fish of temperate and tropical seas.

Behavior Lives in schools which tend to remain near the surface and about 15–20 miles from the coasts.

Feeding Small fish (anchovy, mackerel, and small cod) and squid, caught for preference at the surface.

Fishing methods A typical fish for light and medium trolling. In the Mediterranean it is most common from April to November. Baits, artificial or natural, alive or dead, are positioned near the surface and trolled quite slowly about 165 ft (50 m) from the boat, preferably using wire leaders.

Common name
Channel bass

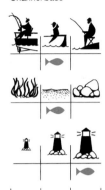

Description   Large elongated body, slightly compressed with a fairly straight ventral profile. The mouth, horizontal and inferior, is furnished with bands of numerous villiform teeth, which are larger in the front part of the upper jaw. Although the species shares the same habitat and bears a bodily resemblance to the sea drum, it is easily distinguished from the latter by the absence of barbels under the chin, these being replaced by 5 pores, and the presence of 10 pores on the snout. Coloration is silver-gray with clear touches of red which are darker on the back. Other distinctive features of the color are black eye spots at the rear of the body between the end of the dorsal and the caudal fin.

Average dimensions   32–40 in (80–100 cm), max. 60 in (155 cm).

Distribution   American Atlantic coasts from Maine to southern Florida and south to Laguna Madre zone of Mexico.

Habitat   Coastal waters and estuaries with beds of sand or mud and sand.

Behavior   Gregarious species, tending to gather in schools. Apparently carries out seasonal migrations but no precise information is available.

Feeding   Crustaceans, mollusks, and small fish.

Fishing methods   Bottom fishing, surf-casting and slow trolling. Use natural baits (crabs, shrimp, and bivalves) or artificial lures (jigs, plugs, feathers, spoons, and streamers). Larger specimens are as a rule caught off reefs, among schools of mollusks or in intertidal channels at high tide.

Common name
King mackerel

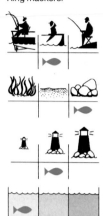

Description Elongated, strongly compressed body. The head is large but the snout, by comparison, is short with a broad mouth. The two dorsal fins touch and are followed by 8–9 finlets. Similarly, 9–10 finlets follow the anal fin. The characteristic lateral line turns sharply downward at the level of the second dorsal fin, and terminates near the tail in a fleshy keel, flanked by the other two, one to each lobe of the caudal fin. Coloration is iridescent blue-green on the back, silvery on flanks and belly. The first dorsal is uniformly blue.

Average dimensions 20 in (50 cm), max. 40 in (100 cm).

Distribution Western Atlantic. From the waters off Florida and in the West Indies, it ranges north to Maine and Massachusetts (in summer) and south to Brazil, although always in water with temperatures of 70°–88°F (21°–31°C).

Habitat Tropical and subtropical waters, especially near reefs and rocks in the open sea.

Behavior Potentially gregarious fish which forms small schools at depths of 65–330 ft (20–100 m), even though solitary individuals are also found. Migratory species. In winter, when the more northerly waters of its range register temperatures below 70°F (21°C), schools of king mackerel congregate densely in the sea off Florida and then, as summer approaches, gradually return northward and westward.

Feeding Small pelagic fish.

Fishing methods Trolling and drifting on surface or bottom. Baits may be either artificial or natural, live or dead.

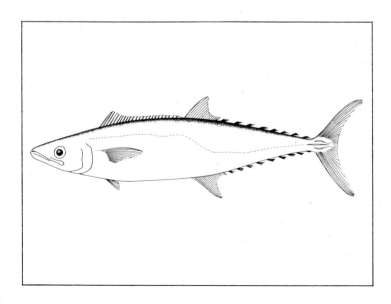

Common name
Spanish mackerel

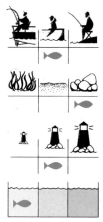

Description Elongated body, somewhat compressed on flanks, which terminates in a pointed snout. The mouth is large and furnished with big, strong teeth. There are two dorsal fins, close together: the first is long and low while the second is short and taller. Both the dorsals and the anal fin are followed by 8–10 finlets. The caudal fin is lunate and characterized by three keels, the middle one being very large and extending to the caudal peduncle. Coloration of the back is iridescent dark blue with gray tones. The lower part of the flanks and the belly are silvery. Along the flanks run wavy, irregular vertical stripes, more plentiful in adults.

Average dimensions 24–28 in (60–70 cm), max. 72 in (180 cm).

Distribution Pacific Ocean from Japan to Australia and to the Red Sea, from where it has penetrated the eastern Mediterranean.

Habitat Tropical and temperate warm coastal waters down to a depth of 650 ft (200 cm).

Behavior Gregarious, tending to form more or less numerous schools. Bigger individuals exhibit a solitary tendency. Undertakes migrations, moving along coasts in spring and summer.

Feeding Small fish (sardines, anchovies).

Fishing methods Trolling with live bait (squid, mullet, garfish, flying fish) and artificial lures. A particularly effective method is to troll near rocky bottoms at dusk or dawn as the tide turns. After being hooked, it fights furiously, swimming rapidly but seldom leaping from the water.

Common name
Spanish mackerel

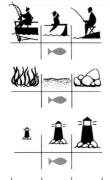

Description Elongated, fusiform, compressed body. Head conical and snout proportionately short. The two dorsal fins are very close to each other. The second dorsal fin and the anal fin are each followed by 8–9 finlets. The pectoral fins have no scales. The lateral line does not turn down sharply as in *Scomberomorus cavalla* but curves gradually to the caudal peduncle, which bears a middle and two lateral keels. Coloration is iridescent blue-green on the back and silvery on belly and flanks where there are also numerous yellow or bronze spots, these being fairly distinctive to the species. The front part of the first dorsal is black. Sometimes the tips of the second dorsal and the pectorals are also black. The anal fin is white.

Average dimensions 16–20 in (40–50 cm), max. 36 in (90 cm).

Distribution Atlantic Ocean from Maine to Yucatan. Sightings reported in waters farther south (South American coasts to Rio de Janeiro) relate to very similar species.

Habitat Tropical and subtropical coastal waters above the continental platform.

Behavior Gregarious, tending to form schools which are hunted by professional fishermen because of the species' importance as a food fish.

Feeding Small fish, especially sardines and anchovies.

Fishing methods Trolling or fly fishing. Ideal lures appear to be light jigs, retrieved by fits and starts. Good results are also obtained with feathers and spoons. Preferred natural baits are small fish or shrimp.

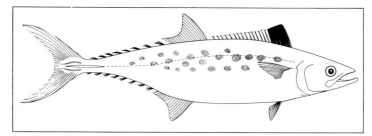

Right: Detail of the ventral fin. The two dorsal fins are very close together. The caudal peduncle bears three keels and the anal fin is white.

Common name
Amberjack

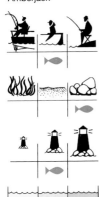

Description Probably the best known and most widely distributed of the Carangidae. The body is elongated and slightly compressed. The eyes, in proportion, are small. The mouth contains rows of numerous small teeth. There are two dorsal fins: the first is short and composed of 7 spiny rays, the first of which is typically covered by epidermis in adult fish; the second is very long, extending to the caudal peduncle. The anal fin is preceded by two isolated spines, likewise covered in adults. The caudal fin is deeply notched. Coloration is blue or olive on the back, silvery white with pink tints on flanks and belly. A dark band runs down the head from the eyes to the base of the first dorsal. An amber-yellow band (from which the common name of the fish is derived) runs along the flanks from the eyes to the center of the body. The lower edge of the pectoral fins is white.

Average dimensions 20–32 in (50–80 cm), max. 76 in (190 cm).

Distribution Cosmopolitan in temperate and tropical waters. It is present in the Indo-Pacific (Japan, China, Hawaii), in the Atlantic and the Mediterranean.

Habitat Pelagic species. It lives at depths of 65–230 ft (20–70 m) but may dive to more than 1,000 ft (300 m).

Behavior Lives in fairly small schools or can be solitary.

Feeding Fish and various invertebrates.

Fishing methods Medium trolling, drifting and sometimes bottom fishing. Either artificial lures (plugs, spoons, and jigs) or natural bait, particularly live, may be used. Trolling speed should be steady at around 2–4 knots.

Common names
California yellowtail
South African amberjack

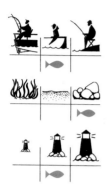

Description Elongated, fusiform body, both fish being very similar to the typical amberjack (*Seriola dumerili*) of the Atlantic and Mediterranean. The snout, however, is more pointed in these Pacific subspecies. The dorsal fin is elongated and the second half appears taller. The caudal peduncle has a small keel on either side. Coloration is very typical and characteristic. The back is generally dark, bluish with purple reflections, while the lower part of the flanks and the belly are silver. Along the lateral line is a clear golden band that extends from the tip of the snout to the tail. The caudal fin is bright yellow while the other fins are opaque yellow or yellow-green.

Average dimensions 16–24 in (40–60 cm), max. 64–68 in (160–170 cm).

Distribution There are three subspecies of *S. lalandi* which are distinguished mainly by their range: the California yellowtail (*S. l. dorsalis*) is found from Baja California in Mexico to Los Angeles; the South African amberjack (*S. l. lalandi*) lives south of the equator in the Atlantic, from Argentina to South Africa, and in the Pacific in Australia and New Zealand. The third subspecies is *S. l. aureovittata*, from the coasts of Asia.

Habitat Mainly coastal waters.

Behavior Gregarious when young, forming schools. The adults tend to be more solitary and sedentary.

Feeding Small fish, various invertebrates, and crustaceans.

Fishing methods Trolling and surf-casting with live bait or artificial lures. Prior to striking, the fish should be allowed a few moments to swallow the entire bait.

Common name
Great barracuda

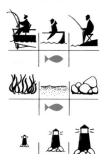

Description   Largest representative of the numerous barracuda family. The body is characteristically elongated and sub-cylindrical. The snout is long and pointed, and the lower jaw prominent, with a fleshy forward lobe which makes the shape of the fish more streamlined when the mouth is closed. The numerous canine-form teeth are present not only in the jaws and on the palate. The two dorsal fins are clearly separated. Coloration varies from grayish to greenish-brown on the back, while the flanks and belly are silvery. Adults have dark, irregular spots on the lower flanks and particularly close to the tail.

Average dimensions   36–48 in (90–120 cm), max. 72 in (180 cm).

Distribution   Tropical and subtropical worldwide, except for eastern Pacific.

Habitat   Pelagic and coastal species.

Behavior   The smallest individuals tend to gather in schools along the coasts and even to enter lagoons, while the larger adults are for the most part solitary. The species is considered potentially dangerous to humans. Take care with the flesh, which is often toxic and even fatal to humans because of the poisons contained in the prey on which the barracuda feeds.

Feeding   Fish, cephalopods, and crustaceans.

Fishing methods   Medium trolling, surf-casting, casting, and fly fishing. Use either artificial lures (spoons, plugs) or natural bait, e.g. live fish. Reel in the line with rapid, irregular jerks. Always use wire leaders to prevent the sharp teeth of the fish cutting through the line.

Common names
Hammerhead shark
Great hammerhead
shark

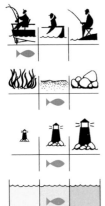

Description Of all sharks, those that belong to the genus *Sphyrna* are certainly the easiest to identify because the head is transformed into the characteristic hammer shape. The body of *Sphyrna zygaena* is long and fairly streamlined. The head is flattened, the forward edge is convex and smooth, whereas in the similar species, *S. mokarran*, it is straight, with a distinctive central notch. The spiny prolongation of the second dorsal fin does not extend to the caudal fin, and the rear edge is almost straight, as in *S. mokarran*. Coloration is olive-brown on the back, shading gradually to grayish-white on the belly.

Average dimensions *S. zygaena*: 120 in (300 cm), max. 160 in (400 cm); *S. mokarran*: 140–160 in (350–400 cm), max. 240 in (600 cm).

Distribution Cosmopolitan, in tropical and temperate warm waters.

Habitat Coastal pelagic species.

Behavior May form schools which, particularly in the case of the hammerhead, can contain more than a thousand individuals. *S. zygaena* regularly travels north as the water gradually warms up and stays there until the temperature dips below 68°F (20°C). *S. mokarran*, which requires a higher average temperature of 75°F (24°C), has a more confined range.

Feeding Fish, especially sting-rays.

Fishing methods Slow trolling or drifting. To attract the sharks, it is essential to strew chum, consisting of very oily food particles that contain food. As a rule they prefer natural bait such as mackerel, small carangids, and squid.

Diagram of the large groove in front of the nostril of the hammerhead shark. Above: The head seen from below. The head is squashed, with a smooth, convex front edge.

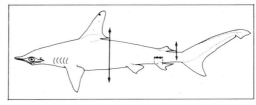

Common name
Giant sea bass

Description   Although at first glance its appearance may point to a relationship with the grouper, this fish belongs to an entirely different family, the Percictidae. The body is sturdy, with a short, high head. The snout is blunt and the lower jaw slightly projecting. The first dorsal fin is very low and contains 11 spiny rays. The second, which is larger, has just 10 soft rays. The caudal fin is slightly concave. Coloration is brownish-black on the back and lighter on the lower part of the flanks and on the belly. All the fins are black. The young are reddish with large black and yellow spots, and the fins are black or almost transparent.

Average dimensions   24–36 in (60–90 cm), max. 72–80 in (180–200 cm).

Distribution   Northeast Pacific from California to Mexico. This species has also been sighted off the Asiatic coasts of the Indian Ocean.

Habitat   Tropical and subtropical coastal waters near rocky bottoms or vast beds of *Laminaria* which offer excellent opportunities both for finding shelter and capturing prey. It prefers water temperatures of 64°–79°F (18°–26°C).

Behavior   Mainly solitary. The young live at a depth of 30–80 ft (10–25 m) then gradually descend to 100–165 ft (30–50 m), like the adults.

Feeding   Principally crustaceans and fish.

Fishing methods   Bottom fishing or drifting. Given the size to which it may grow, this species should be fished with appropriate tackle and live or dead bait, provided it is large, at depths of 65–165 ft (20–50 m).

Common names
Tautog
Blackfish

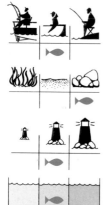

Description   Large representative of family Labridae, characterized by a sturdy body and rounded back. The head is blunt and compact, terminating in a mouth with very thick lips. The dorsal fin is very long and consists predominantly of spiny rays. The caudal fin is square. Scales cover parts of the dorsal and anal fins, and there is an isolated zone of small scales close to the eyes. Coloration is dark, ranging from gray to black. The belly and throat are white or pale gray, sometimes spotted. The eyes are greenish. A typical feature of this fish is its ability to change color to blend with its surroundings. The young are generally brown or olive with dark markings on the flanks.

Average dimensions   12–20 in (30–50 cm), max. 36 in (90 cm).

Distribution   Atlantic Ocean from Nova Scotia to South Carolina. They are most abundant in the coastal belt between Cape Cod and Delaware.

Habitat   Temperate coastal waters, at a depth of not more than 100–135 ft (30–40 m), on beds of rock or detritus, or around reefs and wrecks.

Behavior   Between May and October, peaking in June, tautog gather in bays and estuaries to spawn. They prefer temperatures of 46°–71°F (8°–22°C) and this is an important factor in their movements.

Feeding   Mainly crustaceans and mollusks.

Fishing methods   Casting and bottom fishing from shore or from anchored boat. Bottom fishing is advisable in late spring and the fall, using natural baits (mussels, crabs or shrimp).

Common name
White marlin

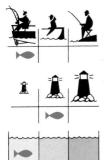

The white marlin's body is characterized by small overlapping scales furnished by a single spine.

Description Elongated, compressed body. The upper jaw is prolonged to form the typical rostrum with circular cross-section. The first of the two dorsal fins is almost the height of the body and has a rounded edge, as do the anal and pectoral fins. The ventral fins are long but very narrow, being constituted merely of 3 rays (1 spiny and 2 soft). The caudal fin is broad and falcate, with a pair of keels, one per lobe, at the base of the peduncle. The body is covered with small overlapping scales furnished with a single spine. Coloration is dark blue or brown with greenish tints on the back, silver-brown on the flanks and silver-white on the belly. The first dorsal has a blue-black inter-radial membrane with a scattering of small but numerous black spots. The other fins are brown-black. With only rare exceptions, there are no bands or stripes on the flanks.

Average dimensions 100 in (250 cm), max. 120 in (300 cm).

Distribution Mediterranean and Atlantic, from Nova Scotia to Argentina. It is most abundant off the Florida coasts, in the West Indies and along the coasts of Brazil and Argentina.

Habitat Pelagic tropical and subtropical waters, rarely temperate seas, and as a rule always above the thermocline.

Behavior It gathers in small groups. Undertakes regular migrations toward warmer parts of its range during the winter.

Feeding Any species of fish, crustacean or cephalopod that is locally plentiful.

Fishing methods Trolling. Despite its size, it is regarded as a fish to be caught with medium tackle. Both live and dead natural bait and artificial lures (spoons, jigs, and feathers) are used.

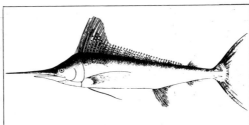

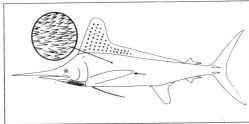

Common name
Striped marlin

Description Body elongated, stout, and much compressed on flanks. In this species, too, the upper jaw is prolonged to form a rostrum. The first dorsal fin is so large that it almost equals the height of the body. The pectoral fins are pointed, highly mobile, and capable of being folded over the flanks. The lateral line is straight, single, and clearly visible. The caudal fin is broad and falcate, bearing a pair of keels, one per lobe, at the base of the peduncle. Coloration is steel-blue on the back and becomes gradually silver-blue and white on the flanks and belly. The fins have blue spots and there are 10–14 vertical light blue stripes on the flanks which persist even after the death of the fish, whereas in other marlins they tend to disappear.

Average dimensions   100–120 in (250–300 cm), max. 160 in (400 cm).

Distribution   Indo-Pacific.

Habitat   Pelagic tropical and temperate warm waters with temperatures of 61°–86°F (16°–30°C).

Behavior   It forms small groups. During the winter months striped marlin tend to concentrate near the equator and then disperse in summer to northern and southern waters.

Feeding   A large variety of fish (anchovies, sardines, mackerel, and flying fish) and squid.

Fishing methods   Typical big game fish, caught with either artificial or natural baits. During the initial fighting phases, after being hooked and dragged into surface waters, it performs series of leaps, more frequently than other marlin, above the waves.

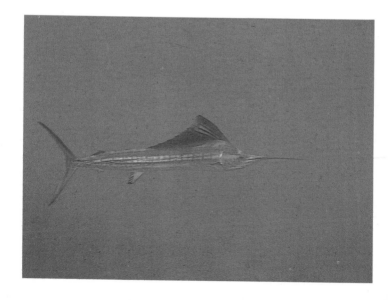

Common name
Mediterranean spearfish

Similar species
Tetrapturus albidus
Tetrapturus angustirostris
Tetrapturus pfluegeri

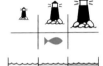

Description Elongated and more or less compressed body. The snout, with its short, rounded rostrum, confirms the affinity of this species to marlins and sailfish. The dorsal fin, relatively low and uniform for much of its length, has a high anterior lobe. Its height is midway between that of marlins and the sailfish. The pectoral fins are short and when folded over the flanks do not extend further than the lateral line. The ventral fins are each constituted of a single ray. The lunate caudal fin displays two basal keels on either side. Coloration is blue-gray on the back and white on the belly. The dorsal fin is usually a variable shade of blue.

Average dimensions 60–72 in (150–180 cm), max. 96 in (240 cm).

Distribution Mediterranean and Adriatic. It is most frequent along the shores of Africa and Sicily. It appears that its distribution is presently confined to the Mediterranean. The related species *Tetrapturus albidus* (see plate 29) and *T. pfluegeri* are found in the Atlantic; and *T. angustirostris* lives in the Indo-Pacific.

Habitat Pelagic species which may dive to a depth of 650 ft (200 m) but prefers to remain between the thermocline and the surface.

Behavior Solitary.

Feeding Fish especially saury pike (*Scomberesox saurus*).

Fishing methods Trolling with light tackle, since these fish, despite appearances, are not that powerful, weighing no more than 65–80 lb (20–25 kg).

Common name
Albacore

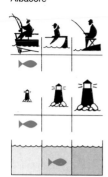

Description Large tuna with fusiform, elongated body which is highest at the attachment point of the second dorsal fin. The latter is separated briefly from the first dorsal and is followed by 7–9 finlets, as is the anal fin. The long pectoral fins extend beyond the dorsals, terminating at the level of the first finlets, a feature which also easily distinguishes the fish from other species of tuna. The body is covered with small scales. The caudal peduncle is thin with a distinct central keel and two other smaller ones on either side. Coloration is metallic dark blue on the back, white on flanks and belly; and there is an iridescent band along the flanks. The yellow color of the first dorsal fin is brighter than that of the second dorsal and anal fins. The finlets are dark. The rear edge of the caudal fin is white.
Average dimensions 24–36 in (60–90 cm), max. 48 in (120 cm).
Distribution Cosmopolitan. Lives in all oceans and seas of tropical and temperate zones.
Habitat Pelagic species. Lives in surface waters, diving to about 330 ft (100 m) at most.
Behavior Lives in schools. Migratory species, the schools following regular routes associated with reproduction. It spawns from July to September.
Feeding Mainly fish, crustaceans, and squid.
Fishing methods Classic prey of big game fishing and medium trolling. It is caught with artificial lures (spoons, jigs, and other baits) or by baiting the hooks with sardines, mackerel, mullet or squid.

The albacore's eyes are quite large. The main feature are the long pectoral fins that extend beyond the dorsals.

Common name
Yellowfin tuna

Description   Typical tuna with huge, fusiform, elongated body. Its distinctive features are the adults' very large, high second dorsal and anal fins, which are crescent-shaped and measure about one fifth of the length of the entire fish. They are followed, respectively, by 8–10 and 7–10 finlets. The very narrow caudal peduncle bears three keels, one central and two laterals. The body is covered by tiny scales which become larger in the corselet area behind the head. The metallic dark blue coloration of the back turns gradually to silver-yellow on the flanks and belly, the latter exhibiting some 20 broken vertical stripes. A golden yellow or iridescent blue band runs along the flanks from the eye to the tail. The dorsal and anal fins are yellow, as are the finlets, which have a black margin. Overall, the yellowfin tuna is the most colorful member of the family.

Average dimensions   56–60 in (140–150 cm), max. 80 in (200 cm).

Distribution   Tropical species present in the Atlantic and Indo-Pacific.

Habitat   Pelagic species of tropical and temperate seas.

Behavior   Gregarious, forming numerous schools that tend to remain below the thermocline. Carries out migrations, few details of which are known. Approaches shore in summer months.

Feeding   Wide range of fish, crustaceans, and cephalopods.

Fishing methods   Essentially trolling with natural and artificial baits. Drifting can be attempted with a regular scattering of small fish as chum.

Common name
Blackfin tuna

Description   Small tuna with fusiform, slightly compressed body. The second of the two dorsal fins is low and small, followed by 7–9 finlets; the anal fin is followed by 6–8 finlets. The pectoral fins are long but never extend beyond the second dorsal. The body is entirely covered by small scales. Coloration is quite characteristic: metallic dark blue back, silver-gray flanks and whitish tail. The fins are dark and the finlets uniformly black, even though they show a faint yellow tint. On the flanks, but only with live specimens, there is a broad golden band; and on the lower part of the flanks, too, there are pale bars alternating with light spots.

Average   dimensions   28–32 in (70–80 cm), max. 36 in (90 cm).

Distribution   Western Atlantic from Massachusetts to Brazil.

Habitat   Pelagic tropical and temperate warm waters.

Behavior   Gregarious species which forms schools consisting of several thousands of individuals that often mingle with skipjack. The favorite spawning grounds seem to be the areas bounded by the Florida Current, the Gulf of Mexico, and the Caribbean. During the summer months the species heads north but still keeps to water with a temperature of not less than 68°F (20°C).

Feeding   Principally fish that live in the surface ocean layers, and also cephalopods and crustaceans.

Fishing methods   Mainly trolling or drifting with natural and artifical baits, at the surface, some miles from shore, over high seabeds.

The whole body of the blackfin tuna is covered by small scales. There is a broad gold band on the flanks, but only in live specimens.

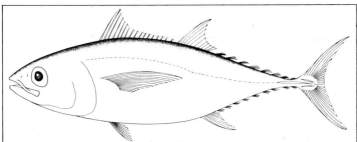

Common name
Southern bluefin tuna

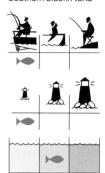

Description The largest of all the Pacific tuna. The body is fusiform, almost rounded in cross-section and much heavier at the front. Of the two dorsal fins, separated by a brief gap, the second is higher and followed by 8–10 finlets. The anal fin is followed by 7–9 finlets. The pectoral fins are short and never reach the vertical, being positioned in the gap between the dorsals. The caudal peduncle is narrow and bears three keels, a large central one and two laterals at the base of the tail, which is large and lunate. Coloration is dark blue, almost black, on the back, and silver-white on the flanks and belly where there are also transverse lines and translucent spots. The finlets are opaque yellow, bordered black. The keels are bright yellow.

Average dimensions 32–48 in (80–120 cm), max. 60–72 in (150–180 cm).

Distribution Indian and Pacific Oceans in the belt between latitudes 30° and 50°S.

Habitat Pelagic and coastal subtropical and temperate warm waters, preferably with a temperature of about 68°F (20°C).

Behavior Gregarious species which forms large schools. Young aged 1–2 years assemble in summer off the coasts of Western Australia; those aged 3–4 years gather off the coasts of South Australia in summer and New South Wales in winter.

Feeding Crustaceans, cephalopods, and fish.

Fishing methods Trolling or drifting, principally with live natural bait (mackerel, mullet, squid, and little tuna) but also with artificial lures (Kona Heads, spoons, jigs, and feathers).

Common name
Bigeye tuna

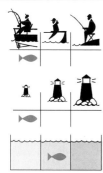

The finlets of the Bigeye tuna are yellow but bordered black.

Description   Huge tuna with fusiform body, the flanks slightly depressed. The lower jaw projects, and the eye, as the common name suggests, is very big. The two dorsal fins are separated by a short space and the second is followed by 8–10 finlets; the anal fin is followed by 7–10 finlets. The pectoral fins are quite long, measuring just under one third of the length, and situated above the juncture, of the second dorsal fin. The caudal fin is lunate and the very narrow caudal peduncle has three keels on either side, the central one being the largest. Coloration is dark blue on the back, whitish on the lower part of the flanks and on the belly. An iridescent bluish band runs along the flanks. The first dorsal fin is bright yellow, the second dorsal fin and the anal fin paler yellow. The finlets are also yellow but bordered black.

Average dimensions   60–72 in (150–180 cm), max. 93 in (236 cm) recorded for one Pacific specimen.

Distribution   Western Atlantic, Pacific, and Indian Oceans in waters with temperatures of 61°–81°F (16–27°C).

Habitat   Tropical pelagic waters, from the surface to a depth of 850 ft (250 m).

Behavior   Typically gregarious, it forms large schools. During the day, these schools remain for preference in deep water, unlike other tuna species which tend to move up to shallower layers. Migratory species, like other tuna, moving toward warmer waters of its range when about to spawn.

Feeding   A wide variety of fish, cephalopods, and crustaceans.

Fishing methods   Deep trolling with natural bait (squid, mackerel, mullet), live or dead, and artificial lures.

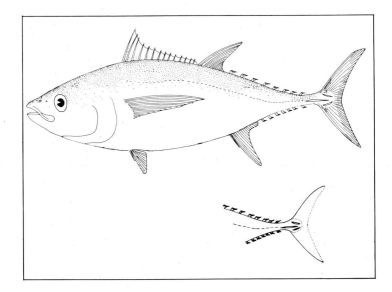

Common name
Bluefin tuna

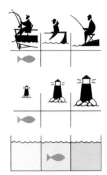

Description The largest of all the tuna, it is distinguished by its fusiform body, almost round in cross-section and heavier at the front. The two dorsal fins are separated by a short gap, the second being taller and followed by 8–10 finlets. The anal fin is followed by 7–9 finlets. The short pectoral fins never reach the vertical, being positioned in the gap between the dorsals. The caudal peduncle is narrow, with three keels, a large central one and two laterals at the base of the broad, lunate tail. Coloration is dark blue, almost black, on the back, and silvery-gray on the flanks and belly, where there are also transverse lines and translucent spots. The first dorsal fin is yellow or bluish, the second reddish-brown. The finlets are opaque yellow.

Average dimensions 28–80 in (70–200 cm) according to population, max. 120 in (300 cm).

Distribution Mediterranean and Atlantic.

Habitat Pelagic subtropical and temperate waters with a temperature of not less than 50°–54°F (10°–12°C).

Behavior Typically gregarious. Spawning occurs, as a rule, from May to July, when the adults make for warmer, shallower waters within their range of distribution. Young and immature individuals then remain in these zones while the adults move off to colder waters in search of food.

Feeding Fish, crustaceans, and cephalopods.

Fishing methods Trolling or drifting. Use is made principally of natural bait, live or dead (mackerel, mullet, squid) but artificial lures are also suitable for trolling only. For drifting, a constant strewing of chum, based on small fish, is necessary.

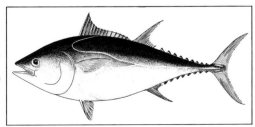

Above: Detail of the pelvic fin. The second of the two dorsal fins is the higher, followed by 8–10 finlets. The flanks and belly are silver-white.

Common name
Longtail tuna

Description Tuna with small, fusiform body characterized by a caudal peduncle longer and narrower than that of other tuna, with numerous finlets, 8–9 positioned dorsally, 7–8 ventrally. The body is almost wholly covered by tiny scales, except for the zone around the pectoral fins, the so-called corselet, where the scales are larger. Coloration is dark blue or black on the back, progressively paling to silver-gray on the flanks and belly. The ventral area between the pectoral fins and the anal fin appears to be sprinkled with translucent spots. The tip of the second dorsal and the anal fin is yellow. The finlets are also yellow but with a gray border. The caudal fin is blackish with greenish-yellow tints.

Average dimensions 16–24 in (40–60 cm), max. 40 in (100 cm).

Distribution Central Pacific and Indian Ocean from the coasts of Southeast Asia to the Gulf of Aden.

Habitat Coastal tropical and subtropical waters with temperatures around 66°–68°F (19°–20°C) and characterized by constant salinity.

Behavior Gregarious fish which forms schools.

Feeding Crustaceans, cephalopods, and fish.

Fishing methods Trolling, casting, and fly fishing. This is by no means an easy prey for it is not always possible to induce it to bite. As a rule experts advise trolling bait close to ciliates, where the bottom slopes rapidly, and near barrier reefs at high tide. Baits may be natural, preferably live, or artificial.

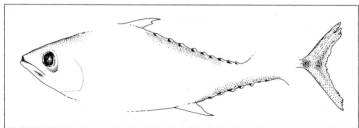

Common name
Permit

Description Short, high, and compressed body. The front of the snout is high and obtuse, terminating in a small mouth which in young individuals only is furnished with small teeth. The adults, in fact, have no teeth but develop a stout internal lining of the mouth, similar to leather. The dorsal fin is preceded by 6 spines. Typically, this fish has over-large second, third, and fourth ribs which are easily identifiable by touching the flanks. Coloration is basically silver or blue-gray.

Average dimensions 12–20 in (30–50 cm), max. 48 in (120 cm).

Distribution Western Atlantic from Massachusetts to southern Brazil.

Habitat Coastal tropical and subtropical waters which are not too deep, 6–135 ft (2–40 m), near muddy or sandy bottoms.

Behavior As a rule, the fish form small schools of a few dozen individuals, although sometimes numbers may be much higher. The young are much more gregarious whereas the adults tend to become solitary.

Feeding Principally mollusks, crustaceans, sea urchins, and small fish.

Fishing methods Casting, surf-casting, fly fishing, bottom fishing from a boat or from piers and rocks. The strike may have to be repeated several times. Natural baits are best. Immediately after it is hooked, the fish makes a quick dive for the bottom, seeking shelter among the rocks and coral, grinding its mouth against them in attempts to break free. In most cases this maneuver results in the line breaking.

XIPHIAS GLADIUS

Common name
Swordfish

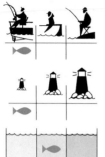

Description Huge fish with elongated, subcylindrical body, the front part being stronger. The snout terminates in a long, pointed rostrum, the longest beak to be found in any fish so equipped. There are two dorsal fins, the second being very small and underdeveloped in comparison with the first, situated right behind the head, which is very high, stiff, and falciform. In young and immature specimens the two fins are, however, joined by a membrane. The pectoral fins are also stiff and falciform. There are no ventral fins. The very high caudal fin is preceded by a keeled peduncle on either side, recessed above and below. Coloration is dark brown, almost black, on the back and flanks, shading gradually to a lighter color on the belly.

Average dimensions 32–84 in (80–220 cm), max. 180 in (450 cm). In many countries the species is protected.

Distribution Cosmopolitan in all tropical and temperate oceans and seas.

Habitat Temperate, pelagic waters although the species may dive to a depth of 2,100 ft (650 m) or more.

Behavior Generally solitary, it sometimes congregates in small groups. It forms pairs in the spawning period. Occasionally, in the spawning season (from June to September), when surface waters reach 73°–75°F (23°–24°C), swordfish travel from colder, deeper waters toward warmer zones of their range, where they remain to feed for the rest of the year.

Feeding Cephalopods, crustaceans, and mainly fish of varied species, both pelagic and demersal (bottom-dwelling).

Fishing methods Trolling, but only after they have been sighted. During the night it is best to practice bottom fishing or drifting. The best bait seems to be squid but mullet, mackerel, and skipjack appear to give good results. The swordfish is cautious, so the bait must be prepared with special care.

Opposite: the three drawings in the center, from bottom to top, show the modified appearance of the swordfish during growth. The snout terminates in a long, flattened rostrum which may reach a length of 15 ft (4.5 m).

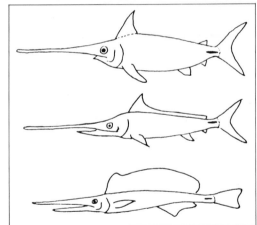

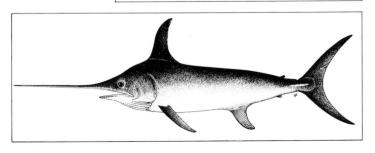

Common names
Atlantic wolf fish
Spotted wolf fish
Similar species
Anarhicas minor

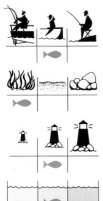

Description Elongated body, narrow and compressed at the rear. The head is huge while the snout is short and rounded in outline. The mouth is large, provided with strong canine teeth that are partially visible when the jaws are closed. There are no ventral fins. The dorsal fin extends along the back for almost the entire length of the body. The caudal fin is small and square. Coloration is grayish, olive with purple reflections on back and flanks. The belly is whitish. A dozen or so vertical dark bands, partly merging together to form a geometrical pattern, run along the flanks. The skin of these species is very tough; in areas where they are caught commercially it is used and worked as if it were leather. Both species share the same waters and are quite similar in appearance, but *Anarhicas minor* is smaller.
Average dimensions 20–24 in (50–60 cm), max. 60 in (150 cm).
Distribution North Atlantic, along the coasts of America and northern Europe, from about latitude 45°N to Greenland and the northern shores of Norway, and the North Sea.
Habitat Coastal and pelagic waters or rocky and sandy bottoms with an abundance of algae.
Behavior Solitary and aggressive. They spawn from October to January.
Feeding Principally mollusks, crabs, and other crustaceans, echinoderms and small fish.
Fishing methods Bottom fishing, especially with natural bait such as crabs and mollusks. It is best to use metal leaders because the strong teeth may snap softer nylon lines.

Common name
Eel

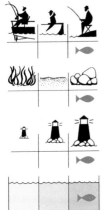

Description Very common, well-known fish with an elongated, snakelike body, rounded at the front and flattened behind. The dorsal, caudal, and anal fins are linked. There are well-developed pectoral fins but no ventral fins. The lower jaw, longer than the upper one, and the juncture of the dorsal, positioned well back in comparison with the pectorals, distinguish this eel immediately from the conger eel (see plate 13). Coloration varies with age and surroundings. In general the back is dark while the flanks and belly are lighter, white or grayish with silvery reflections.

Average dimensions 12–32 in (30–80 cm), max. 60 in (150 cm). Females are longer.

Distribution Fairly widespread in coastal waters of Mediterranean, North Sea, and eastern Atlantic from Scandinavia to the shores of Africa up to latitude 25°N. The American eel *Anguilla rostrata* lives off the Atlantic coasts of the United States. Other species inhabit the Indian and Pacific Oceans (e.g. *A. japonica*).

Habitat Marine coastal and brackish waters, lagoons, and estuaries over muddy bottoms.

Behavior Aggressive and voracious, it may be very abundant in some places. It is most active at night. Very familiar as a migratory fish.

Feeding Fish, crustaceans, and mollusks.

Fishing methods Bottom fishing with sliding and floating sinker, baiting the hook with small fish, worms or crustaceans. Keep it away from the bottom to prevent it hiding in a cleft. The best spots for angling are river mouths, lagoons, and canals.

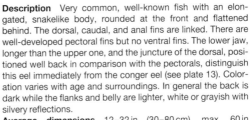

Common name
Sheepshead

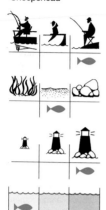

Description Oval, compressed, and fairly high body. The snout is rounded at the front, this feature being more marked in older individuals. The mouth is quite small but there are 8 broad, sharp teeth at the front of either jaw. The forward part of the dorsal fin has a series of strong spines. The pectoral fins are long and extend almost to the attachment of the anal fin, this being characterized by a second very strong spiny ray. The caudal peduncle is broad and the caudal fin is slightly bifurcate. The body is covered by large scales that become smaller in front of the pectoral and ventral fins. Coloration is silver-gray or greenish-yellow, with 5–6 broad, dark vertical bands on the flanks that are clearer in the young.

Average dimensions 14–16 in (35–40 cm), max. 30 in (75 cm).

Distribution Western Atlantic from North Carolina to Texas. Some experts are of the opinion that this species is divided into three subspecies that occupy an overall range from Nova Scotia to south of Rio de Janeiro.

Habitat Coastal and brackish waters near bays and canals over beds of mixed sand and rocks down to a depth of 270 ft (80 m).

Behavior Lives in groups that may in places consist of quite a few individuals.

Feeding Principally mollusks and crustaceans.

Fishing methods Bottom fishing and casting, preferably from piers and bridges. Either natural or artificial baits can be used, but the fish will not always bite, being suspicious of bait.

Common name
Meager

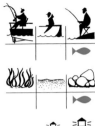

Description Sturdy, elongated, and slightly compressed body. The mouth is large, oblique, and terminal. The pre-opercular margin is dentate. The dorsal fin is divided into two parts by a deep notch. The anterior part is higher, with spiny rays. The second dorsal fin is much longer, but low. The first ray of the anal fin is spiny, the second soft. The caudal fin is truncate and almost quadrangular in shape. The lateral line extends to the posterior margin of the caudal fin. Coloration is silvery, darker and duller on the back, with golden-bronze reflections on the flanks. The mouth cavity is golden-yellow.

Average dimensions 12–40 in (30–100 cm), max. 80 in (200 cm).

Distribution Mediterranean, eastern Atlantic from southern Scandinavia to Senegal. Similar species are found along the American coasts and in the Indo-Pacific.

Habitat Coastal waters at depths of 50–650 ft (15–200 m), near sandy or rocky bottoms but also in midwater and surface waters. Ventures into brackish lagoons.

Behavior Tends to be solitary but becomes gregarious in the reproductive period. The young usually gather in large schools. It spawns from March to June.

Feeding Pelagic fish, particularly mullet, sardines, and anchovy (following the schools), and crustaceans.

Fishing methods Bottom fishing or very slow trolling at depth. Hooks should for preference be baited with crustaceans, pieces of mackerel or sardines. Once hooked, the meager offers stout resistance and is thus an excellent game fish.

Above: A detail of the gills. The meager has a dorsal fin divided into two parts by a deep notch, the forward part being higher, with spiny rays.

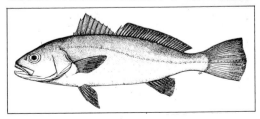

Common names
Kahawai
Australian salmon

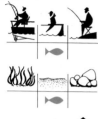

Description Fairly low, fusiform body. The head is pointed and the mouth, terminal, has a slightly protruding lower jaw. The single dorsal fin has the overall appearance of two triangles separated by a small notch. The anterior part is shorter, with 9–11 spiny rays. The anal fin is short and terminates just behind the dorsal. The caudal fin is deeply notched and markedly lobate. Coloration is olive with gray tones on the back, paler on the flanks and belly, where there is a faint golden-yellow tint. The upper parts of the head are adorned with irregular markings while 3–4 rows of circular golden spots appear on the flanks, above the lateral line.

Average dimensions 16–20 in (40–50 cm), max. 36 in (90 cm).

Distribution Pacific Ocean, particularly along the coasts of Australia and New Zealand and neighboring islands.

Habitat Tropical coastal waters near sandy bottoms or rocky shoals.

Behavior Fish with gregarious habits which tends to form quite large schools composed mainly of 4–7 -lb (2–3-kg) specimens. Larger individuals are less sociable.

Feeding Small fish and crustaceans.

Fishing methods Casting with artificial lures or live natural bait (ideally garfish), with light tackle. The best technique is to be guided by sea birds which always hover around schools of kahawai and, once the fish are sighted, to let the boat drift with the current into their midst. At this point, the bait is cast and rapidly retrieved. As a rule, kahawai are ready to bite.

Common name
Mediterranean flagfin

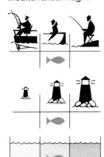

Description Slender body, subcylindrical in cross-section, but compressed on caudal peduncle and entirely covered by close-fitting scales. The head is quite high and sturdy with a long snout. The mouth, broad and terminal, is equipped with sharp, erectile teeth scattered over the jaws and mouth cavity. The eyes are large and elliptical. None of the fins has spiny rays. The wide dorsal fin begins almost above the ventrals, and in the males the first 3–4 rays are very long, with filamentous tips. There is a small adipose fin after the dorsal fin and above the anal fin. The caudal fin is bifurcate and partly covered by scales. Coloration is reddish on the back and flanks, which are variously streaked, and silver-gray on the belly. The tip of the dorsal bears a black spot. There are reddish-yellow bands, of varying clarity, on all the fins. The iris is a mixture of yellow and sky-blue.

Similar species *Chlorophthalmus agassizil* and *Synodus saurus*.

Average dimensions 8–16 in (20–40 cm), max. 18 in (45 cm).

Distribution Mediterranean and eastern Atlantic from coasts of Portugal to those of Senegal and to the Canaries and Madeira.

Habitat Lives at depths of 500–1,000 ft (150–300 m), max. 3,300 ft (1,000 m), close to muddy bottoms.

Behavior Spawns from March to June.

Feeding Carnivorous predator of fish, cephalopods, and crustaceans.

Fishing methods Bottom fishing with naturally baited hooks.

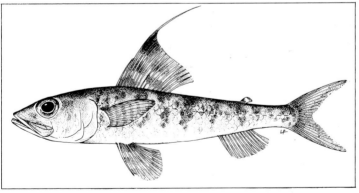

The snout of Chlorophthalmus agassizil *(far right) and that of* Synodus saurus *(right).*

Common name
Bullet tuna

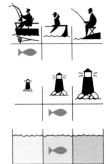

Description Sturdy, fusiform body, round in cross-section. The snout is short and pointed, the mouth provided with tiny teeth. The two dorsal fins are well separated, the first, consisting of spiny rays, being higher than the second. The second dorsal and the anal fins are followed respectively by 8 and 7 finlets. The caudal fin is small and falcate with 3 keels on the caudal peduncle, one in the middle and one to each lobe. The body has no scales except for the corselet and the lateral line. Coloration is bluish on the back, the rear part displaying some 15 dark bands that extend to the lateral line. The flanks are silver and the belly is white. The anal fin is whitish.

Average dimensions 12–16 in (30–40 cm), max. 20 in (50 cm).

Distribution Mediterranean and Atlantic where it mingles with the related *Auxis thazard*, also found in the Pacific.

Habitat Normally pelagic waters but often nearer the coast.

Behavior Gregarious and migratory, it forms large schools comprising individuals of the same size. Spawns from May to November, at which period it is seen offshore.

Feeding Fish (basically Clupeidae), crustaceans, and squid.

Fishing methods Trolling with light tackle, preferably with artificial lures such as feathers, chrome spoons combined with feathers or imitations of squid and octopus. Pieces of mackerel or anchovy are the best of natural baits. All bait should be trolled at moderate speed through the middle of the school. The species can also be used as bait for larger tuna, marlin, etc.

Common name
Gafftopsail catfish

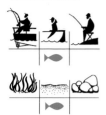

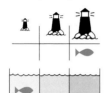

Description Long body with curved and slightly depressed head. The snout is short and rounded. There are two pairs of barbels, the first being short, on the chin, the other, longer and flattened, on either side of the mouth. The dorsal and pectoral fins are notable for a very long spiny ray, filamentous and erectile, the front part of which is serrated. The dorsal is followed by a small adipose fin. The caudal fin is deeply notched, the upper lobe being longer. Coloration varies from gray-blue to brown on the back, becoming a lighter silver-white on the belly. The body is typically devoid of scales and thus appears smooth.

Average dimensions 16–20 in (40–50 cm), max. 40 in (100 cm).

Distribution Western Atlantic from the Carolinas to Brazil; it is abundant in the Gulf of Mexico and the Caribbean.

Habitat Coastal waters, lagoons, and estuaries, from which it sometimes ventures upriver.

Behavior Tends to be gregarious. The males are noted for brooding the eggs in their mouth from the time they are fertilized to the moment they hatch, a period of about three months.

Feeding Principally small fish and invertebrates which it dislodges from the bottom with its sensitive barbels.

Fishing methods Bottom fishing, surf-casting and slow trolling. Both natural and artificial baits can be used. Once hooked, the catfish defends itself fiercely, particularly if the tackle is light. When removing the fish from the water, care needs to be taken because the strong spines are capable of inflicting painful wounds.

Common names
Gar

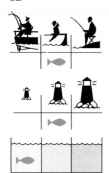

Description Elongated, slightly compressed body, almost cylindrical in cross-section. The snout is characterized by two long, slender jaws (the lower one more so than the upper one), furnished with many sharp teeth. The dorsal and anal fins, similar in appearance and size, are positioned far back near the caudal peduncle. The caudal fin is falcate and the lower lobe is slightly larger than the upper lobe. Coloration is dark blue on the back and silver-white on the flanks and belly. There is an opaque blue band on the sides. A characteristic feature, astonishing to anyone catching the fish for the first time, but quite natural, is the green coloration of the bones and flesh.

Average dimensions 12–24 in (30–60 cm), max. 36 in (90 cm).

Distribution Mediterranean and Black Sea, eastern Atlantic from coasts of Morocco to Scandinavia and Iceland, North Sea, and Baltic Sea.

Habitat Coastal surface waters.

Behavior Gregarious species which lives in schools of varying numbers. In spring and summer it is found close to rocky shores but returns to deeper waters as winter approaches.

Feeding Principally small fish such as anchovy and sardines.

Fishing methods A typical species for light trolling. The tackle should be light if the aim is to have a bit of fight when reeling in. Artificial lures are best, e.g. small silver spoons and the classic feather. The feather is fixed to the hook with colored wire to simulate the head of a fish but should not project more than 4–5 mm beyond the hook point to ensure the strike.

Common name
Bogue

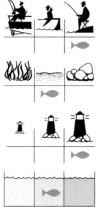

Description   Fairly short body, tapering and slightly compressed. The eye is quite big, occupying most of the short snout area. The mouth is small and terminal. The dorsal fin is well developed, higher toward the front and capable of being retracted into a groove. The caudal fin is notched, with pointed lobes. Coloration of the back is olive-green with metallic tints while the flanks are silver with 3–4 longitudinal golden lines. The ventral and anal fins are white. There is a black spot at the base of the pectoral fins.

Average dimensions   4–10 in (10–25 cm), max. 14 in (36 cm).

Distribution   Mediterranean and Atlantic along European shores (from Norway to Angola) and American coasts (Caribbean and Gulf of Mexico).

Habitat   Bottoms of various types (rocky, sandy, muddy, with *Posidonia*) in coastal waters up to a depth of 1,200 ft (350 m).

Behavior   Gregarious species that forms schools, with semipelagic habits, liable to make fairly regular migrations along the coasts. During the night it moves upward to surface waters; but in stormy weather it heads for the depths.

Feeding   Virtually omnivorous, feeding on small crustaceans, planktonic organisms and vegetable matter. The young are more carnivorous than the adults.

Fishing methods   Casting at surface or on bottom. The fish is frequently caught even though it is not always eager to bite. Hooks should be baited with pieces of shrimp, mollusks, shreds of fish or mixed preparations. Strewing mushy chum is also recommended for keeping the school intact.

Common name
Ray's bream

Similar species
Brama japonica

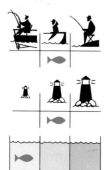

Description Front of body rounded and high, narrowing toward the tail. The head is very flat with a short snout and a wide, oblique mouth, furnished with numerous sharp, conical teeth arranged in several lines. The long dorsal and anal fins, similar in shape, are raised at the front. The pectoral fins are long and when they are spread close to the body they overlap the apical lobe of the anal fin. The ventral fins are inserted at the base of a large spine-shaped scale. The caudal fin is deeply notched. Coloration is silvery-black and fairly uniform over the whole body. The unpaired fins are rather lighter in color while the rest are pale yellowish-gray. The mouth is entirely black.

Average dimensions 12–16 in (30–40 cm), max. 28 in (70 cm).

Distribution Mediterranean, northern and central Atlantic, South Africa, Indian Ocean, and southern Pacific from Australia to Chile. In the northern Pacific there is a similar species, *Brama japonica*, very widespread in Japanese waters.

Habitat Principally oceanic in surface waters although occasionally this fish dives to a depth of 2,500 ft (800 m).

Behavior Tends to be solitary. Undertakes annual migrations northward during the summer, remaining in waters with a temperature range of 54°–75°F (12°–24°C). It spawns in August–September, usually when the water is around 68°F (20°C).

Feeding Small fish, pelagic crustaceans, and cephalopods.

Fishing methods Bottom fishing and sometimes trolling. Crustaceans, small fish or pieces of squid make the best bait.

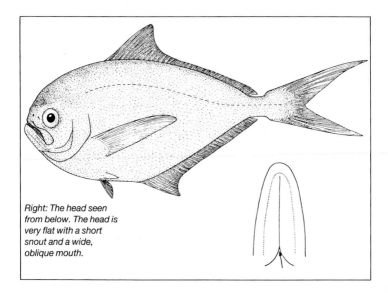

Right: The head seen from below. The head is very flat with a short snout and a wide, oblique mouth.

Common name
Blacktip shark

Description Rather stockier than other Carcharinidae, the blacktip shark is notable for its long, pointed snout. The mouth is large with triangular, finely serrated teeth, those of the lower jaw being narrower and sharper, with an almost straight base. The first dorsal fin is averagely high and begins just behind the pectoral fins. Both dorsals and the anal fin have a basal spine at the rear. The upper lobe of the caudal fin is much larger than the lower lobe. Coloration of the back is dark gray with bronze or bluish tints, and the belly is yellowish-white. Typically, the color of the tip of the dorsal, pectoral, and anal fins and of the lower lobe of the caudal fin is black.

Average dimensions 60–72 in (150–180 cm), max. 102 in (255 cm).

Distribution Present in much of the Mediterranean, except apparently in the Adriatic and along the Greek coasts. In the Atlantic it is distributed in the tropical belt from Madeira to the Cape Verde Islands and from Brazil to Florida and north to Cape Cod. It has been sighted in the Pacific from Baia California in Mexico to Peru.

Habitat Pelagic and coastal waters, quite near the surface.

Behavior Lives both on its own and in schools. It often leaps from the water. It is reputed to be dangerous to humans.

Feeding Principally fish but also mollusks and crustaceans.

Fishing methods Trolling. In some places it may be abundant even though caught accidentally. Tackle is the normal type for sharks (strong hooks, metal leaders). Offers fair resistance and is particularly combative when wounded.

Common name
Atlantic gray shark

Description Stout, strongly curved body, highest at level of first dorsal fin, convex in shape at the front. The first dorsal fin, situated well forward above the pectorals, is very large. A fold of skin runs along the middle of the back as far as the second dorsal which has a free rear margin. The snout is broad and oval, narrowing into a rounded tip. The teeth of the lower jaw are smaller and sharper than those of the upper jaw, triangular and serrated from base to apex. The caudal peduncle is quite short and the upper lobe of the caudal fin is about twice the size of the lower lobe. Coloration is slate-gray to brownish-gray on the back and white on the belly.

Average dimensions 76–84 in (190–210 cm), max. 120 in (300 cm).

Distribution Common in Mediterranean and throughout the Atlantic, both on the east coasts (from Portugal to the Cape Verde and Canary Islands) and west coasts (from United States to Gulf of Mexico and West Indies to Brazil).

Habitat Tropical and temperate warm coastal and oceanic waters from the surface to a depth of 900 ft (280 m). It often enters brackish waters.

Behavior Gregarious. Lives in schools which may be numerous in places. It is considered relatively harmless to humans.

Feeding Fish, crustaceans, and mollusks, with a clear preference for the last.

Fishing methods Trolling. Hooks should preferably be baited with mollusks and trolled at a depth of 15–65 ft (5–20 m) where the species appears to be found most frequently.

Common name
Musselcracker

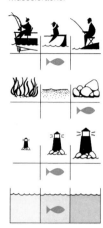

Description Tall, sturdy body which resembles that of the gilthead. The head is huge and in larger individuals the snout becomes very thick and fleshy, typically projecting above the upper lip. The teeth, 4 in the upper jaw and 6 in the lower jaw, are strong and conical. The fish uses them to crack the shells of the organisms on which it feeds. The pectoral fins are long and the caudal fin is slightly notched. The body is covered by large scales. Coloration varies with age, although most individuals are gray or blackish. The ventral fins are dark or pink. The margin of the tail is yellow. The young are lighter in color with 2 or more bands along the flanks.

Average dimensions 16–24 in (40–60 cm), max. 40 in (100 cm).

Distribution South Africa along the shores of the Indian Ocean and in part of the Atlantic Ocean.

Habitat Coastal waters close to reefs and cliffs down to a depth of 230–270 ft (70–80 m).

Behavior A typically solitary species. The numbers of musselcrackers increase in coastal waters during the winter months.

Feeding Crustaceans, sea-urchins, and mollusks.

Fishing methods Bottom fishing and drifting from a boat. The best zones are those where the bottom is characterized by rocks and cliffs, and off reefs. Recommended baits are crustaceans (whole shrimp). Catching the species is difficult because larger specimens put up stout resistance and may even snap lines with their powerful teeth.

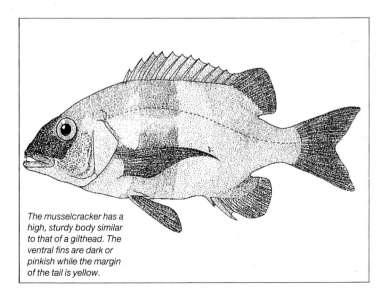

The musselcracker has a high, sturdy body similar to that of a gilthead. The ventral fins are dark or pinkish while the margin of the tail is yellow.

Common name
Dentex

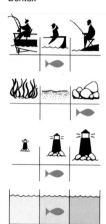

Description Robust, oval body, quite high and slightly compressed. The head is enormous with an inclined, convex profile. The snout is long and pointed. Both jaws carry well-developed canine teeth. The pectoral fins are rather long. The caudal fin has pointed lobes. Coloration is iridescent gray-blue on the back, more silvery with pinkish tints on the flanks and belly. There are scattered dark spots on the flanks, more numerous on the head. The dorsal and caudal fins are pinkish-brown, the ventral and anal fins yellowish and the pectorals pink.

Average dimensions 12–20 in (30–50 cm), max. 40 in (100 cm).

Distribution Mediterranean and eastern Atlantic from British Isles to Senegal.

Habitat Coastal waters close to rocky bottoms, generally 50–165 ft (15–50 m) deep, at most 500–650 ft (150–200 m), reefs and promontories. The young settle more often on sandy-muddy bottoms or among *Posidonia* prairies.

Behavior Solitary as adults but gregarious when young. Spawns from April to June.

Feeding Fish and cephalopods, which it attacks after lying patiently in wait.

Fishing methods Deep trolling. An infrequent although not altogether rare quarry, it is one of the few Mediterranean species which offers a chance of setting a record and appearing in the annual IGFA lists. Artificial lures may include spoons, while natural baits are virtually restricted to garfish and cuttlefish, possibly live. Choice of grounds is determined by the preference of the dentex for *Posidonia* prairies, reefs, and waters around promontories, trolling slowly and hoping to induce the fish to attack.

The drawing on the right shows the front canines and the lateral teeth of the dentex. The dorsal and caudal fins are pinkish-brown, the ventral and anal fins yellowish.

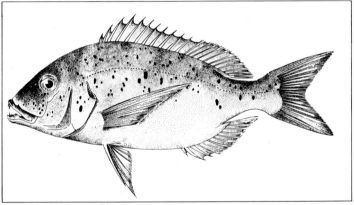

Common names
Annular sea bream
White sea bream
Two-banded sea bream

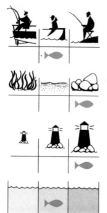

Similar species
Diplodus sargus
Diplodus vulgaris

Description Relatively high, compressed body. The head is slightly protractile and characterized by large notched teeth, somewhat inclined forward. All three species are very similar in morphology, the differences being mainly associated with coloration. *Diplodus annularis* is grayish-yellow with silvery reflections and 5 vertical not very evident light brown bands. There is a black spot on the caudal peduncle which does not extend, however, to the lower side of the peduncle. The color of *D. sargus* is similar to the preceding species but it is darker on the back. There are 6–8 vertical stripes on the flanks which are more evident in the young. The margin of the operculum and of the unpaired fins is black. The caudal peduncle also displays a black spot. *D. vulgaris* is the same color as the above. There are 7–9 longitudinal golden lines on the flanks. A dark band extends along the nape from the insertion of the dorsal fin to the pectoral fins. There is a complete black band on the caudal peduncle which may stretch to the rear extremities of the anal and dorsal fins.

Average dimensions *D. annularis*, 3–7 in (8–18 cm), max. 10 in (24 cm); *D. sargus*, 6–12 in (15–30 cm), max. 18 in (45 cm); *D. vulgaris*, 7–10 in (18–25 cm), max. 18 in (45 cm).

Distribution All are present in the Mediterranean. *D. annularis* and *D. vulgaris* are also found in the Atlantic, the former from the Bay of Biscay to Gibraltar, the Canaries and Madeira, the latter southward to Angola.

Habitat Sea bream all live in coastal waters. The annular sea bream prefers beds of sand and *Posidonia*, at a depth of up to 300 ft (90 m). The other two species are found more frequently on rocky and neighboring sandy bottoms. *D. annularis* and *D. sargus* also venture into brackish water, adapting well to this environment.

Behavior May be solitary or part of small schools. The young are more gregarious. The annular sea bream spawns from February to September, depending on the water temperature within its range. The white sea bream spawns from January to June and the two-banded sea bream in the fall.

Feeding Quite varied and based mainly on invertebrates (worms, crustaceans, mollusks, and echinoderms) and algae.

Fishing methods Bottom fishing. The bait should be suspended some way from the bottom and thus the line must be mounted with a terminal lead. Natural baits are best, and given the feeding habits of the three species, there is a wide choice, although the preference goes to worms, mollusks, and pieces of squid.

Sea bream have a slightly protractile mouth with incisor-like teeth. The three species are differentiated mainly by coloration.

Common name
Ladyfish

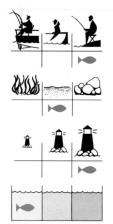

Description Elongated, fusiform body, pointed snout and large mouth. The eyes have a well-developed adipose lid. The dorsal fin, higher at the front, starts just beyond the body's half-way mark. The anal fin is placed far back. The caudal fin is deeply notched. The body is covered by very small scales. Coloration is silver-blue on the back and silver on the flanks and belly. The dorsal and caudal fins are variably dark while the others are paler.

Average dimensions 20–24 in (50–60 cm), max. 40 in (100 cm).

Distribution Western Atlantic from New England to Gulf of Mexico, Brazil, and South Africa.

Habitat Coastal waters of seas and lagoons. Often ventures into brackish water and freshwater, e.g. mangrove swamps and rivers.

Behavior It lives in schools of varying size which come nearer to shore at high tide. Moves north at the end of the summer. It probably spawns in late spring in waters of the Gulf Stream off the American coasts. From here the larvae, very similar to those of eels, head for zones of mangrove swamps and coastal lagoons to complete their growth.

Feeding Principally crustaceans and small fish.

Fishing methods Surf-casting, either with natural or artificial baits. Once hooked, the fish defends itself fiercely, leaping above the surface and swimming away rapidly. Its energetic, combative attitude is reminiscent of the bonefish (*Albula vulpes*) and the tarpon (*Megalops atlanticus*).

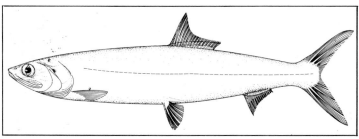

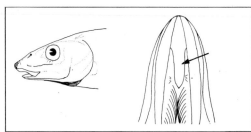

Right: the head seen from the side and from below. The dorsal fin is higher at the front. Coloration is silver on the flanks and belly.

Common names
Dusky grouper
Atlantic weakfish

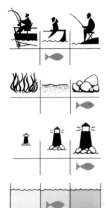

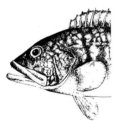

Description   The dusky grouper has a large, robust body with a high, rounded outline. The head is huge and the mouth broad, with distinctively thick lips. The fairly large, long dorsal fin has very strong, spiny first rays which can be raised and locked in an upright position. A series of three spines is also present along the edge of the operculum. The caudal fin is broad and rounded. Coloration varies from opaque brown to reddish with irregular white spots and stripes on the flanks. The rear margin of the caudal fin is distinctively white. The Atlantic weakfish differs in having a head that is concave in outline, a longitudinal crest along the upper part of the operculum, otherwise devoid of spines, and reddish-brown or bluish coloration.

Similar species   *Polyprion americanum*

Average dimensions   *Epinephelus guaza*, 12–32 in (30–80 cm), max. 60 in (150 cm); *Polyprion americanum*, 32 in (80 cm), max. 80 in (200 cm).

Distribution   Mediterranean and Atlantic.

Habitat   Coastal waters on rocky bottoms with caves and clefts in which to hide. The Atlantic weakfish may descend to about 1,400 ft (420 m), although it is more common at 330–660 ft (100–200 m).

Behavior   Solitary, territorial species that occupy burrows to which they return regularly and when in danger.

Feeding   Voracious predators which feed essentially on fish, cephalopods, and crustaceans.

Fishing methods   Almost exclusively bottom fishing although they may occasionally be caught by deep trolling, using live or dead natural baits. The strike must be quick and decisive.

The head of the dusky grouper is huge, with a broad mouth and thick lips. The first spiny rays of the dorsal fin can be raised and fixed in an upright position.

Common names
Gray gurnard
Sapphirine gurnard

Similar species
Triglia lucerna

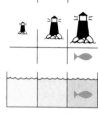

Description Small, elongated body. The large head is covered by bony plates. In *Eutriglia gurnardus* the snout is blunt whereas in *Triglia lucerna* it is pointed. There is a strong backward-facing spine behind the operculum and above the pectoral fins. The two dorsal fins are separated, the second being virtually identical in shape and position to the anal fin. In both species the first 3 lower rays of the pectorals are free. Coloration of the gray gurnard is as a rule grayish-brown, more or less reddish, on the back and flanks, whitish on the belly. The first dorsal fin has a large black spot. The sapphirine gurnard, on the other hand, is redder and more markedly streaked on the back, golden-white on the belly. The outer surface of the pectorals is violet-pink, dappled white or green and with a light blue or red margin; the inner side has a blue patch with lighter spots.

Average dimensions *Eutriglia gurnardus*, 6–16 in (15–40 cm), max. 24 in (60 cm); *Triglia lucerna*, 8–16 in (20–40 cm), max. 30 in (75 cm).

Distribution Mediterranean and eastern Atlantic from Norway to Senegal.

Habitat Bottoms of sand, mud and sand or detritus between depths of 65–1,000 ft (20–300 m), more frequently 165–500 ft (50–150 m).

Behavior Both these species tend to be gregarious. When removed from the water they may emit grunting sounds caused by contractions of the swim-bladder. The gray gurnard spawns from December to April, the sapphirine gurnard from February to August. In summer both species come nearer to shore and frequent shallower water.

Feeding Crustaceans and fish. The gray gurnard appears to feed more widely on crustaceans.

Fishing methods Bottom fishing. Because both species live on seabeds that are generally smooth and flat, hooks can be baited with shrimp, pieces of squid, and fish, and leaders allowed to bob freely along the bottom to attract the attention of any fish in the vicinity. The gurnards described here are more active at night.

The head of the gurnard is covered by bony plates. The two dorsal fins are separated. In both species the first 3 lower rays of the pectoral fins are free.

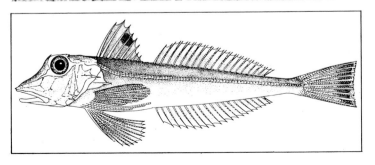

Common names
Giant goby
Grass goby

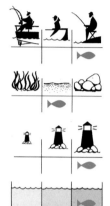

Description In both species the body is rather stocky, but in *Zosterisessor ophiocephalus* the head is compressed, while in *Gobius cobitis* it is depressed, so that the back and belly are flattened. The upper jaw of the latter species does not project beyond the lower jaw, as is the case with its relative. The two dorsal fins are separated, the second being longer and similar to the anal fin. Coloration of the giant goby ranges from brown to green and yellow, with irregular bands or large blackish spots. The margins of the dorsal fins are often bordered white, like those of the caudal and anal fins. The grass goby is olive-yellow with brown streaks. A dark spot is always present on the caudal peduncle. The anal fin is sky-blue or yellowish.

Average dimensions *Gobus cobitis*, 6–8 in (15–20 cm), max. 11 in (27 cm); *Zosterisessor ophiocephalus*, 6–8 in (15–20 cm), max. 10 in (24·5 cm).

Distribution *G. cobitis*, Mediterranean and eastern Atlantic from Norway to Mauritania; *Z. ophiocephalus*, along Mediterranean coasts, particularly abundant in Venetian lagoons.

Habitat *G. cobitis*, coastal waters on rocky bottoms with eelgrass; *Z. ophiocephalus*, muddy bottoms and lagoons.

Behavior Social during reproductive period between May and June when they form pairs.

Feeding Crustaceans, mollusks, worms, and small fish.

Fishing methods Bottom fishing, the most effective baits being worms, mollusks, and crustaceans. On muddy beds it is best to reel in the line jerkily. In the vicinity of algae and eelgrass, it is possible to fish in midwater, supporting the line with a float.

Common name
Squirrelfish

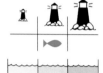

Description Fairly elongated, high, compressed body with a long snout. The wide mouth is notable for its thick, rounded lips. The dorsal fin is higher at the front where there are 12 spiny rays. The coloration is very characteristic. The head and the body bear alternating blue and yellow stripes which increase in number but diminish in size (especially the yellow ones) as the fish grows. The inside of the mouth is red. The unpaired fins are dark, often black in the rear part. There is often a red spot near the operculum.

Average dimensions 10–12 in (25–30 cm), max. 20 in (50 cm).

Distribution Western Atlantic from South Carolina to the Gulf of Mexico and Brazil.

Habitat Shallow coastal waters near barrier reefs.

Behavior The squirrelfish lives in groups, often mingling with individuals of other species but of the same genus, e.g. *Haemulon plumieri*, easily distinguished by having stripes on the head alone. With the aid of sonar or an underwater microphone, it is a fairly simple matter to identify a school of these fish, for they are capable of producing grunting noises by scraping their pharyngeal teeth and using the complex swim-bladder as a sound-box. Spawns in late spring and summer.

Feeding Small fish and various invertebrates (mollusks, crustaceans, and worms) which it hunts and catches on the bottom.

Fishing methods Bottom fishing or slow trolling in midwater. It bites readily and is regarded as an excellent quarry because of its appetizing flesh.

Common names
Ballan wrasse
Cuckoo wrasse
Rainbow wrasse

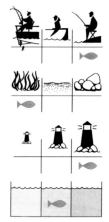

Similar species
Coris julis
Labrus bimaculatus

Description The ballan wrasse has a fairly large and compact body with a sturdy but comparatively short head. The snout is pointed and the mouth, of average size, has thick lips and strong teeth. At the front of the dorsal fin is a long series of spiny rays. The rear part, with soft rays, is higher. The cuckoo wrasse, however, is longer and moderately compressed. The head, too, is longer. The dorsal fin is elongated and of the same height overall. The rainbow wrasse is decidedly slimmer, its snout pointed and the mouth small. The first dorsal fin is higher at the front. Coloration of the ballan wrasse, like that of all the Labridae, is extremely variable, although in this species the livery shows no sexual dimorphism. In general the dominant color is green or reddish-brown with numerous small white spots. The dorsal and anal fins are often striped blue. The coloration of the male cuckoo wrasse is brownish-yellow with blue stripes on the back, flanks, and fins; the head and front part of the back are greenish. Young and female cuckoo wrasse, however, are orange-red or red with three black spots on the back between the end of the dorsal and the caudal peduncle. The male rainbow wrasse has a blue-green back and a longitudinal red or orange, blue-bordered band. The front part of the dorsal is distinguished by a red spot. The young and the females have a violet-brown back and a pinkish-white longitudinal band on the flanks.

Average dimensions Labrus bergylta, 12–20 in (30–50 cm), max. 24 in (60 cm); L. bimaculatus, 6–10 in (15–25 cm), max. 16 in (40 cm); Coris julis, 4–8 in (10–20 cm), max. 10 in (25 cm).

Distribution L. bergylta, rare in Mediterranean but widespread in eastern Atlantic from Morocco to Scandinavia; L. bimaculatus, Mediterranean (rarer in eastern part) and eastern Atlantic from Senegal to Scandinavia; C. julis, Mediterranean and eastern Atlantic from the Canaries to Scandinavia.

Habitat Coastal waters on beds of rocks or eelgrass. L. bergylta is more of a surface species while the other two are found at greater depths, L. bimaculatus up to 650 ft (200 m).

Behavior These are interesting marine fish, most species having the additional peculiarity of changing sex with age. At spawning time, between spring and early summer, males of the two Labrus species described here build a nest in which the females lay their eggs. Rainbow wrasse often behave like cleaner fish for larger species.

Feeding Crustaceans, mollusks, worms, and other invertebrates. Larger individuals also catch small fish.

Fishing methods Bottom fishing close to rocky coasts or above beds of eelgrass. The line should be equipped with a terminal sinker and can carry two or three small hooks baited for preference with mollusks or crustaceans. The touch is delicate and requires fairly sensitive tackle.

The dorsal fin bears a long row of spiny rays at the front, and in the ballan wrasse, the rear part, with soft rays, is higher (central drawing). The rainbow wrasse is markedly slimmer.

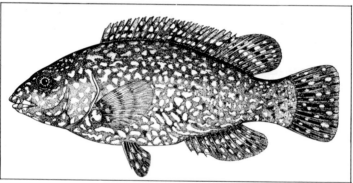

Common name
Scabbard fish

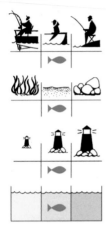

Description   Very long and markedly compressed body which both in shape and coloration resembles a metallic ribbon. The head is very large with a prominent crest on the nape. At the front of the broad mouth are strong hooked teeth. The lower jaw is larger and longer than the upper jaw. The dorsal fin is low but extends along the entire length of the body. The anal fin is very long although the first 40 rays are almost invisible. The ventral fins are reduced to a tiny spine. The caudal fin is small and bifurcate. The skin is bare and the coloration uniformly silver.

Average dimensions   20–60 in (50–150 cm), max. 84 in (210 cm).

Distribution   Virtually cosmopolitan. It is found in the Mediterranean, the Atlantic, and the Indo-Pacific.

Habitat   Deep waters of 330–1,000 ft (100–300 m), max. up to 2,000 ft (600 m), close to sandy bottoms. The fish also lives near the coast, especially where strong currents rise from the depths.

Behavior   Fairly gregarious, it may form large schools, particularly in the spawning period, which is from late winter to spring in the south of its range, and from summer to the fall in the north. At these seasons it approaches the shore.

Feeding   Fish, crustaceans, and cephalopods.

Fishing methods   Bottom fishing and sometimes deep trolling as well. The hooks, baited with pieces of mackerel or squid, should be mounted on wire leaders to prevent the line being torn away by the fish in its attempts to break free.

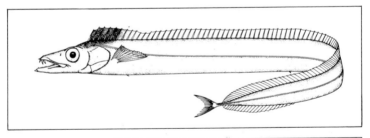

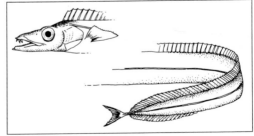

The scabbard fish has a much flattened body, metallic in color. The front of the wide mouth is furnished with strong, hooked teeth. The dorsal fin is low and extends along the entire body.

Common name
Leer fish

Description Elongated body, averagely high and compressed. The top of the head in outline is almost straight and the snout is pointed. There are two dorsal fins, the first composed of 7 very short spiny rays, interlinked at their base by a membrane; the second is initially high and then dips sharply. The anal fin, similar in appearance to the second dorsal, is preceded by 2 spines. The caudal fin is deeply notched. Coloration of the back is brown; the flanks beneath the lateral line and the belly are silver-white. The fins are light brown and the tips of the second dorsal and the anal fins are black.

Average dimensions 16–40 in (40–100 cm), max. 80 in (200 cm).

Distribution Mediterranean and Atlantic Ocean from the Bay of Biscay to South Africa and along African coasts of the Indian Ocean.

Habitat Coastal waters from the surface to a depth of about 165 ft (50 m). It also enters brackish waters.

Behavior Gregarious when young, tending to be solitary as an adult. At night it approaches the coasts to hunt.

Feeding Almost exclusively fish (mackerel, sardines, mullet, and garfish).

Fishing methods Trolling, preferably with live bait (especially garfish). Artificial lures can also be used, notably spinning chrome spoons combined with white feathers. Baits should be kept at a certain distance, say 165–265 ft (60–80 m), from the boat so as not to arouse the suspicions of the leer fish, always somewhat reluctant to bite, and trolled at 3–6 knots.

The leer fish has a long, tall, and flattened body. There are 2 dorsal fins, the first with 7 spiny rays.

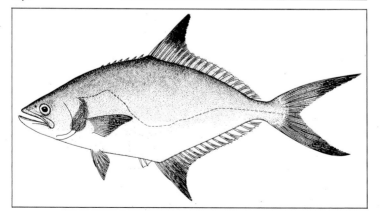

Common name
Dab

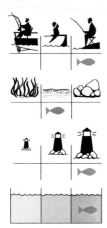

Description　Dextral flatfish with much compressed, oval body. The mouth is relatively small. The large, long dorsal fin starts just above the eyes. The caudal fin is moderately rounded. The body is covered by denticulate scales which make the skin rough to the touch, especially on the colored side. Coloration is brownish with small dark or reddish-yellow spots on the ocular side. The side facing the bottom is whitish.

Average dimensions　12 in　(30 cm), max.　16–18 in (40–45 cm).

Distribution　North Atlantic, from the Bay of Biscay to Norway and Iceland, and North Sea.

Habitat　Very common especially in coastal waters with sandy bottoms at depths of 65–130 ft (20–40 m), at most 500 ft (150 m).

Behavior　Lives in large schools which regularly migrate for spawning. After hatching, and before metamorphosis, the young are carried by the currents toward the coast. Spawns from February to June. Dab congregate in waters closer to shore during the summer to escape the first frosts of the fall.

Feeding　Very varied diet consisting mainly of the most plentiful species. Examinations of stomach contents have revealed that the dab feeds on echinoderms, mollusks, worms, and small fish, but particularly crustaceans.

Fishing methods　Bottom fishing and surf-casting. Given the reduced size of the mouth, it is necessary to use small hooks baited with shrimp, small crabs or mollusks.

Common name
Striped sea bream

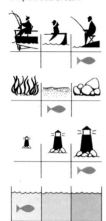

Description Fairly elongated, compressed body. The outline of the head is almost straight. The snout is long and pointed, the mouth low and broad, furnished with tiny teeth that take on a molar shape at the back. The dorsal and pectoral fins are long. The caudal fin is large and deeply notched. The coloration is distinctive: gray with silver and gold tints, darker on the back. There are 15–16 narrow, vertical dark bands which run down from the back but do not reach to the belly, which is white. The upper part of the snout is dark.

Average dimensions 6–12 in (15–30 cm), max. 22 in (55 cm).

Distribution Mediterranean, eastern Atlantic from the Bay of Biscay to South Africa, Red Sea, and southwestern Indian Ocean.

Habitat Coastal waters, preferably at depths of around 15–65 ft (5–20 m) and at most 265 ft (80 m), on beds of sand, mud and sand, and *Posidonia*.

Behavior Tends to be gregarious, living in small schools. Reproduction is in spring or summer.

Feeding Principally small invertebrates (worms, mollusks, crustaceans, and sea urchins).

Fishing methods Surf-casting, bottom fishing, and slow trolling. The best places are sandy beds off beaches and near *Posidonia* prairies. Preferred baits are worms, shrimp, and mollusks. In surf-casting the line should be cast beyond the zone of breaking waves and then wound in slowly so that the lead trails along the bottom, raising clouds of sand that attract the fish in expectation of an easy prey. Fishing is best done at night.

Common name
Tripletail

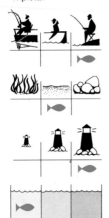

Description　Very tall body, compressed and almost rectangular. The forehead is recessed and the mouth, oblique and turned upward, has a protractile upper jaw and thick lips. The rear margin of the preoperculum is serrated. The dorsal and anal fins are symmetrical and rounded; and because the posterior part of each, with its soft rays, is placed so far back, the fish appears to have a caudal fin with three lobes. Coloration ranges from yellowish-brown to dark brown with indistinct marks on the flanks. The belly is lighter in color. The fins are darker than the body, the pectorals being yellowish. The eye appears to be masked by an oblique dark band. The young are much more yellow but become darker with age. The body is covered by small, rough scales.

Average dimensions　16–20 in (40–50 cm), max. 40 in (100 cm).

Distribution　Cosmopolitan. It is widespread in the Atlantic and the Indo-Pacific, in tropical and temperate warm waters.

Habitat　Coastal waters, estuaries, and lagoons.

Behavior　Lives in schools. The young take advantage of their coloration and shape to float passively on the surface so that they look like leaves, thus deceiving predators.

Feeding　Small fish, crustaceans, and mollusks.

Fishing methods　Bottom fishing, surf-casting, and trolling. Larger specimens are capable of putting up reasonable resistance when hooked. They may also bite at artificial lures (spoons) but the best results are achieved with natural bait such as shrimp or mollusks.

The mouth of the tripletail is oblique and turned upward. The upper jaw is protractile and the lips are thick. Coloration of the body varies from yellowish-brown to dark brown.

Common names
Anglerfish
Monkfish

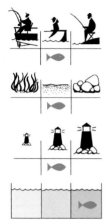

Description   The head and front part of the body are very broad and flattened. The rear part, however, gradually narrows toward the tail. The enormous mouth is directed upward. There are two dorsal fins, the first being composed of spiny rays separated from one another. The highly distinctive first ray, enlarged at the base and situated close to the upper jaw, is movable and is used by the fish as a lure to attract prey. There are numerous spines and small fleshy appendages on the back and the flanks. Coloration of the back is brown with violet and green tints, adorned with lighter spots and irregular streaks. The belly is whitish. *Lophius budegassa* is very similar to but smaller than *L. piscatorius*, has fewer rays on the second dorsal fin (9–10 instead of 11–12), and a shorter third spiny ray.

Average dimensions   8–40 in (20–100 cm), max. 80 in (200 cm).

Distribution   Mediterranean and Atlantic Ocean from Gibraltar to Iceland and Scandinavia, and North Sea.

Habitat   Coastal waters on muddy or sandy bottoms to a depth of 1,300–2,000 ft (400–600 m).

Behavior   Solitary and rather aggressive species. Spawning occurs between February and July.

Feeding   Principally fish and, in surface waters, diving seabirds.

Fishing methods   Bottom fishing with natural bait. Given their habits, they are not often caught; moreover, the bait has to end up very close for them to be tempted to bite.

Common name
Louvar

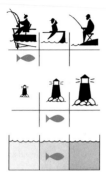

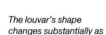

The louvar's shape changes substantially as it grows.

Description   Oval, elongated body, laterally flattened. The head is enormous, almost vertical at the back. The mouth is small, lacking teeth in the adults, and situated at the same level as the tiny eyes. There is one dorsal fin, similar and opposite to the anal fin, positioned at the rear of the body and provided with weak spinelike rays, spaced well apart. The pectoral fins are long while the ventral fins, larger in the juvenile stage, are rudimentary in the adults. The large, falcate caudal fin has a thin peduncle with a short keel on either side. The skin is roughened by the presence of spiny scales. Coloration is metallic blue on the back, silver with golden reflections on the flanks and belly.

Average dimensions   24–60 in (60–150 cm), max. 80 in (200 cm).

Distribution   Cosmopolitan. Tends to be found in waters between latitudes 17°N and 14°S, although it sometimes goes beyond these bounds. It is also present in the Atlantic, the Indian Ocean and the Pacific.

Habitat   Oceanic warm temperate waters, mesopelagic, in open sea off the continental platform.

Behavior   Solitary. Spawns late spring and summer.

Feeding   Feeds on planktonic organisms (salpa, ctenophores, and jellyfish), vegetation, and possibly also small fish and cephalopods.

Fishing methods   Bottom fishing or deep trolling. It is caught accidentally, however, because of its rarity and the difficulty in choosing suitable bait (pieces of squid and small fish alternating with green vegetation are advised).

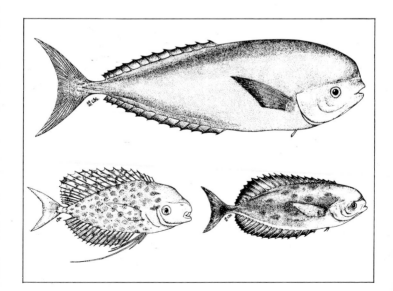

Common name
Hake

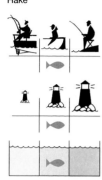

Hake is widely fished for commercial purposes.

Description Elongated body, narrow and laterally compressed. The back of the head is flattened and characterized by a raised V-shaped crest which is a distinguishing mark of all the family Merlucciidae. The mouth is wide and the lower jaw more developed than the upper jaw. The chin bears no barbels. There are two dorsal fins, quite distinct and lacking spiny rays: the first is high whereas the second is lower and longer. The anal fin is very similar in shape and size to the second dorsal. The caudal fin becomes progressively more notched as the fish grows. Coloration is steel-gray on the back, paler on the flanks and white on the belly. The inside of the mouth is black.

Average dimensions 12–24 in (30–60 cm), max. 52 in (130 cm) in Atlantic, max. 44 in (110 cm) in Mediterranean.

Distribution From Mediterranean to North Sea and northeast Atlantic from Mauritania to Norway and Iceland.

Habitat Deep coastal or pelagic waters with average depth of 230–1,200 ft (70–350 m), although sometimes up to 3,330 ft (1,000 m).

Behavior Lives in schools like the majority of Gadiformes. During the day it remains near the bottom, ascending toward the surface at night.

Feeding Highly voracious species that feeds mainly on crustaceans and small school fish.

Fishing methods Bottom fishing with natural and artificial bait. It is often seen emerging with a white mass protruding from its mouth. This is the swim-bladder, abnormally swollen as a result of the fish rising too rapidly from the depths.

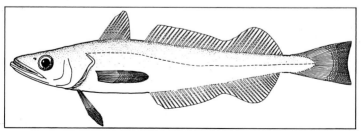

Common name
Ling

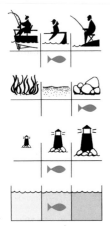

Description   Long, slender body that terminates in a small, pointed head. The upper jaw is larger and more prominent, which enables the fish to be distinguished easily from others of the same genus. The lower jaw is notable for the long, clearly visible barbel on the chin. The two dorsal fins have no spiny rays: the first is small and rounded, the second long. The anal fin is similar to the second dorsal, but shorter. The caudal fin is rounded. Coloration is reddish, bronze or olive-green with variable marbling. The flanks are lighter beneath the lateral line and the belly is white. The dorsal and anal fins are bordered white and all three have a dark spot on their rear tip; the ventral fins are white and the caudal fin gray-black.

Average dimensions   48–60 in (120–150 cm), max. 72 in (180 cm).

Distribution   Eastern Atlantic from Gibraltar to Barents Sea and Iceland.

Habitat   Coastal waters on rocky bottoms at depths of about 330–2,000 ft (100–600 m).

Behavior   Gregarious species which forms large schools, these being fished abundantly by trawlers from many countries.

Feeding   Aggressive and extremely voracious species that feeds mainly on fish (small cod, herring, and flatfish) but also on crustaceans and, strangely, starfish.

Fishing methods   Bottom fishing from boat on rocky beds, near wrecks and deep reefs. Natural baits are used, sometimes with artificial additions of spoons.

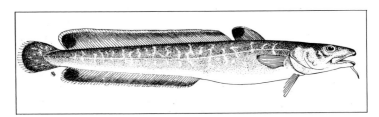

The dorsal and anal fins of the ling are edged in white and the caudal fin is rounded. The flanks are paler beneath the lateral line and the belly is white.

Common names
Striped mullet
Thin-lipped gray mullet

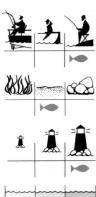

Description The striped mullet has a long body, subcylindrical in cross-section. The head is large and flattened on top. The eyes are partly covered by an adipose lid. The mouth is broad and the jaws are packed with teeth. The two dorsal fins are set well apart, the first being made up only of spiny rays. The thin-lipped gray mullet, however, has a slimmer shape, its head is covered with scales to the tip of the snout, and the eyes have no lid. Coloration of the striped mullet is gray-blue or greenish on the back, uniformly gray on the flanks and silver-gray on the belly. The head is darker than the rest of the body which displays yellow reflections. There is usually a dark spot at the base of the first pectoral fin. The thin-lipped gray mullet has a golden spot on the operculum, surrounded by a darker zone.

Similar species *Liza ramada*

Average dimensions *Mugil cephalus*, 12–16 in (30–40 cm), max. 24 in (60 cm); *Liza ramada*, 12–14 in (30–35 cm), max. 28 in (70 cm).

Distribution The striped mullet is cosmopolitan in temperate and warm waters; the thin-lipped gray mullet is present only in the Mediterranean, the Black Sea and the Atlantic from Scandinavia to Morocco.

Habitat Coastal waters at a depth of no more than 100 ft (30 m) near sandy bottoms covered with eelgrass. The fish also inhabit brackish water and freshwater.

Behavior Gregarious species which form small schools.

Feeding Crustaceans, worms, and mollusks.

Fishing methods Casting or bottom fishing with floats in shelter of cliffs, canals, and lagoons . Use natural baits.

Common names
Red mullet
Striped mullet

Description Slightly compressed body, higher at the front. The head is short, and one of the main distinguishing features of the two species is that the forward part is more vertical in the red mullet than in the striped mullet. There are two barbels beneath the mouth, larger and longer in the striped mullet. The two dorsal fins are well separated. The caudal fin is bifurcate with two rounded and slightly convex lobes. The red mullet is pink without any spots and stripes; the striped mullet is redder with a dark red longitudinal stripe on the flanks which extends from the eye to the caudal fin, plus a number of yellow lines. The first dorsal fin is yellowish with a series of black stripes.

Average dimensions *Mullus barbatus*, 4–8 in (10–20 cm), max. 12 in (30 cm); *Mullus surmuletus*, 4–10 in (10–25 cm), max. 16 in (40 cm).

Distribution Mediterranean and eastern Atlantic from Norway to Senegal, and North Sea.

Habitat The red mullet tends to live on muddy bottoms, the striped mullet among rocks, but also close to beds of sand or mud and sand.

Behavior The red mullet is more gregarious than the striped mullet, adults of which tend to live isolated or in small groups. Both spawn between April and August.

Feeding Mainly small organisms that live on the bottom such as crustaceans, mollusks, and small fish.

Fishing methods Bottom fishing. Baits can be worms, crustaceans, mollusks or slivers of fish. The best seasons for fishing mullet are summer and the fall.

Common name
Moray eel

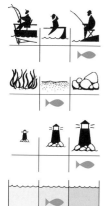

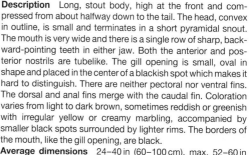

Description Long, stout body, high at the front and compressed from about halfway down to the tail. The head, convex in outline, is small and terminates in a short pyramidal snout. The mouth is very wide and there is a single row of sharp, backward-pointing teeth in either jaw. Both the anterior and posterior nostrils are tubelike. The gill opening is small, oval in shape and placed in the center of a blackish spot which makes it hard to distinguish. There are neither pectoral nor ventral fins. The dorsal and anal fins merge with the caudal fin. Coloration varies from light to dark brown, sometimes reddish or greenish with irregular yellow or creamy marbling, accompanied by smaller black spots surrounded by lighter rims. The borders of the mouth, like the gill opening, are black.

Average dimensions 24–40 in (60–100 cm), max. 52–60 in (130–150 cm).

Distribution Mediterranean and eastern Atlantic from British Isles to Senegal.

Habitat Coastal waters on rocky beds with plenty of caves.

Behavior Solitary. It is mainly active at night.

Feeding Carnivorous predator, feeding principally on cephalopods as well as crustaceans and small fish.

Fishing methods Bottom fishing among rocks, using mainly pieces of squid or octopus as bait. The strike should be quick and decisive. When dead, care has to be taken with its blood, which is toxic and can cause problems if it comes into contact with hand injuries, but cooking the flesh banishes such risks.

Common name
Smooth hound

Similar species
Mustelus asterias
Mustelus canis

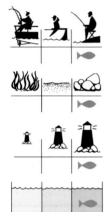

Description　Medium-sized shark with streamlined body. The head is long and flat. The teeth are blunt, resembling small slabs with more or less wavy edges. The eyes are markedly oval. A distinct fold of skin runs along the back from the tail to the gill openings. The dorsal fins are fairly small and set well apart, both terminating in a sharp posterior spine. The anal fin has the same feature. The lower lobe of the caudal fin is very short. Coloration is uniformly gray on the back and flanks, whitish on the belly. *Mustelus asterias* is quite similar but is easily distinguished by its rough skin, the forward-positioned dorsal fin and the larger caudal peduncle.

Average dimensions　24–48 in (60–120 cm), max. 64 in (160 cm).

Distribution　Mediterranean and eastern Atlantic from Angola to north of Scotland. This species has also been reported in American waters but such sightings actually refer to the very similar smooth dogfish (*Mustelus canis*).

Habitat　Coastal waters over bottoms of sand or mud and sand and near prairies of eelgrass. It may dive to a depth of 1,500 ft (450 m) but is more commonly found at 15–165 ft (5–50 m).

Behavior　Tends to be gregarious.

Feeding　Principally crustaceans but also small fish.

Fishing methods　Bottom fishing or surf-casting. It is advisable to use metal leaders and natural bait. The best time for fishing this shark appears to be at night.

Above: Head of the smooth hound, seen from below. The two dorsal fins are quite small and separated from each other, both terminating in a sharp spine at the rear.

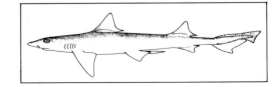

Common name
Pilot fish

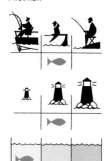

Description Elongated body, not very high and slightly compressed. The snout is typically obtuse. The mouth is not very large and is provided with fairly small teeth. Of the two dorsal fins, the first is reduced to 4–5 spines. The anal fin, similar in shape to the second dorsal, is preceded by 2 spines, the first of which is not always easily visible. The caudal peduncle is keeled on the sides and exhibits a superior and inferior groove. The body is rough to the touch because it is densely covered by small ctenoid scales. Coloration is gray-blue, darker on the back. On the flanks there are 6–7 dark vertical bands that also extend to the fins. The tips of the caudal lobes are white as are the tips of the second dorsal and anal fins.

Average dimensions 12–16 in (30–40 cm), max. 28 in (70 cm).

Distribution Cosmopolitan in all the world's tropical oceans and seas from the Mediterranean to the Atlantic and the Indo-Pacific.

Habitat Pelagic tropical and temperate waters.

Behavior Closely associated with sharks and other big pelagic fish such as manta and devil rays, playing a virtually obligatory commensal role. For this reason it is known as the pilot fish, so called because at one time it was believed that it literally guided the shark in its search for prey.

Feeding Feeds as a rule on the remains of prey caught by the species which it accompanies, as well as small fish and invertebrates.

Fishing methods Trolling with natural bait.

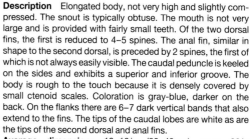

The caudal peduncle of the pilot fish, as seen in the drawing above, is strongly keeled at the sides and exhibits an upper and lower groove.

Common name
Saddled bream

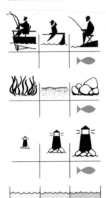

Description Elongated, oval-shaped, slightly compressed body, the back and belly being equally curved. The snout is short, with fairly large eyes. The lower jaw protrudes slightly. The teeth are tiny and numerous. The elongated dorsal fin can be lowered so as to disappear into a dorsal groove. The pectoral fins are pointed and almost twice the length of the ventral fins. The caudal fin is bifurcate with pointed lobes. Coloration is silver-gray, darker and with bluish reflections on the back. More or less visible on the flanks are longitudinal gray stripes and the dark lateral line. The caudal peduncle bears a characteristic white-bordered black spot in the shape of a saddle.

Average dimensions 6–8 in (15–20 cm), max. 12 in (30 cm).

Distribution Mediterranean and eastern Atlantic from the Bay of Biscay to Angola.

Habitat Coastal waters close to rocky bottoms with plenty of cracks and crevices or *Posidonia* prairies, at a maximum depth of about 130 ft (40 m).

Behavior Gregarious species that forms fairly large schools. During the day it tends to stay well away from shore, coming nearer between dusk and dawn. It spawns from April to June. In the winter months it makes for deeper waters than those where it normally lives for the rest of the year.

Feeding Omnivorous, including small invertebrates (worms, mollusks, and crustaceans) and algae.

Fishing methods Bottom fishing from shore or from a boat, or trolling with light tackle. The last is considered the classic technique for saddled bream, and use should be made exclusively of artificial lures such as spoons and feathers, the former for fishing the bottom, the latter for surface work. Trolling should be slow, skimming the rock bottom just before dawn and at dusk, the two periods of day judged most effective for catching these fish. The ideal times for bottom fishing are when the water is quite rough and slightly murky.

The drawing opposite, below, shows the upper jaw of the saddled bream. The elongated dorsal fin can be lowered to disappear in an apposite dorsal groove. The caudal fin is bifurcate with pointed lobes.

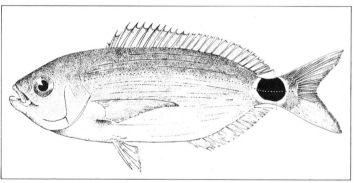

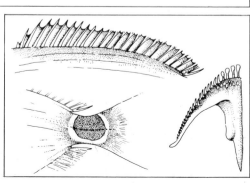

Common names
Red sea bream
Pandora

Description *Pagellus bogaraveo*: elongated body, round head and short snout with large eyes. The last soft ray of the dorsal fin and the anal fin is enlarged and partially covered by scales. Coloration is gray with pinkish tints, darker on the head and paler on the belly. Above the pectorals, where the lateral line begins, there is a large black spot. The fins are pink and the inside of the mouth orange-red. *P. erythrinus*: oval, compressed body with straight head. The eyes are small. The pectoral fins are pointed and as long as the head. Coloration is pinkish-red with silver tints and blue spots on the upper part of the flanks. The fins are pink and the inside of the mouth blackish.

Average dimensions *Pagellus bogaraveo*, 6 in (15 cm), max. 28 in (70 cm); *P. erythrinus*, 4–12 in (10–30 cm), max. 24 in (60 cm).

Distribution Both live in the Mediterranean, although the red sea bream appears not to be found in the eastern part. Also the Atlantic from Norway to the coasts of North Africa.

Habitat They live on bottoms of varied nature (rocks, sand, mud, and detritus). The red sea bream ranges deeper, to 2,600 ft (800 m), the pandora to 1,000–1,200 ft (300–350 m).

Behavior Gregarious. They spawn from spring to the fall.

Feeding Small fish and various invertebrates.

Fishing methods Bottom fishing. The recommended baits are crabs, sandworms, pieces of sardine, anchovies or squid. In order to catch larger specimens it may be necessary to fish at greater depths, over 330 ft (100 m). The best times of day to look for these species appear to be morning and early afternoon.

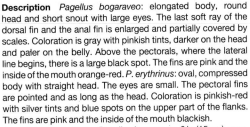

Common name
Forkbeard

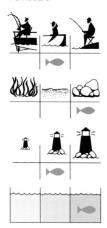

Description Relatively high, compressed body. The head is large with a well-developed upper jaw and a lower jaw furnished with a long barbel on the chin. The jaws are characterized by thick, fleshy lips. The fins are devoid of spiny rays. There are two dorsal fins: the first is short and triangular, the second long, extending to the insertion of the caudal rays. The anal fin is symmetrical and similar in shape to the caudal fin. The ventral fins are characteristically formed of only three rays, the longest being bifid, reaching to or just beyond the juncture of the anal fin. The caudal fin is narrowly spatulate with a rounded rear margin. Coloration varies from dull brown to reddish-brown on the back. The belly is lighter. The unpaired fins all display a dark band parallel to the margin, duplicated by a lighter one.

Average dimensions 8–16 in (20–40 cm), max. 26 in (65 cm).

Distribution Throughout the Mediterranean, except for most southerly coasts, and in the eastern Atlantic from Mauritania to the Bay of Biscay.

Habitat Coastal waters near rocky bottoms. Mostly found at 330–660 ft (100–200 m).

Behavior Forms denser schools at night while in daytime it displays a certain tendency to remain motionless among the rocks on the seabed. Spawns from January to March when it makes for shallower waters.

Feeding Small fish, worms, mollusks, crustaceans.

Fishing methods Bottom fishing from boat on rocky beds and near deep reefs and wrecks. Natural baits are generally used but sometimes artificial lures as well (e.g. spoons).

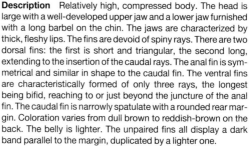

Common names
Plaice
Flounder

Similar species
Platichthys flesus

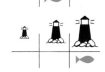

Description Both are dextral fish with a high, oval body, the outline of the head being more or less concave above the eyes. The mouth is small. In the plaice, there are 4–7 bony tubercles between the eyes and the upper corner of the operculum. The fins have no spiny rays. The dorsal and anal fins are more rounded in the plaice than in the flounder. The latter has a series of bony tubercles at the base of the above-mentioned fins and along the forward part of the lateral line. The coloration of the plaice is grayish-brown with red or orange, brown-bordered spots in larger individuals. Similar markings are also present on the dorsal, anal, and caudal fins. The flounder is grayish-brown or olive with darker streaks and sometimes with orange or red spots.

Average dimensions *Pleuronectes platessa*, 14–18 in (35–45 cm), max. 40 in (100 cm); *Platichthys flesus*, 4–12 in (10–30 cm), max. 20 in (50 cm).

Distribution *Pleuronectes platessa*, eastern Atlantic from Norway to Iceland and south to Spain, Morocco, and Spanish Mediterranean coasts; *Platichthys flesus*, eastern Atlantic and Mediterranean. There are two subspecies of flounder, one of which, *P. flesus luscus*, is present only in the Adriatic and the Black Sea.

Habitat Coastal waters on sandy, muddy or mixed bottoms. Both fish freely enter estuaries and lagoons. Flounder may even venture some dozens of miles upriver.

Behavior Both species tend to form large groups on the bed, where conditions are suitable. They remain resting on the bottom, partially buried in the sediment and well camouflaged. They are quite active at dusk and during the night. Flounder feed by day on the bottom and hunt for prey in midwater at night. They spawn in winter and spring.

Feeding Worms, crustaceans, mollusks, and small fish.

Fishing methods Bottom fishing and surf-casting where coastal features permit. Either live or artificial baits can be used, reeled in by fits and starts to simulate a fleeing prey. During the night fishing in midwater may prove rewarding, for both species then leave the bottom to hunt. In such circumstances it is best to use natural bait such as worms and crustaceans.

The central drawing opposite shows how the eyes of the plaice shift during the juvenile and adult phases. The coloration of the fish is gray-brown.

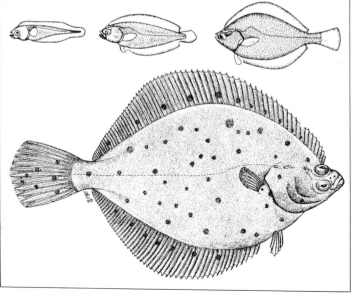

Common names
Pollock
Saithe
Coalfish

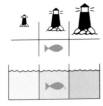

Description　Body somewhat fusiform, higher at the front and tapered at the back. The lower jaw is larger, projecting beyond the upper jaw. On the lower side of the mouth is a small barbel that disappears with age. There are three dorsal fins, none with spiny rays; the middle one is the longest and largest. There are two anal fins, and the small ventral fins are positioned in front of the pectorals. The caudal fin is slightly notched. Coloration is greenish-brown on the back, lighter on the flanks, and silver-gray on the belly. The ventral fins are white with a reddish tint.

Average dimensions　24–28 in (60–70 cm), max. 52 in (130 cm).

Distribution　North Atlantic from Greenland to North Carolina, to Iceland and Norway, and to the English Channel and the North Sea.

Habitat　Pelagic waters or near the bottom, from the surface to a depth of 330–660 ft (100–200 m). Adults prefer colder waters of 35°–52°F (2°–11°C), whereas the young favor temperatures of 59°–65°F (15°–18°C).

Behavior　Gregarious species which forms large schools and therefore much sought after commercially as a food fish. The fish spawn at great depth in very salty waters and at temperatures of 43°–46°F (6°–8°C) from early winter to spring.

Feeding　Pollock are highly voracious and feed principally on herring and other small pelagic fish.

Fishing methods　Bottom fishing or casting with natural bait (pieces of mackerel or small fish) and artificial lures close to rocky beds. At dusk it is best fished at the surface.

Common name
Turbot

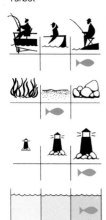

Description　Almost circular and rather thick body. The eyes are situated on the left side. The mouth is very wide with the upper edge slightly recessed. The dorsal fin begins in front of the upper eye and terminates at the caudal peduncle, above the end of the anal fin. The caudal fin is rounded. There are no scales but bony tubercles are present on the ocular side only, easily visible and sensitive to touch. Coloration of the upper side varies from gray to reddish-brown and yet other tints, given the notable ability of the species to blend with the surroundings. The blind side is generally whitish with scattered dark spots.

Average dimensions　16–20 in (40–50 cm), max. 40 in (100 cm).

Distribution　Mediterranean, coasts of eastern Atlantic from Morocco to the British Isles and Norway, the North Sea, and the Baltic Sea. The species has also been introduced, apparently with success, to the waters of New Zealand.

Habitat　Beds of sand, gravel or detritus, down to about 330 ft (100 m) deep.

Behavior　Gathers in variable numbers according to the availability of food on the bottom. With time, older individuals move toward the lower limits of its bathymetric range.

Feeding　Fish, mollusks, crustaceans, and worms.

Fishing methods　Bottom fishing. Strong tackle is recommended because the turbot offers stout resistance when hooked, thanks to its flat shape. Either live or artificial bait is suitable. There are international agreements which do not permit the catching of specimens measuring under 12 in (30 cm).

Common names
Starry ray
Flapper skate

Similar species
Raja batis

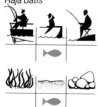

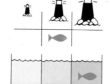

X

Description Typical bottom fish with flat body shaped like a rhomboid disk, with slightly wavy forward edges. The rostrum is short and obtuse. Curiously, the teeth of the male are sharp while those of the female are blunt. The skin is rougher in the middle of the body and on the tail. There are spines, sparse or in groups, near the eyes, in the center of the disk, on the tail and on the fins. *Raja batis* is distinguished by its sharp rostrum, the concave anterior margin of the disk and the three series of strong spines on the tail. Coloration is olive or yellowish with the thinnest of white margins. There are large numbers of dark spots, except on the snout and around the edges of the disk. The color of *Raja batis* is gray-brown or yellowish-gray with varying numbers of whitish circular spots.

Average dimensions *Raja asterias*, 16–20 in (40–50 cm), max. 28 in (70 cm); *Raja batis*, 32–48 in (80–120 cm), max. 100 in (250 cm).

Distribution *P. asterias*, Mediterranean and part of the Atlantic near Gibraltar; *R. batis*, eastern Atlantic from Portugal to Iceland and Scandinavian peninsula, western Mediterranean.

Habitat Bottoms of sand or mud and sand and eelgrass; *R. asterias*, 35–1,000 ft (10–300 m); *R. batis*, 100–2,000 ft (30–600 m).

Behavior Although they cannot be described as gregarious, they may gather locally in some numbers where conditions are suitable. They appear along the coasts from late fall to spring, but most frequently in winter.

Feeding All varieties of organism to be found on the bottom. *R. batis*, because of its larger dimensions, feeds for preference on fish.

Fishing methods Bottom fishing from anchored boat or surfcasting with strong enough tackle to pull to the surface a fish which, under traction, becomes a flat kite capable of considerable resistance. It is best to use metal leaders. Pieces of mackerel would seem to constitute the best bait.

The photograph opposite is of a ray displaying its ventral surface. There are spines in groups or thinly scattered around the eyes, in the center of the dish, on the tail and on the fins.

Common name
Oilfish

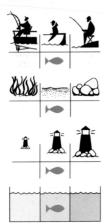

Description Fusiform and slightly compressed body. The snout is pointed and the large mouth furnished with strong teeth and a prominent lower law. The first of the two dorsal fins, composed of spiny rays, is long and low, the second is higher and followed by 2 finlets, as is the anal fin. The caudal fin is bilobate and moderately bifurcate. Underneath, between the ventral and anal fins, there is a marked denticulate keel. The skin is characterized by numerous small, bony tubercles, furnished with spines. Coloration is uniformly brown with purple or violet reflections. In the young, the second dorsal and anal fins are bordered white.

Average dimensions 24–60 in (60–150 cm), max. 80 in (200 cm). In the Pacific, where this species is present, it apparently reaches as much as 120 in (300 cm) in length.

Distribution Western and central Mediterranean in all tropical and temperate seas.

Habitat Pelagic waters near the continental platform at depths of 330–2,500 ft (100–800 m).

Behavior Usually swims near the bottom alone or in pairs. It may ascend to midwater.

Feeding This rapidly swimming carnivore chases and catches a wide variety of fish, crustaceans, and cephalopods.

Fishing methods Bottom fishing and also deep trolling given that the species sometimes rises to midwater nearer the surface. Lines should be baited mainly with pieces of fish and cephalopods. The bite may be decisive but considering the depth at which the fish lives, it must be sensitive to the touch.

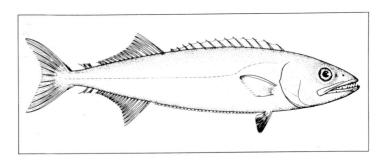

The skin of the oilfish, as can be seen from the drawing on the right, is notable for the presence of many small bony tubercles with spines.

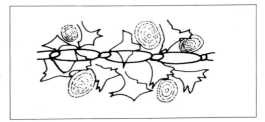

Common name
Atlantic salmon

Description   Large fish with tapering, streamlined body, similar to that of a trout. The head is small, the mouth and jaws large. Males in the spawning phase are notable for their size. The dorsal fin is followed by the adipose fin which distinguishes all the Salmonidae. The caudal peduncle is slender and slightly compressed. The caudal fin is concave. Coloration is gray-green on the back, silver on the head and flanks, white on the belly. Above the lateral line is a cross-shaped series of black spots.

Average dimensions   28–36 in (70–90 cm), max. 60 in (150 cm).

Distribution   European Atlantic coasts, North Sea, Baltic Sea, Iceland, Greenland, and North American Atlantic coasts.

Habitat   Pelagic and surface waters.

Behavior   Gregarious, living in schools of varying numbers, these becoming increasingly dense at the mouths of rivers prior to the journey to the spawning grounds. According to latitude and to individual population, salmon approach the coasts from early to late spring, heading for the mouths of rivers, swimming upstream and spawning between September and February.

Feeding   Almost exclusively pelagic fish, especially Clupeidae (sardine and herring) and crustaceans.

Fishing methods   Fly fishing or casting along coasts and estuaries, using strong tackle. In addition to submerged flies, artificial lures such as plugs, rotating silver or gold spoons can be used. The best time for sea angling is when they near the coasts and enter estuary waters.

Common names
Salema
Saupe

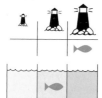

Description   The body is flatter and taller than that of the bogue, with which it may be confused. The head is small and the snout rounded and obtuse. The upper jaw protrudes slightly and has teeth with two equal, blunted cusps; the teeth of the lower jaw have only a single cusp. The dorsal and anal fins are fairly low, with very slender spiny rays. The caudal fin is notched. Coloration is bluish-gray, darker on the head and lighter on the belly. The flanks bear 10–11 horizontal stripes that are gold with orange tints. At the base of the pectoral fins is a small black spot.

Average dimensions   6–12 in (15–30 cm), max. 20 in (50 cm).

Distribution   Mediterranean and eastern Atlantic from North Sea to South Africa.

Habitat   Fairly shallow coastal waters, at most 65 ft (20 m) in depth, near various types of bed (rocks, sand, mud and sand) but always with rich plant growth, either algae or *Posidonia*.

Behavior   Gregarious species that forms large schools. Some individuals that are caught in summer have toxic flesh as a result of ingesting particular algae.

Feeding   Very varied although the young appear to be mainly carnivorous and the adults herbivorous.

Fishing methods   Bottom fishing either from a boat or from shore. The line should be cast into midwater and baited with worms or fish pulp, perhaps mixed with algae and vegetable matter. The best conditions for fishing are at high tide and in rough seas. The touch is light and sensitive rods may be needed in order to strike at the first sign of a bite.

Common name
Brown meager

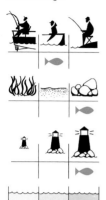

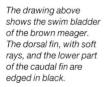

Description Compact, high body, the back strongly arched. The snout is short and rounded. The mouth faces downward and is almost horizontal, provided with 3–4 rows of small teeth arranged along either jaw and another row toward the outside. The dorsal fin is very high at the front and divided into two parts by a deep notch. The second part of the dorsal and the anal fin are covered at the base by scales. The margin of the caudal fin is slightly convex. Coloration is uniformly dull brown with metallic and golden reflections. The anterior rays of the ventral and anal fins are white. The dorsal fin with soft rays and the lower part of the caudal fin are bordered black.

Average dimensions 8–16 in (20–40 cm), max. 28 in (70 cm).

Distribution Mediterranean and eastern Atlantic from English Channel to Senegal.

Habitat Shallow coastal waters at most 500–600 ft (150–180 m) deep on rocky bottoms with plenty of clefts and caves or sandy bottoms mixed with *Posidonia*.

Behavior Forms small schools comprising a few individuals that are often found in or outside caves during the day. The species is more active at night. Spawns from March to August and at these times it comes much nearer shore.

Feeding Small fish, crustaceans, mollusks, and worms.

Fishing methods Bottom fishing. The line must be strong with a sliding lead and a single hook. This should be baited with pieces of squid, crustaceans or worms, perhaps mixed with algae, and lowered close to rocks or prairies of *Posidonia*, especially at night.

The drawing above shows the swim bladder of the brown meager. The dorsal fin, with soft rays, and the lower part of the caudal fin are edged in black.

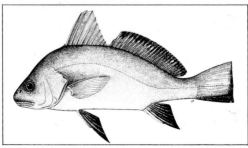

Common name
Mackerel

Description Long, fusiform body with a pointed snout and thin caudal peduncle. The mouth is large. The anterior and posterior borders of the eye are characteristically covered by an adipose lid. The two dorsal fins are set well apart: the first is high and subtriangular while the second is lower and followed by 5 pinnules, as is the anal fin. The caudal fin is deeply notched and bears two small keels at the base. Coloration is bright blue-green on the back with darker narrow, wavy lines. The lower part of the flanks and the belly are silver-white. The scales are very small and adherent so that the skin, overall, looks smooth.

Average dimensions 8–12 in (20–30 cm), max. 20 in (50 cm).

Distribution Mediterranean and Black Sea, eastern Atlantic from the African coasts to Scandinavia. It is also present along the American coasts from Labrador to North Carolina.

Habitat Pelagic and coastal waters down to a depth of 800 ft (250 m).

Behavior Gregarious species that live in schools.

Feeding Pelagic crustaceans as well as fish such as herring, anchovy, and sardines.

Fishing methods Trolling or casting when schools are sighted. In trolling, baits may either be natural or artificial, or combined, and kept some feet below the surface. A very useful procedure for retaining the school within the fishing zone and prevent it from dispersing is to scatter chum, composed of pieces of fish and mollusks ground very small so that the fish do not lose interest in the bait.

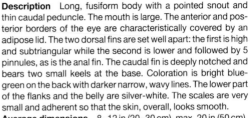

Above: detail of the ventral fin of the mackerel. The coloration of the fish is bright blue-green on the back with darker stripes. The lower parts are silver-white.

Common name
Brill

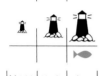

Description   Oval body, the length about twice that of the height. The eyes are situated on the left side. The mouth is large and markedly oblique, reaching to a level in line with the rear edge of the eyes. The dorsal fin begins well forward (between the eye and the mouth) and the first rays are longer as well as free and ramified at their tip. The caudal fin is rounded. The scales are smooth, without tubercles. Coloration is gray-brown with a scattering of numerous irregular dark markings and light, black-bordered zones. Among the margins, at the base of the fins, are small white spots of varying clarity. The blind side is white with sparse dark spots.

Average dimensions   8–16 in (20–40 cm), max. 30 in (75 cm).

Distribution   Mediterranean, European coasts of the Atlantic up to latitude 64°N, and partially along the North African coast, the North Sea and the Baltic Sea.

Habitat   Typical inhabitant of sandy bottoms down to a depth of 400–430 ft (120–130 m), but most frequent at 230–265 ft (70–80 m).

Behavior   Between February and April, the spawning season, mature specimens move to surface waters of 30–45 ft (10–20 m) where the young later remain for a couple of years.

Feeding   Small fish and invertebrates, especially benthic species.

Fishing methods   Bottom fishing and surf-casting where coastal features permit. Live and artificial baits that can be maneuvered and retrieved in a manner that imitates a small creature in flight will trigger the aggressive instincts of the fish.

Common names
Black scorpionfish
Red scorpionfish

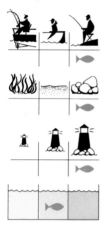

Similar species
Scorpaena scrofa

Description   Both species are similar in shape, the body being sturdy and the head large with an assortment of crests and spines. The black scorpionfish has a shorter snout than the red, and the latter has a lower jaw furnished with numerous frills of skin which are also present near the eyes and along the lateral line. Both species, too, have many spines on the fins and opercula. Coloration is the quickest, although not necessarily the most certain, means of identification. The body and fins of *Scorpaena porcus* are reddish-brown with darker streaks, and the caudal fin is adorned with three vertical dark bands. The color of *S. Scrofa* is reddish or yellowish-pink with dark streaks, and there is usually a black spot in the center of the dorsal fin.

Average dimensions   *S. porcus*, 4–8 in (10–20 cm), max. 12 in (30 cm); *S. scrofa*, 8–12 in (20–30 cm), max. 26 in (66 cm).

Distribution   Mediterranean and eastern Atlantic from British Isles to Senegal.

Habitat   Coastal waters on rocky bottoms or among *Posidonia* prairies. The red scorpionfish also lives on muddy bottoms and settles at greater depths of 65–330 ft (20–100 m).

Behavior   Tend to be solitary and are more active at night. During the day they remain mostly immobile, resting on the bottom, relying on their perfect camouflage to catch any prey that passes by. Both species spawn between May and August.

Feeding   Fish, crustaceans, mollusks, and various invertebrates.

Fishing methods   Bottom fishing, using natural bait such as small fish, shrimp, and pieces of octopus and squid. Given the sedentary habits of these fish, chances of catching them depend on dangling the bait immediately before the snout. At night, scorpionfish are more active, which makes them easier to catch. Specimens must be handled with care because the numerous spines are capable of inflicting painful wounds.

The black scorpionfish has a shorter snout than that of the red scorpionfish, the lower jaw of the latter being provided with many frills of skin.

Common names
Redfish
Black rockfish

Similar species
Sebastodes melanops

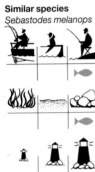

Description Oval, compact, fairly tall body. The head is enormous, distinguished by a series of spines that confirm the relationship of these species to scorpionfish. The outline of the snout is slightly concave and this feature becomes more accentuated with age. The single dorsal fin is large, with a notch at the level of the last spiny rays. The anal fin also possesses large spiny rays. The pectoral fins, too, are well developed, whereas the caudal fin is comparatively small. Coloration of the redfish is normally orange, red or reddish-brown. The belly is lighter. Dark spots are sometimes present on the opercula, the back, and along the dorsal fin. The black rockfish, on the other hand, is olive-brown on the back and paler on the flanks and belly. The head is black on the nape and there are black stripes across the cheeks. Some of the pectoral rays are often orange.

Average dimensions *Sebastes marinus*, 12–18 in (30–45 cm), max. 38 in (95 cm); *Sebastodes melanops*, 10–14 in (25–35 cm), max. 24 in (60 cm).

Distribution *Sebastes marinus*: North Atlantic along European, Canadian, and American coasts. *Sebastodes melanops*: Pacific Ocean from Alaska to California.

Habitat Coastal waters at depths from 100–165 ft (30–50 m) to 2,000 ft (600 m) near rocky or muddy bottoms.

Behavior They tend to form fairly large groups. By day they remain close to the bottom, ascending at night. They spawn from late spring to end summer, showing a preference for cold water at a temperature of not more than 50°F (10°C), for which reason they make for zones nearer the surface in winter.

Feeding Small fish and crustaceans, both benthic and pelagic, which they catch in the course of moving up and down through the water.

Fishing methods Bottom fishing and drifting. For obvious reasons, the species spends more time at depth during the day than at night. It is best to use natural bait such as shrimp and crabs or small whole fish.

The coloration of the redfish is generally orange, red or reddish-brown. The black rockfish, however, is olive-brown on the back and lighter on the flanks and belly.

Common name
Painted comber

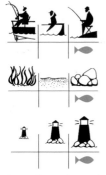

Description Long and slightly compressed body. The head is pointed, terminating in a large mouth. The opercular bones bear three sharp spines close to the rear margin. The single dorsal fin, relatively long and tall, is furnished at the front with spiny rays. The caudal fin is supported by a short, high peduncle, and the rear edge is straight or slightly convex. Coloration is reddish-brown on the back and gray with violet tints on the belly. There are several dark vertical streaks on the flanks. According to one legend, the numerous thin, wavy blue lines on the top of the head represent Arabic lettering in praise of Allah. The dorsal and anal fins are gray-red, the caudal fin yellow, the ventral fins blue-brown and the pectorals gray-red or yellow.

Average dimensions 4–10 in (10–25 cm), max. 14 in (36 cm).

Distribution Mediterranean and eastern Atlantic from the Bay of Biscay to South Africa.

Habitat Coastal species near beds of rock, mud or eelgrass, seldom more than 100 ft (30 m) deep, max. depth 500 ft (150 m).

Behavior Tends to be solitary, not much liking the company of others of the species. It often hovers around the burrows of octopi, feeding on the remains of their meals. Reproduces from April to September. The species is hermaphroditic.

Feeding Active and voracious predator which feeds on small fish, crustaceans, and mollusks.

Fishing methods Bottom fishing, where it is one of the most frequently caught species. Lures may consist of small spoons, white feathers or, in the case of natural bait, pieces of fish, mollusks, and crustaceans.

Common name
Parrot fish

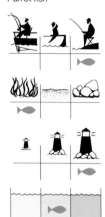

Description Oblong, compact and slightly compressed body. The head is conical and the mouth is characterized by short jaws furnished with teeth that are linked to form a kind of beak, which explains why the Scaridae are known as parrot fish. The caudal fin is rounded. The whole body is covered by large scales that even extend to the cheeks. Coloration is quite variable: it may, in fact, be gray-brown, purple, greenish or red with longitudinal rows of whitish spots along the flanks. The females are reddish with a black spot after the operculum and a yellow spot between the caudal peduncle and the tip of the dorsal fin. The males are brown with white spots on the back and flanks.

Average dimensions 4–12 in (10–30 cm), max. 20 in (50 cm).

Distribution Central-western and eastern Mediterranean, eastern Atlantic from Portugal to Senegal.

Habitat Coastal waters on rocky or sandy bottoms, with *Posidonia* growth within 165 ft (50 m) from the surface.

Behavior Lives in groups comprising a variable number of individuals. During the night, as happens with other members of the family, the fish normally sleep on the bottom, lying on one side. Spawns from August to October.

Feeding Algae and small invertebrates (mollusks and crustaceans) which it grinds up with its strong beak.

Fishing methods Bottom fishing. It is caught only occasionally but seems to be more common off Cyprus and the coasts of Turkey and Morocco.

Common name
Gilthead

Description High and markedly compressed oval body, the front part of which is strongly convex. The sturdy head terminates in a mouth furnished with teeth powerful enough even to crack the largest shells. At the base of the dorsal fin is a groove into which the front portion of the fin can be folded. The pectoral fins are very long. Coloration is gray with reflections that are blue-gold on the back, silver on the flanks. Above the eyes there is a golden band encircled by a black patch that breaks off at the nape and reappears on the opercula. A red spot of variable intensity is noticeable on the pectoral fins.

Average dimensions 8–20 in (20–50 cm), max. 28 in (70 cm).

Distribution Mediterranean and eastern Atlantic from British Isles to Senegal.

Habitat Fairly shallow coastal waters, seldom more than 100–130 ft (30–40 m), at most 500 ft (150 m) in depth, preferably close to *Posidonia* prairies mingled with sand and rocks. It also enters lagoons and zones of brackish water.

Behavior The young are gregarious whereas larger specimens tend to become solitary. On its daily journeys it usually follows the same routes. Spawns in winter.

Feeding Principally mollusks but also crustaceans, echinoderms, worms, and small fish.

Fishing methods Bottom fishing and surf-casting. Hooks should be baited with mollusks (e.g. mussels) which are the gilthead's favorite prey. The fish is fairly diffident and is liable to abandon the bait if it senses unusual resistance, so that leads should be positioned a fair distance from the hook.

The drawing opposite, below, shows the upper and lower jaws of the gilthead. The dorsal fin can be folded into an apposite groove at the base of the fin.

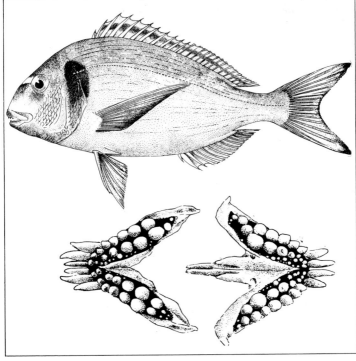

Common name
Northern puffer

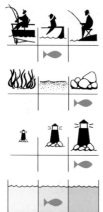

Description   Heavy, tapering body, higher at the front. This shape changes dramatically when the fish swells itself up for self-defense by swallowing water or air. This process accentuates the many spines that cover the body. The mouth is equipped with strong jaws that are transformed into a kind of beak resulting from the fusion of the upper and lower teeth. The dorsal and anal fins are very small and placed far back. There are no ventral fins. The caudal fin is rounded. Coloration of the back is gray or olive-brown with paler spots. The belly is yellow or white. Small dark spots similar to pepper grains are visible on the flanks and snout. The lower part of the flanks bears a series of vertical dark bands.

Average dimensions   8 in (20 cm), max. 14 in (35 cm).

Distribution   Western Atlantic from Newfoundland to Florida. The related species *S. cutaneus* has recently been reported in the Mediterranean.

Habitat   Coastal waters and in bays and estuaries at a depth of about 200 ft (60 m).

Behavior   Not a gregarious species even though it may often collect in groups; however, these display irregular behavior and tend to disperse quite rapidly. It spawns in summer but little is known of its biology and movements; these are likely to be limited since the species is not a very strong swimmer.

Feeding   Mainly crustaceans and mollusks, which it cracks with its strong teeth, and occasionally fish.

Fishing methods   Bottom fishing and casting with natural baits, the most effective of which are crustaceans. It is not difficult to catch and increasingly popular because of its appetizing flesh.

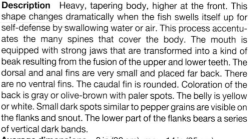

The northern puffer, which has an enormous, tapering body, can change shape dramatically, swelling itself up into a ball by swallowing air and water and displaying its spines in self defense.

Similar species
Spicara flexuosa
Spicara smaris

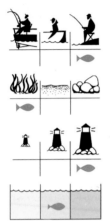

Description Elongated, slightly compressed body. The head, especially of larger specimens, is humped in front at the nape. The upper jaw projects strongly. The upper outline of the dorsal fin is almost straight. Coloration is bluish-gray or greenish on the back and silver on the flanks, where there are also small dark spots and invariably a large black rectangular mark in a central position. The operculum has blue stripes. In the spawning period, the fish is adorned with blue and yellow lines and spots, darker on the body than on the fins. All three species mentioned here are equally well distributed, quite similar and identifiable as members of the same genus by the constant presence of the rectangular patch on the flanks.

Average dimensions 5–8 in (12–20 cm), max. 10 in (25 cm).

Distribution Mediterranean and eastern Atlantic from Portugal to Morocco and the Canaries.

Habitat Coastal waters on rocky bottoms or among *Posidonia* prairies.

Behavior Gregarious, living in schools of varying size. At the time of spawning, the females move upward and all gather together at a point higher than the males. Spawning is from spring to fall, depending on the zones. Eggs are laid in holes dug by the males in the midst of *Posidonia*.

Feeding Principally small crustaceans, mollusks, and plant matter.

Fishing methods Bottom fishing from the shore or from a boat, using bait such as shrimp, mollusks, pieces of fish or pulp of bread and cheese. Spring to summer is the best time.

Common name
Black sea bream

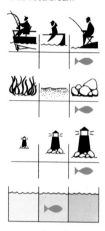

Description　Oval, compressed body. The upper part of the head at eye level is recessed, the snout is short and the mouth terminal, with large, pointed front teeth followed by several rows of tiny ones. The dorsal fin can be folded into an appropriate groove. The caudal fin is concave. Coloration is silver-gray with blue, green, pink or whitish tints in mature females. The head is more opaque and darker. Broken longitudinal golden-yellow stripes run along the flanks. The dorsal, anal, and ventral fins are blackish with lighter base and margins. The rear margin of the caudal fin is black.

Average dimensions　8–12 in (20–30 cm), max. 24 in (60 cm).

Distribution　Mediterranean and eastern Atlantic from Norway to Angola.

Habitat　Coastal waters on bottoms of rock, sand or *Posidonia*, at a depth of 300–500 ft (10–150 m).

Behavior　Gregarious, sometimes forming good-sized schools. Spawns from February to May, depositing eggs on sandy bottoms, unique among Mediterranean Sparidae.

Feeding　Omnivorous, principally algae, small crustaceans, and other invertebrates.

Fishing methods　Bottom fishing. Recommended baits are the flesh of mollusks or small crustaceans. Chum is useful for keeping the school close by. Catches are most frequent in late winter and early spring off cliffs and pebble beaches. In summer it is best to fish at night.

Above: Side view of the jaw of the black sea bream. There are broken longitudinal golden-yellow stripes along the flanks.

Common name
Spiny dogfish

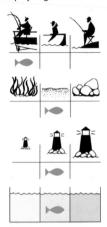

Description Long, fusiform body. The head is flattened, the snout is rounded and the mouth almost straight. The teeth of the two jaws are very similar, typical in shape with the tip strongly backward. Each of the dorsal fins is preceded by a spine, that of the first being shorter. The species has no anal fin and this feature, together with the dorsal spines, makes for easy identification. The pectoral fins are well developed and almost triangular in shape. The upper lobe of the caudal fin is larger than the lower lobe. A longitudinal fold of skin runs along either side of the caudal peduncle. Coloration is usually slate-gray with bluish tints on the back, white on the belly. There are small, irregular pale spots along the flanks.

Average dimensions 24–36 in (60–90 cm), max. 80 in (200 cm). The largest individuals are always females.

Distribution Cosmopolitan (Mediterranean, North Atlantic, and Pacific) within the temperature limits mentioned below.

Habitat A bottom species which prefers muddy beds down to a depth of 3,000 ft (900 m). It is nevertheless more commonly found at 30–650 ft (10–200 m).

Behavior Gregarious, forming schools comprising thousands of individuals.

Feeding Devours enormous quantities of pelagic and benthic fish as well as squid and crabs.

Fishing methods Bottom fishing and sometimes trolling. Much care must be taken when boating it, for it arches its back in defense to expose the spines, which are believed to be poisonous.

The dorsal fins of the spiny dogfish are each preceded by a spine, that of the first being shorter. The snout is blunt and the mouth almost straight.

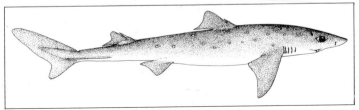

Common name
Pompano

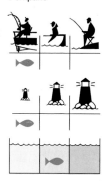

Description Although the species belongs to the same genus as the permit (*Trachinotus falcatus*, see Plate 30), its body is lower, albeit still oval and compressed. The snout is short, the mouth small and slightly oblique, the teeth tiny, conical, and curved. The first dorsal fin consists of 6 short spiny rays. The second dorsal fin is almost identical in shape and length to the anal fin. The caudal fin is clearly notched with long, sharp lobes which ideally extend to the tips of the dorsal and anal fins, forming a large X. Coloration is gray-green on the back, silver on the flanks. There are 3–5 vertical, dark green spots along the front part of the lateral line. The tips of the caudal lobes and of the dorsal and anal fins are black.

Average dimensions 8–14 in (20–35 cm), max. 28 in (70 cm).

Distribution Mediterranean and eastern Atlantic from the Bay of Biscay to Angola.

Habitat Pelagic waters, but often appears in large numbers offshore.

Behavior Gregarious, forming schools that may number hundreds of individuals. Spawns in spring and summer.

Feeding Small invertebrates (mollusks and crustaceans) and small fish.

Fishing methods Surface or midwater trolling. Baits can be natural (small fish such as anchovy, mullet or smelt) or artificial (feathers and spoons). The latter should be trolled in midwater whereas feathers yield better results on the surface. Trolling speed should not be more than 2–3 knots and the best places to fish are on rocky bottoms or close to reefs and promontories.

The first dorsal fin of the pompano consists of 6 short spiny rays, while the second is identical in shape and length to the anal fin.

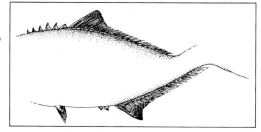

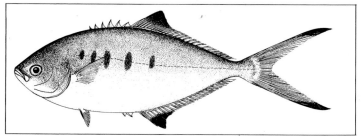

Common name
Greater weever

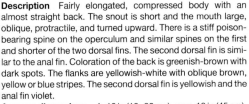

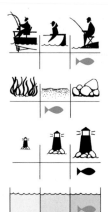

Description Fairly elongated, compressed body with an almost straight back. The snout is short and the mouth large, oblique, protractile, and turned upward. There is a stiff poison-bearing spine on the operculum and similar spines on the first and shorter of the two dorsal fins. The second dorsal fin is similar to the anal fin. Coloration of the back is greenish-brown with dark spots. The flanks are yellowish-white with oblique brown, yellow or blue stripes. The second dorsal fin is yellowish and the anal fin violet.

Average dimensions 4–12 in (10–30 cm), max. 18 in (45 cm).

Distribution Mediterranean and eastern Atlantic from Norway to Morocco.

Habitat Coastal waters on sandy or muddy bottoms up to a depth of 1,000 ft (300 m).

Behavior Tends to be solitary. It stays buried in sediment awaiting possible prey, allowing only its head, eyes and part of the dorsal fin to protrude. Spawns in spring and summer.

Feeding Mainly small invertebrates and small fish.

Fishing methods Deep or midwater trolling, or bottom fishing. The best form of lure is the spoon, but good results can also be achieved by baiting the line with pieces of fish, mollusks, and worms. For bottom fishing the bait should be reeled in by skimming it along the seabed in order to stimulate the aggressive instincts of the fish, evidence of which is shown by reports of spontaneous attacks against swimmers and scuba-divers. Great care must be taken, in any event, because of the poison-bearing spines.

Common name
Atlantic horse mackerel

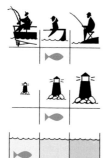

Description Elongated and moderately compressed body. The head is broad and the mouth fairly wide. The large eyes are provided with a well-developed adipose lid. There are two dorsal fins, the first being higher than the second and formed of 8 spiny rays. The anal fin, similar in appearance to the second dorsal, is preceded by 2 spines. The caudal fin is bilobate. On the flanks is a characteristic clear lateral line, composed of tall, narrow scales, those in the rear part bearing spines. The grayish-black coloration of the back, with blue-green tints, gradually lightens to silver-white on the flanks and belly. There is a small spot near the upper margin of the operculum.

Average dimensions 8–16 in (20–40 cm), max. 24–28 in (60–70 cm).

Distribution Mediterranean and Atlantic Ocean from Norway to South Africa and from Brazil to Argentina.

Habitat Pelagic waters from the surface to a depth of 2,000 ft (600 m). It is more frequent in the first 330–660 ft (100–200 m) above the sandy bottom. It sometimes enters estuaries.

Behavior Gregarious, migratory fish which forms large schools. It shows a tendency in summer to settle at a depth of 15–65 ft (5–20 m). Spawns from January to April.

Feeding Sardines, anchovies, crustaceans, and squid.

Fishing methods Trolling either on the surface or in midwater with light tackle in order to heighten the interest. It is best to use only artificial lures such as feathers, spoons or minnows.

Along the flanks of the Atlantic horse mackerel is a visible lateral line composed of high, narrow scales, those toward the rear being furnished with spines.

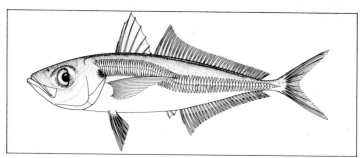

Common name
Shi drum

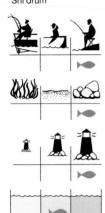

Description Elongated, tall, laterally compressed body, with a ventral outline that is practically horizontal. The snout is prominent and rounded, and the lower jaw bears a very short, stiff barbel, perforated at the tip. The dorsal fin is long and higher at the front with its spiny rays. The caudal fin is truncate with a slightly more pronounced upper tip. The lateral line extends to the rear edge of the caudal fin. Coloration is silver-gray or brownish with metallic tones and many oblique, slightly wavy stripes; these are golden-yellow with blue-violet borders on the back and upper part of the flanks. The operculum has a black margin.

Average dimensions 12–32 in (30–80 cm), max. 40 in (100 cm).

Distribution Mediterranean and eastern Atlantic from the Bay of Biscay to Senegal.

Habitat Fairly shallow coastal waters, max. 330 ft (100 m), preferably close to beds of rocks, sand or detritus. It also frequents brackish lagoons, particularly in the juvenile stages.

Behavior Lives alone or in small groups. Spawns in spring and summer.

Feeding Fish and seabed invertebrates as well as algae.

Fishing methods Bottom fishing or surf-casting. The fish is only caught by accident. Natural baits can include sardines, mollusks, and worms. Night and dusk are the best times to come across them, following high tide when the sea is still rough and the water murky, casting for preference near river mouths or at the base of cliffs.

Common name
Stargazer

Description   Rather large body, particularly at front. The head is huge and flattened on top. The eyes, positioned at the back, are directed forward. The large mouth is furnished with a retractile tentacle situated in front of and under the tongue. On the head and behind the opercula are strong spines capable of inflicting painful stings. The two dorsals touch each other, the first being rounded. Coloration is yellowish-brown on the back and flanks with small white spots. The belly is yellowish-white and the first dorsal is black.

Average dimensions   6–12 in (15–30 cm), max. 14 in (35 cm).

Distribution   Mediterranean and Atlantic from the Bay of Biscay to Morocco.

Habitat   Sandy or muddy bottoms from a few feet to about 800 ft (250 m) in depth, most frequently at 35–350 ft (10–100 m).

Behavior   Sedentary fish which for most of the time remains buried on the bottom, the only visible parts being the eyes, the top of the head and the mouth with its rectractile tentacle. This tentacle acts as a lure for other fish which, when they venture near the mouth, are immediately seized and swallowed. Spawns between April and August. Has a liking for warm water and comes to the surface in the summer months.

Feeding   Principally fish although also worms and crustaceans.

Fishing methods   Bottom fishing. It is best to use hooks with terminal bait so as to give the line as natural an appearance as possible when lowered to the bottom and, ideally, close to where the fish is buried.

Common name
Saint Peter's fish

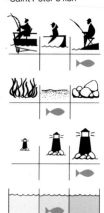

Description   High body with noticeably flattened flanks. The head is large, the top straight and convex. The lower jaw protrudes and the mouth, which is protractile, can be extended slightly forward when the fish is about to seize its prey. The dorsal fin is characterized by very long spiny rays that are transformed almost into filaments near the tip. There are rows of spinelike bony plates at the base of the soft rays of the dorsal and anal fins; and there is a prominent keel on the belly. The caudal fin is large and spatulate with a rounded posterior margin. Coloration is greenish-gray with golden reflections. There is a circular black spot with a white edge on the flanks.

Average dimensions   8–20 in (20–50 cm), max. 26 in (66 cm).

Distribution   Fairly widespread, in Mediterranean, eastern Atlantic from South Africa to Norway, and in Pacific along the coasts of Australia, New Zealand, Japan, and Korea.

Habitat   Coastal waters, most frequently at a depth of 165–500 ft (50–150 m), over muddy bottoms or prairies of eelgrass.

Behavior   Tends to be solitary but sometimes joins with several conspecifics. Individuals of this species are poor swimmers and move slowly in fits and starts. Moves out to open sea to spawn. This occurs from March to May in the Mediterranean and from June to August in the Atlantic.

Feeding   Wide variety of fish which it catches by thrusting out its protractile jaws, as well as mollusks and crustaceans.

Fishing methods   Bottom fishing. The most suitable baits seem to be shrimp and small live fish. Catches may be accidental but there is much satisfaction because of the rarity of the species and excellence of the flesh.

Saint Peter's fish, noted for its particularly delicate flesh, has a protractile mouth that can be extended forward when the fish is after a prey.

GLOSSARY
BIBLIOGRAPHY
INDEX

GLOSSARY

Artificial   Name applied to a bait which, apart from its shape and composition, is not found in nature.

Backing   The length of wire on the spool preceding the fly line.

Barb   Metal projection close to the hook point, designed to prevent the latter slipping from the mouth of the fish.

Barbel   Fleshy, filiform organ rich in nerve endings, found on the chin or on the sides of the mouth (mullet, cod, meager, etc).

Benthonic   Name for all organisms living on the bottom of the sea, whether sessile or drifting.

Brake   Reel mechanism which controls the unwinding of the line according to the pull of the fish. In reels for deep-sea fishing brakes may be either of the lever or star type.

Breaking strain   Maximum strength limit of nylon.

Caudal   The fin at the rear end of a fish's body, supported by a peduncle.

Compressed   Applied to the body of a fish which is flattened sideways (as in the sole family).

Condrichthyes   Cartilaginous fish or Selachii (rays, sharks, etc).

Corslet   Front part of body of tuna family, which alone is covered by scales.

Ctenoid   Type of partially rough surface scale.

Cycloid   Type of smooth surface scale.

Depressed   Applied to the body of a fish which is flattened from top to bottom (rays, etc).

Dorsal   Generally referring to the back of a fish. More specifically it indicates the dorsal fin, single, double or even triple (cod family).

Finlets   Small fins, more or less stiff, separated from one another and situated above and below the caudal peduncle.

Fly line   Type of line narrowing in cross-section, used in fly-fishing.

Foot   The part of a deep-sea fishing rod that bears the reel. It may be straight or curved but according to IGFA standards must not measure more than 27 in (68.6 cm).

Gaff   Solid hook used for recovering very large fish. It may be fixed or flying, depending on whether or not it is attached firmly to a shaft.

Heterocercal   Applied to a caudal fin with unequal lobes (e.g. that of sharks).

Heterothermal   Applied to animals which, like fish, cannot independently control their body temperature.

Homocercal   Applied to a caudal fin with equal lobes.

Infralittoral   The sea zone situated between the lower limit of low tide and the point where *Posidonia* disappears.

Interradial membrane   The membrane that links the rays of fins.

Keel   Laminate body structure, of variable size, typical of very fast-moving fish (sharks, tuna, sailfish, swordfish, etc.), situated between the caudal peduncle and caudal fin.

Knot   Interlacement of one or more ropes, cords, etc. for binding objects together. Used in angling in special forms (e.g. Palomar knot, Blood knot, etc.)

Lateral line   Characteristic sense organ of fish formed of scales well furnished with pores and arranged in a line along the flanks.

Mobile bottoms   Applied to sea beds composed of gravel, sand, mud or a combination of these, so called because they can be mixed and shifted by the currents, in contrast to rocks.

Neritic   Applied to the part of the sea closest to the coast and particularly the entire belt covering the continental shelf.

Nutrients   Collective term used mainly for compounds containing phosphorus and nitrogen, on which algae and the entire marine food chain depend for growth.

Pectoral girdle   Part of the fish skeleton that supports the pectoral fins.

Pelagic   Applied to the entire area commonly known as "open sea," and more specifically to the sea zone above the continental shelf and the deep trenches.

Pelvic girdle   Part of the fish skeleton that supports the ventral fins.

Phanerogams   Group of specialized plants represented in the sea by *Posidonia*; they are in fact true plants (not algae) with flowers and fruit.

Placoid   The scale of a fish belonging to the Condrichthyes (*q.v.*), similar to a backward-turned tooth and responsible for the rough skin typical of most of these fish.

Planktonic   Any organism that is carried more or less passively by the ocean currents.

Plug   Imitation small fish made of various materials.

Popper   Artificial lure of varying shape and size, with a flat head and surface.

Pulley   Metallic device enabling two different lengths of line to rotate freely without becoming entangled.

Rings   Typical elements of rods for casting and surf-casting. They must be sufficiently numerous and evenly distributed along the rod, and smooth enough to allow the line to run out perfectly.

Sinker   Large weight that carries the bait to the desired depth. It is often equipped with a downrigger release mechanism which lets it go when the fish bites.

Streamer   Imitation small fish made of feathers.

Strength   Applicable to rods, the weight in grams necessary, with the rod held horizontally, to bring the tip to a right angle with the ground.

Strike   Sharp pull on the line by the angler when the fish bites to ensure the hook is embedded in its mouth.

Thermocline   The layer of water that separates the warm surface waters from the colder waters below, in which the temperature descends very rapidly in relation to increasing depth.

Tip   The part of a deep-sea fishing rod through which the line runs. According to IGFA norms it must measure at least 40 in (101.6 cm).

Trophic   Everything that concerns the nutrition of animals, as for example, trophic behavior, trophic chain (food chain).

BIBLIOGRAPHY

Bussani, M. *La pesca marittima*, Edagricole, Bologna, 1987.

IGFA, *World Record Game Fishes*, 1983 onward.

Keybook to world map of fisheries, Scandinavian Fishing Yearbook, 1976.

Laevastu, T. and Hela, I. *Fisheries Oceanography*, Fishing News Books Ltd, 1970.

Lyman, H. *Blue Fishing*, Lyons & Burford, New York, 1987.

McClane, A.J. *Mclanes Field Guide to Saltwater Fishing of North America*, Holt, Rinehart & Winston, New York, 1965.

Millman, M. *Boat Fishing*, Crowood, Malborough, 1991.

Mosetti, F. *Il volto degli oceani*, Mondadori, Milan, 1978.

Muus, B.J. and Dahlstrom, P. *Collins Guide to the Sea Fishes of Britain and North-Western Europe*, Collins, London, 1977.

Pérès, J.M. *Precis d'océanographie biologique*, PUF, 1976.

Pullen, G. *Sea Fishing Baits*, Oxford Illustrated Press, Yeovil, Somerset, 1988.

Prescott, J.R.V. *Maritime Political Boundaries of the World*, Methuen, London, 1985.

Schultz, K. *Fishing*, Hamlyn, London, 1990.

Sosin, M. and Kreh, L. *Fishing the Flats*, Lyons & Burford, New York, 1983.

Stoker, H. *The Modern Sea Angler*, Hale, London, 1987.

Yasuda, F. and Hiyama, Y. *Pacific Marine Fishes*, Vol. 1, T.F.H. Publications Inc., Neptune City, N.J., 1972.

INDEX OF ENTRIES

Common names are given in roman, Latin names in italic. The numbers are those of the entries.

Acanthocybium solanderi 1
African pompano 3
Albacore 59
Albula vulpes 2
Alectis ciliaris 3
Alopias vulpinus 4
Amberjack 50
Anarhicas lupus 68
Anarhicas minor 68
Anguilla anguilla 69
Archosargus probato cephalus 70
Argyrosomus regius 71
Arripis trutta 72
Anglerfish 95
Annular sea bream 83
Atlantic bonito 45
Atlantic cod 23
Atlantic halibut 27
Atlantic gray shark 80
Atlantic horse mackerel 128
Atlantic sailfish 28
Atlantic salmon 112
Atlantic weakfish 85
Atlantic wolf fish 68
Aulopus filamentosus 73
Auxis rochei 74

Bagre marinus 75
Ballan wrasse 89
Belone belone 76
Black marlin 32
Black rockfish 118
Black sea bass 11
Black sea bream 124
Black scorpionfish 117
Black skipjack 21
Blackfin tuna 64
Blackfish 55
Blacktip shark 79
Bluefish 42
Blue marlin 33
Blue shark 43
Bluefin tuna 64
Bogue 77
Bonefish 2
Boops boops 77
Brama brama 78
Brama japonica 78
Brill 116
Brown meager 114
Bullet tuna 74

California halibut 38
California yellowtail 51
Caranx caninus 6
Caranx hippos 6
Caranx ignobilis 7
Caranx latus 6
Caranx sexfasciatus 8
Carcharinus limbatus 79
Carcharinus plumbeus 80
Carcharodon carcharias 9
Centropomus striatus 1
Centropomus undecimalis 10
Channel bass 46
Coalfish 108
Cobia 4
Conger conger 12
Conger eel 12
Coris julis 89
Coryphaena hippurus 113
Crevalle jack 6
Cubera snapper 31
Cuckoo wrasse 89
Cymatoceps nasutus 81
Cynoscion nebulosus 14
Cynoscion regalis 15

Dab 92
Dentex 82
Dentex Dentex 82
Dicentrarchus labrax 16
Diplodus annularis 83
Diplodus sargus 83
Diplodus vulgaris 83
Dogtooth tuna 26
Dolphinfish 13
Dusky grouper 85

Eel 69
Elagatis bipinnulatus 17
Elops saurus 84
Epinephelus guaza 85
Epinephelus itajara 18
Euthynnus affinis 19
Euthynnus alletteratus 20
Euthynnus lineatus 21
Euthynnus pelamis 22
Eutriglia gurnardus 86

Flapper skate 110
Flounder 107
Forkbeard 106

Gadus morhua 23
Gafftopsail catfish 75
Galeocerdo cuvieri 24
Galeorhinus galeus 25
Gar 76
Giant goby 87
Giant kingfish 7

Giant sea bass 54
Gilthead 121
Gobius cobitis 87
Grass goby 87
Gray gurnard 86
Great barracuda 52
Great hammerhead shark 53
Great trevally 8
Great weever 127
Gymnosarda unicolor 26

Haemulon sciurus 88
Hammerhead shark 53
Hake 97
Hippoglossus hippoglossus 27
Horse-eye jack 6

Istiophorus platypterus 28
Isurus oxyrhynchus 29

Jewfish 18

Kawahai 72
Kawakawa 19

Labrus bimaculatus 89
Labrus bergylta 89
Ladyfish 84
Lamna nasus 30
Leer fish 91
Lepidopus caudatus 90
Lichia amia 91
Limanda limanda 92
Ling 98
Lingcod 37
Lithognathus mormyrus 93
Little tuna 20
Liza ramada 99
Lobotes surinamensis 94
Longtail tuna 65
Lophius piscatorius 95
Louvar 96
Lutjanus analis 31
Lutjanus cyanopterus 31
Lutjanus sebae 31
Luvarus imperialis 96

Mackerel 115
Makaira indica 32
Makaira nigricans 33
Mako shark 29
Meager 71
Mediterranean flagfin 73
Mediterranean spearfish 58
Megalops atlanticus 34
Megalops cyprinoides 34
Merluccius merluccius 97
Molva molva 98
Monkfish 95
Moray eel 101
Morone saxatilis 35
Mugil cephalus 99
Mullus barbatus 100

Muraena helena 101
Musselcracker 81
Mustelus asterias 102
Mustelus canis 102
Mustelus mustelus 102
Mutton snapper 31

Naucrates ductor 103
Nematistius pectoralis 36
Northern puffer 122

Oblada melanura 104
Oilfish 111
Ophiodon elongatus 37

Pacific bonito 45
Pacific cod 23
Pacific crevalle jack 6
Pacific halibut 27
Pacific snapper 31
Pagellus bogaraveo 105
Pagellus erythrinus 105
Painter comber 119
Pandora 105
Paralichthys californicus 38
Paralichthys dentatus 39
Parrot fish 120
Permit 66
Phycis phycis 106
Pilot fish 103
Plaice 107
Platichthys flesus 107
Pleuronectes platessa 107
Pogonias cromis 40
Pollachius pollachius 41
Pollachius virens 108
Pollack 41
Pollock 108
Polyprion americanum 85
Pomatomus saltatrix 42
Pompano 126
Porbeagle shark 30
Prionace glauca 43
Psetta maxima 109

Rainbow runner 17
Rainbow wrasse 89
Rachycentron canadum 44
Raja asterias 110
Ray's bream 78
Red mullet 100
Red scorpionfish 117
Red sea bream 105
Redfish 118
Roosterfish 36

Saddled bream 104
Saint Peter's fish 131
Saithe 108
Salema 113
Salmo salar 112
Sapphirine gurnard 86
Sarda australis 45

Sarda chilensis 45
Sarda orientalis 45
Sarda sarda 45
Sarpa salpa 113
Saupe 113
Scabbard fish 90
Sciaena umbra 114
Sciaenops ocellatus 46
Scomber scombrus 115
Scomberomorus commerson 48
Scomberomorus maculatus 49
Scophthalmus rhombus 116
Scorpaena porcus 117
Scorpaena scrofa 117
Sea bass 16
Sea drum 40
Sebastes marinus 118
Sebastodes melanops 118
Seriola dumerili 50
Seriola lalandi dorsalis 51
Serranus scriba 119
Sheepshead 70
Shi drum 129
Skipjack 22
Smooth hound 102
Snook 10
South African amberjack 51
Southern bluefin tuna 62
Spanish mackerel 48, 49
Sparisoma cretense 120
Sparus aurata 121
Sphyraena barracuda 52
Sphyrna mokarran 53
Sphyrna zygaena 53
Sphoeroides maculatus 122
Spicara flexuosa 123
Spicara maena 123
Spicara smaris 123
Spiny dogfish 125
Spondyliosoma cantharus 124
Spotted sea trout 14
Spotted wolf fish 69
Squalus acanthias 125
Squirrelfish 88
Stargazer 130
Starry ray 110
Stereolepsis gigas 54
Striped bass 35

Striped mullet 100
Striped marlin 57
Striped sea bream 93
Summer flounder 39
Swordfish 67

Tarpon 34
Tautog 55
Tautoga onitis 55
Tetrapturus albidus 56
Tetrapturus angustirostris 58
Tetrapturus audax 57
Tetrapturus belone 58
Tetrapturus pfluegeri 58
Thin-lipped gray mullet 99
Thunnus alalunga 59
Thunnus albacares 60
Thunnus atlanticus 62
Thunnus maccoyii 62
Thunnus obesus 63
Thunnus thynnus thynnus 64
Thunnus tonggol 65
Tiger shark 24
Tope 25
Trachinotus falcatus 66
Trachinotus ovatus 126
Trachinus draco 127
Trachurus trachurus 128
Triglia lucerna 86
Tripletail 94
Turbot 109
Two-banded sea bream 83

Umbrina cirrosa 129
Uranoscopus scaber 130

Wahoo 1
Weakfish 15
White marlin 56
White sea bass 5
White sea bream 83
White shark 9

Xiphias gladius 67

Yellowfin tuna 60

Zeus faber 131

PICTURE SOURCES

The abbreviations a, b, c, l, r, refer to the position of the photograph on the page (above, below, center, left, right).

Introduction

Overseas: 10, 12, 20, 28, 45b, 56, 74.
Overseas: 64, 90–91 (Animals–Animals); 58 (Alistair Black); 57 (Bernhart); 37, 40, 41, 46, 50, 51, 59, 82, 83, 85, 86, 87, 90–91 (Bimarine); 18, 29, 42, 75, 88, 92 (L. Bonfanti); 39, 53 (C. Sergi); 78, 84 (G. Caliero); 44a (Campbell); 44a (S. De Cenzo); 73 (J. Dupont); 23, 24–25, 63 (P. Equisetto); 14 (Explorer-A. Baudry); 15, 44b, 48, 49, 72 (Oxford Scientific Films); 11 (V. Pigazzini); 55 (R. Polo); 2 (Schuster).

Chapter opening pages

Overseas: 8–9 (Schuster); 98–99 (Animals–Animals); 170–171 (Bimarine).

Entries

Animals–Animals: 44 (Zig Leszczynski); 55 (Earth Scenes).
P. Arnold/N. Wu, 1988: 28;
Game Fish: 22, 72l;
Odyssey: 37 (Frerck); 29, 125 (Seaborn)
Overseas: 20; 7 (Ashod); 32l, 82c (Bimarine); 2 (Bonfanti); 68, 74, 104, 119, 123, 130 (A. Calegari); 59l, 61 (De Marpillero); 87, 99, 122b (C. Galasso); 85, 100, 101 (A. Ghisotti), 32r, 71 (Giango); 14 (Okapa); 9 (C. Roessle); 105, 108, 117a (H. Schmidbauer); 62r, 64, 67 (I. Sonnino); 27, 57 (M. Snyderman)
Overseas/Animals–Animals: 19 (R. Radden); 34b; Zig Leszczynski); 38 (J. Scott); 33 (I.D. Watt); 70, 79 (F. Whitehead); 118b (J. Wilburn)
Overseas/Oxford Scientific Films: 86, 95, 110 (G. Bernard); 107 (J.A.L. Cooke); 34a, 52 (L. Gould); 127 (F. Ehrenstrom); 8, 51, 131 (R. Kuiter); 72r (K. Westerskov); 43 (N. Wu Wun)
Overseas/Explorer: 42 (Y. Gladu)
Overseas/Jacana: 48, 114 (Annunziata); 12, 89 (H. Chaumeton); 45, 69, 76; 97, 113, 115, 129 (J.L.S. Dubois); 93 (J. Dupont); 24 (Eliot); 13, 83a, 120 (Y. Gladu); 118a (Kerneis); 2, 68, 77, 106, 109 (R. König); 4, 26, 31, 50, 103 (Laboute); 16, 23, 41, 82a, 83b, 112, 121 (Lanceau); 53 (Moisnard); 1 (M. Neumann, 1984); 92 (F. Sardou); 6, 24, 66, 75, 94, 102, 116, 117b, 128 (Varin Visage)

Photo Researchers Inc.: 39, 17 (F. McConnaughey); 2, 5, 35, 54 (T. Mc Hugh); 10 (J. Lidington); 40, 46 (G.S. Grant)
The Wildlife Collection: 60r (H. Hernano); 56, 60l, 62l (F. Lettuss)